TO PAUL
KEEP LIST8
ENJOY THE BOOK.

THE WRECK OF THE COLUMBIA

The
WRECK
of the
COLUMBIA

A BROKEN BOAT, A TOWN'S SORROW & THE END
OF THE STEAMBOAT ERA ON THE ILLINOIS RIVER

Ken Zurski

The Wreck of the Columbia

© Copyright 2012, Ken Zurski

All rights reserved. No part of this book may be used or reproduced in any manner whatsoever without written permission from the publisher, except in the case of brief quotations in critical articles and reviews.

First Edition ISBN 13: 978-1-937484-05-7

AMIKA PRESS

Jay Amberg, President

466 Central Ave STE 6   Northfield IL 60093   847 869 8084

info@amikapress.com   Available for purchase on amikapress.com

Edited by John Manos.

Cover art by Justin Russo, justindavidrusso.com

Title page photograph courtesy Murphy Library University of Wisconsin-La Crosse.

Author photograph by Portrait Innovations.

Book designed by Sarah Koz in Adobe InDesign. Body set in 10.25/14.25 Walbaum Text, designed by Walbaum Justus Erich in 1800, digitized by František Štorm in 2010. Titles set in Metro #2, designed by William Addison Dwiggins in 1939, digitized by Linotype in 2000. Cover titles set in Duke, designed by James T. Edmondson in 2009.

Thanks to Nathan Matteson.

**TO THE VICTIMS OF THE COLUMBIA DISASTER
AND TO THEIR FAMILIES AND DESCENDANTS
WHO KEEP THE MEMORY ALIVE**

This book is a work of narrative nonfiction. The stories included are all true, and the people are real. To the best of my ability I have pieced together the final voyage of the *Columbia* using newspaper accounts, magazine articles, letters, witness testimony and legal documents. With only a few exceptions, such as personal interviews, everything is based on sourced or published material. Where warranted, many of the sources are acknowledged by name within the text. The majority of the dialogue and testimonials indicated by quotation marks are taken from these sources. In some cases, dialogue was recreated to carry the narrative, but always based on actual descriptions. There are names that appear throughout the book that come up frequently and were obtained from multiple sources. In many instances, they were spelled in varying ways. I tried to use the version that appeared most often. If a proper name is misspelled, it is not intentional.

CONTENTS

PROLOGUE THE BOAT WENT DOWN   1

1 TROUBLE AHEAD   5
2 PLACE IN TIME   11
3 STEAMBOATS COMING   19
4 MOVERS   31
5 HIT BOTTOM   45
6 MIDNIGHT CRUISE   55
7 SURPRISE TICKET   63
8 FRANKIE FOLSOM   71
9 AL FRESCO   77
10 FULL AHEAD   85
11 FALLEN BEAMS   91
12 STRAIGHT DOWN   99
13 BLACKING OUT   105
14 CLEAR ALL TRACKS   109
15 MORE HELP   117
16 ON THAT TRAIN   125
17 IN SHOCK   133
18 HE'S TALKING   141
19 DST   149
20 WHEELS OF JUSTICE   157
21 A PAINFUL GROAN   173
22 HOT WATER   181
23 ANOTHER BODY   189
24 HERO DIVER   199

25	THE STORM	205
26	SPECIAL PRAYERS	211
27	PICNIC DAY	219
28	OVER THERE	227
29	THE TRUTH	235
30	SAD SCENARIO	241
31	SHIFTY POSITIONS	253
32	VERY PECULIAR	261
33	THIS THEORY	271
34	ADMIRALTY LAW	279
35	FLANKING IN	291
36	SENSATIONAL ORDER	305
37	DEAD WOOD	317
38	TAKING THE STAND	325
39	THE PLEA	333
40	STICKY ISSUES	339
41	PEGGED AHEAD	349
42	LEGAL BATTLE	357
43	BEYOND CONTROL	369
44	LOCK AND DAMS	375
45	DEAD DOCKET	385
46	NO MORE GOOD MORNINGS	393
EPILOGUE	DO NOT FORGET	405
ACKNOWLEDGEMENTS		413
SOURCES		417

AGNES
TAZEWELL COUNTY GENEALOGICAL AND HISTORICAL SOCIETY (TCGHS)

THE BOAT WENT DOWN

AGNES SOADY NEVER FORGOT that warm July night. Not a moment of it. In fact, she would live to retell it for many years, even some 63 years to the day, in 1981, when a newspaper article featured her amazing story. By then, at the age of 82, Agnes had lived a full life. She married a local man who had served in the war and they started a family together. They stayed rooted in the town she grew up in. A town scarred by the events of that fateful July night. The night everything changed. Agnes Soady, née Smith, would never forget it. It started with a long walk home from work, a full mile-and-a-half hike along the cobbles and rutted dirt roads.

She was exhausted and disappointed.

The pretty but dowdy-by-design 19-year-old had a ticket to go on the steamer *Columbia* for a moonlight cruise on the Illinois River. It was an unexpected invitation from her neighbor John Diepenbrock, who asked Agnes to join him and his family for a night out. The event was sponsored by a local social club to which John belonged.

Agnes liked John, his wife Martha, and their three small boys,

Henry, Melvin, and baby Norman. She enjoyed watching them play in the yard. And they adored her singing. Agnes accepted their gracious offer and told the Diepenbrocks she would meet them around seven that evening at the dock on Court Street. She would have just enough time to make it after work.

For Agnes, her hours at Kreager's Drugstore in Pekin, Illinois, went by quickly as the anticipation of the cruise grew by the minute. Her excitement, however, was about to change to despondency. It was nearing 7 o'clock and Agnes could not leave. Her boss was running an errand, and Agnes had to wait until he returned. She kept looking at the clock on the wall. Time was running out. "Be right back," her boss had told her, heading out the door.

But he never returned. At least, not soon enough.

Agnes would not be going on the *Columbia* that night after all.

Saddened, she walked home and decided to make it an early night. In bed, Agnes kept thinking about all the wonderful stories she would hear about the *Columbia* the next day at work. Then finally, she fell asleep. That is, until the knock at the door jolted her awake.

A MAN AND HIS SON, both dripping wet, were on their way back to Pekin in the back of a taxi. The driver sped along the cobbled roads taking directions from the man in the back seat. The man was holding his son in a tight bear hug. They both looked frightened, the driver noticed. The boy was quiet and shivering.

"Turn here," the man told the driver, "that's my home."

The man asked the driver if he was going back to the river. Yes, the driver answered.

"Wait here then, please," he said, "I'll be right back."

The driver watched as the man and his son ran to a house across the street.

The house was dark, but soon a faint light appeared in the front window.

IT WAS LATE, well past midnight. Agnes thought, *Who would come calling at this hour?*

The knocking came again.

A light flickered on in a bedroom down the hall. Agnes could hear her parents whispering. Then she heard footsteps.

Agnes and her sister Maude sprang from bed and ran toward the door. Frederick Smith, Agnes' father, motioned for the girls to stand back. The knocking was persistent. Then she heard a cry for help. "Hurry, please!" came the voice from the other side of the door.

Agnes froze.

She recognized the voice.

Frederick fumbled for the lock, tensely turned the knob, and swung the door open. Standing on the other side, drenched from head to toe, were John Diepenbrock and his eldest son Henry. Agnes was startled by John's pale, shaken look. Henry appeared scared.

"The boat went down," John said, trying to catch his breath. "All I've got is Henry. Please, watch him for me. I beg of you." He turned and disappeared into the night.

Agnes took hold of young Henry Diepenbrock and watched as her neighbor ran back into the darkness. Then she pressed her hands to her mouth and gasped. A frightening thought ran through her head. She tried to shake it off but couldn't.

Where were Martha and the two other boys?

THE TAXI DRIVER waited and watched as the front door of the house opened and a family appeared. They looked like the sleep was still in them. The man left the boy with the family and ran back to the car alone. "I'm in a hurry to get back," he told the driver, "and find my wife and two sons."

The driver asked him to reconsider. The police were encouraging everyone to go home and stay home, he told him. "They asked me to bring people home safely," the driver exclaimed, "not take anyone back."

"I had my baby in my arms!" the man shouted. "Then the water came," he said, his voice now trembling. But he could not finish the sentence. The man slumped in the seat and said no more.

The driver understood. He turned the car around and headed back to the wreck of the *Columbia.*

THE STEAMER COLUMBIA
MURPHY LIBRARY UNIVERSITY OF WISCONSIN-LA CROSSE

1

TROUBLE AHEAD

IT WAS LATE ON A FRIDAY, the day after the Fourth of July, 1918. Captain Mehl stood near the bow of the *Columbia*, which was filled with passengers on a midnight excursion on the Illinois River. The short, stocky 47-year-old German immigrant with the boyish-looking face wanted a cigar so badly he could taste it, but that would be a pleasure for later. The night's work would soon be over, he thought, another job well done.

The air had been clear upriver–a perfect trip–but now something had stirred up. It wasn't a full-blown fog bank Mehl noticed up ahead, but a slight, mysterious mist, the kind that gives a pilot fits and a captain a good case of the nerves. Mehl looked up at his trusted pilot, George 'Tom' Williams, who stood 40 feet above the water. Williams must have seen it, too, Mehl thought. But it was hard to tell. A steamboat pilot shows few emotions. He stands next to the twelve-foot wheel, always looking straight ahead, rigid like a statue. Mehl considered calling up, but his voice might not carry over the sound of the orchestra in the dance hall. Best not to alarm the passengers, he thought–a yelling captain is bad for business.

There was no other choice. He tipped his hat to a fellow along the rail and hurried to the top deck.

Pilot Williams, universally called Tom for short, was a step ahead of his captain. He had yanked the bell-pull and alerted the engine crew below to ease up. Just then a voice came through the pilothouse door, an unmistakable voice with a thick German accent. "Take it on a slow bell, Tom," Captain Mehl ordered, without hesitation or explanation. But Tom knew.

"Can you see the bridges?" Mehl asked. Williams looked cautiously ahead. Yes, he could see them fine. The mist was not heavy enough to affect his vision, not yet at least. But there was trouble up ahead.

The Wesley City sand bar.

Bar 11 on the navigational map.

Williams hated the blasted thing.

The Wesley City sand bar was a large obstruction in the middle of the Illinois River between Peoria and Pekin. Oftentimes hidden by high water, the danger was present each time a boat passed through. There was only a narrow channel to navigate on either side. It was notorious for testing a pilot's skill–and wits.

More trouble, Williams thought.

The water was up from recent rains, and the current was running fast. This was not going to be an easy end to the night.

William's job as a steamboat pilot was to "read the river and steer the boat." Bar 11 was easy to spot, that was clear, and Williams knew it well, but piloting the boat around it took the skills of a good 'driver.'

"First thing you learn is how to steer the boat," explained steamboat pilot Walter Karnath in the book *The River's In My Blood*. "You stood on one side of the wheel and kept turning it one way or the other. There was a foot brake on the floor underneath the pilothouse. You'd step on that and hold the wheel, instead of holding the spokes all the time."

Some pilots missed the brake, and the spokes would spin back like a whirling fan, snagging the poor man's clothing and sending him flying like a ragdoll against the pilothouse wall, or worse, out the front window. "Once you learned to steer," Karnath continued, "then you had to learn where to go."

Williams ran the scenario in his head as he had a hundred times before. He took his foot off the brake and turned the wheel slightly, testing its pull. Just as he anticipated, the ship's heaviest passenger, a full load of coal—100 tons of it—in the forward part of the main deck made the ship hard to handle, especially hard when turning. The passenger load was just over half-full to capacity, and the dance floor was packing them in up front.

By comparison, the boat's stern was light.

Williams had some decisions to make. A clear run would certainly help, he must have said to himself, as the boat inched closer to the Wesley City sand bar. He needed to see, too.

"Better keep it lit up then," Mehl directed.

Williams agreed. He reached for the knife-switch toggle and opened the electric current. Just in front of the pilothouse between the two smokestacks and directly ahead of the stage mast was the circular electric-arc searchlight. It warmed up, then fizzed on. Suddenly, a brilliant ray of light reached outward like a straight arrow that spread its "noonday glare" against the blackness ahead. Pointing forward, it looked like a rope pulling the ship. Mark Twain called a steamboat searchlight "daylight in a box."

A relatively new invention, the carbon-arc light was introduced at Chicago's Columbian Exposition in 1893. Sitting atop a massive building, the round searchlight was nearly ten feet tall and weighed more than 6,000 pounds. But it was that glorious stream of bright white light that wowed them. The much smaller version for river navigation was considered a safety intervention, and it was used sparingly and cautiously. The round housing itself was as hot as a burning stove on the inside. Even the outside glass envelope could reach 500 degrees F. The beam was so powerful it could stab a fellow sailor's eye blind.

In the prominent days of steamboating, pilots were reluctant to use the newfangled navigation aids, like the searchlight. "It was a question of honor," argued one veteran pilot. "Anybody who used a headlight at night to find out where they were was an old woman!" he wrote.

One stubborn pilot named Captain Jack actually used the sound of a barking dog to navigate through thick fog. At a dangerous spot in the river, Jack would ring the bell, and a farmer's dog would come running along the bank "barking his head off." Jack would listen to the dog's incessant bark and know where he was "to the very inch." One day he rang the bell and got no answer. No dog. No barking. He rang it again and still nothing. He thought they might be running behind schedule so he ordered the engine crew to move faster. Next minute, they were on the rocks. The dog had died the night before.

In time, and after too many unfortunate meetings with the rocky shore, common sense would override reckless bravado, and the use of the searchlight became more widespread.

"Best to just let it burn," Mehl ordered, reluctantly.

There was no other way around it. The Wesley City sand bar was up ahead somewhere in the mist. Williams nodded approval. From inside the pilothouse, Williams had a handle on both the current flow and the gear movement. He pulled the handle. The beam of light trekked across the bow from starboard to the shoreline just off the port side. Then it went back again. The hanging willows on the starboard side stopped the point of light dead. Too soon, Williams thought. The boat was drifting.

Allen L. Davidson was in the engine room when he received the slow bell signal from the pilothouse and ordered the crew to decrease steam and back off speed. As the ship's engineer, his job wasn't to question a pilot's will, only to follow it. But silently he questioned it. He wondered if there was something wrong.

In the cramped quarters of the engine room office, Davidson wiped the sweat from his brow and noticed the shadow of his arm on the wall briefly disappear. He looked up. The swinging light bulb hanging from the ceiling flickered out and then came back on again.

That could only mean one thing.

The searchlight was burning.

A clear sign something was amiss, he thought.

Davidson ran outside to take a look.

CAPTAIN HERMAN F. MEHL
CHILLICOTHE HISTORICAL SOCIETY & MUSEUM

2

PLACE IN TIME

WHAT ENGINEER DAVIDSON, pilot Williams, Captain Mehl, the rest of the crew and passengers of the *Columbia* couldn't know was that in a matter of moments, a little farther downstream just beyond the searchlight's beam, was an underwater hazard that would turn all of them into a footnote in the history of the Illinois River.

Yes, a footnote.

Sadly, the wreck of the *Columbia* is a mostly forgotten chapter on the river today. Some people still know about it, but only a select few. For others, there may be a vague recollection about a boat sinking on the Illinois River–possibly heard passed down from generations–but many can't seem to remember the name, place, or any of the details. In most instances, however, the response is simply, "Steamboat wreck? What steamboat wreck?"

That wasn't always the case, however. Throughout the years, and especially in the mid- to late-20th century, local newspaper articles on the *Columbia* frequently appeared to mark certain milestones like the yearly anniversary of the wreck itself. The articles were mostly feature stories about survivors–many of whom were now in their golden years—recalling that "horrific" night.

In the town of Pekin, annual gatherings commemorated the disaster and remembered those who died that day. One was in 2003, when a state historical marker was dedicated. Several *Columbia* survivors attended the event and threw flowers into the river. The marker is located in a park near the McNaughton Bridge, about a mile south of the actual wreck site.

The very spot where the *Columbia* went down is in an area then known as Wesley City, today known as Creve Coeur. The shoreline is unmarked and unremarkable in appearance, overgrown by brush and accessible only via a gravel road. Without directions or a guide, there is no way of knowing at which point on the river the accident actually occurred. There are no signs, no marker.

In the early '90s, there were plans to build a memorial park on the site and give it some historical significance. "The park will include a bronze marker with a picture of the *Columbia* and a plaque containing the names of those who lost their lives," the *Pekin Daily Times* reported. "A boardwalk with wrought-iron fences and park benches will run the length of the park."

A 60-by-60 foot stretch of privately owned shoreline land was donated to the town of Creve Coeur, and the local Historical Society hoped to break ground and dedicate the site by 1993, the 75th anniversary of the wreck. But the plan—mostly a volunteer effort—went nowhere. There simply wasn't enough interest, money or both. Today, with the Peoria dam and locks nearby, long barges and tugboats line up along both sides of the river obstructing the view.

Still, if you are looking for information on the wreck itself, it's not too difficult to find.

In the Pekin Public Library, a collection of articles, letters and photos on the *Columbia* can be found in a cardboard box tucked away in a pull-out drawer that's easily accessible. In the Peoria Public Library's history room—an impressive space in the basement of the main library building—another box with similar items can be found. You have to ask to see it. The Tazewell County Genealogical and Historical Society along with the Tazewell County Museum, both in Pekin, have folders and vertical files filled with comparable newspaper clippings and articles.

The Peoria Historical Society also has a box of mementos and photos from the wreck. The box is stored in the Special Collections office on the campus of Bradley University, where, by appointment only, a staff member will retrieve resources from a climate-controlled back room while you wait in a cozy but confined study area. No ink pens, they kindly inform.

The history of steamboats themselves is still alive. There are still several good organizations, museums and universities that help to protect and preserve its legacy. Yet, the historical significance of the grand boats, some would argue, gets lost in a generation and century that witnessed great strides in transportation. With the advancement of roads after World War I, the automobile, with its practicality, became a staple for all Americans. And the emergence of the airplane changed how quickly we could move from one place to the other—either across country or overseas.

In time, the convenience of traveling by air overtook the convenience of traveling by rail, which had done the same to traveling by waterway many years before. Soon the aviation industry would have its own record of heroic achievements and tragedies to remember. By comparison, a steamboat wreck, especially one like the *Columbia,* gets lost in the mists of time.

Even for a local story like the *Columbia,* and in a town like Pekin, the path of history evolves. Shortly after the disaster, the 'war to end all wars' came to an end and young men returned home to their small towns. And later that same year another story with even more heartbreak and death would dominate the headlines, eclipsing even a horrific local tragedy.

But let's not get too far ahead of ourselves.

By the summer of 1918, the year the *Columbia* went down, ships and steamboats were very big news, especially those involved in a catastrophe. The sinking of the passenger liner *Lusitania* in 1915—destroyed by a German torpedo—would eventually draw American troops into a mostly European conflict. And before that, in 1912, another liner, the biggest one ever, and one that was considered 'unsinkable,' struck an iceberg and sank in the Atlantic Ocean.

The *Titanic* is the most famous shipwreck of modern times. Its story of human emotion, suspense and great sadness continues to live on through generations, thanks to numerous books, a box office smash of a movie and an amazing documentary that brought vivid pictures of the wreckage from the ocean floor to our living room TV screens.

But between the turn of the century and 1914, when the Great War began in Europe, steamer technology and safety were steadily improving. Thousands upon thousands of people had no reservations about boarding the massive vessels and traveling across the sea or along the coasts.

The Good Years, as they were called, brought prosperity and generally high spirits that even a few spectacular disasters like the Great 1906 San Francisco Earthquake and Fire and the sinking of the *Titanic* couldn't sway. Even after being warned a German submarine attack was imminent, the *Lusitania* still sailed with a full load of happy–albeit somewhat concerned–passengers. The smaller boats that made the shorter jaunts, including the steamers that ran the inland waters, were considered to be more or less safe.

Before the turn of the century, however, safety on America's inland waterways was a different story entirely. "Accidents involving destruction of life and property have become so frequent on Western rivers," wrote one observer in 1840, "that we look as regularly, when we open a newspaper, for a steamboat disaster, as for the foreign news."

"Steam engine explosions were the forerunners of modern-day catastrophic airline crashes," writes author Ed O'Donnell in *Ship Ablaze: The Tragedy of the Steamboat General Slocum*. "Just as a jetliner is utterly vulnerable to the smallest of technological glitches when in flight, so too were steamboats at sea or on rivers and lakes."

This is around the time Samuel Clemens (later known as Mark Twain) became a steamboat pilot. "The golden age of steamboating!" author Roy Morris Jr. wrote about the world young Clemens entered in his early days on the river. "Sam and his fellow pilots were lords of all they surveyed." But death and destruction were a reality lurking around every twisted bend. For Clemens, a personal tragedy almost sank his childhood dream of one day piloting a steamboat down the mighty Mississippi. It provides a good example of the risks endemic to the industry.

In 1858, 18-year-old Henry Clemens was working an unpaid entry-level job on the steamer *Pennsylvania,* thanks to his brother Sam, a cub pilot on the steamboat who reluctantly introduced his little sibling to a life on the river. During a routine trip just below Memphis, the *Pennsylvania*'s boiler exploded, killing 120. Henry survived the initial blast but was badly burnt. He never regained consciousness and died eight days later in a Memphis hospital.

Sam Clemens was not on board at the time. Earlier that summer he was thrown off the boat by the captain after an argument concerning his little brother's work ethic. Though Henry stayed, Sam left to avoid any further confrontations. Several days after the explosion, Sam was on another boat when they floated by the wreck site and past the bloated, decomposing bodies that were still floating in the water. Clemens visited his brother in the hospital. "For 48 hours, I labored at the side of my poor burned and bruised but uncomplaining brother," he wrote as he watched Henry die. "The star of my hope went out and left me in the gloom of despair." Clemens blamed himself for his brother's fate.

"Henry's death permanently haunted Sam," writes Morris Jr.

Still the lure of the river, despite its dangers, was too great for the man who would later write the classic tell-all river book, *Life on the Mississippi.* Clemens became a fully licensed pilot in April the following year.

This tale of tragedy for the Clemens family was by no means unique and far from the worst disaster on the great inland rivers during the steamboat era. In the mid-1800s, steamboats were almost grotesquely dangerous.

The worst shipwreck on America's greater inland waters was the *Sultana,* a large side-wheeler steamboat that exploded and burned in the Mississippi River on April 27, 1865. An estimated 1,800 perished, mostly Union soldiers who had just been released from Confederate prison camps. Even at the time, the wreck itself received somewhat diminished attention because it occurred only a week after President Lincoln was assassinated. In terms of historical importance that year, which included the end of the Civil War, the *Sultana* disaster got bumped down the list.

Today, only steamboat aficionados and Civil Wars buffs recognize its significance by name. Like the *Sultana,* most steamboat wrecks, such as the *Eastland* on the Chicago River, the *General Slocum* on New York's Long Island Sound and the *Columbia* at Pekin are rarely mentioned or remembered. The *Eastland,* where more than 800 lives were lost, is considered "America's forgotten tragedy." Still the *Columbia* deserves a place in history. It is the worst boat wreck, based on loss of life, on the Illinois River. Nothing else comes close.

And the story is remarkable.

It's the tale of a close-knit community suddenly grieving for its dead and seeking restitution and justice. It's about government agencies trying to assess some responsibility and mete out punishment. It's about a proud captain and his crew defending their actions and character. And, of course, it's about the innocent victims who were caught in a situation that required great courage. Many would make it through to tell their stories, but 87 others would not.

The wreck also brought to an end a glorious era on the Illinois River, one that began nearly a century earlier when a skittish pioneer named Hugh Barr in a place called 'Town Site,' soon to be known as Pekin, heard strange sounds coming from the woods near his home. Barr grabbed his rifle, and with his "madly excited" dog by his side, ran in pursuit of the shrill whistle and swooshing oars, ready to fight the Indians. But it was no Native American war chant or canoe paddles that Barr heard that day. The first steamboats had made it up the Illinois River.

That is where this story truly begins—in 1828.

STEAMER PRAIRIE STATE
MURPHY LIBRARY UNIVERSITY OF WISCONSIN-LA CROSSE

3

STEAMBOATS COMING

AS LEGEND HAS IT, a pilot who was unfamiliar with the Illinois River's many channels ran the boat off course and into one of the adjoining oxbow lakes by mistake. This led Barr to come running, rifle in hand and ready to fight. Fortunately, the boat's pilot managed to back out and escape before any shots were fired. A fellow settler named Jacob Tharpe heard the flap of the wheel boards and toot of the whistle that morning, too. He thought the angel Gabriel had finally blown his horn signaling the Day of Judgment. "Get out of bed," he told his frightened family. And he summoned them to prayer.

Undeterred, the steamboats kept coming.

The actual name of the first steamboat to chug up the Illinois River is, as one writer put it, "lost in the grey fog of unrecorded history." However, one of the earliest documented trips was by a small steamer named the *Liberty*, which came up the Illinois as far as Peoria in 1829. It was soon followed by many others. Two years later, there were 17 arrivals and departures in Peoria, and by 1850, 59 steamboats were docking at Peoria, which now saw a total of

1,236 arrivals and departures for the year. When the steamboats came, so did a dramatic change in lifestyle, which James Ayars chronicles in his book, *The Illinois River:*

> With steamboats came changes in outlook, changes in mode of living along the river. People of the Illinois River country now had direct water connections, much faster and much easier that they had known before, with Pittsburgh in the East, New Orleans in the South, and dozens of lesser cities along the way. They were freed from the isolation imposed by arduous journeys between Illinois and the outside world.

The convenient but crude boats were an effective and inexpensive way to travel between St. Louis to the south and LaSalle, Illinois, to the north, the end of the line for the Illinois River at the time. As one writer explained, the river had become the first "veritable super highway." But travelers compromised comfort and safety for time and convenience.

The early packets were "primitive, rude and often dangerous." The flimsy wooden hulls were ripped open by stumps, snags or collisions. The boiler engines were prone to explosions. In 1851, upon boarding one boat, the Reverend J.P. Thompson of New York took one look at the exposed boilers on the first deck and sermonized, "The flaming furnaces would give you rather uncomfortable hints of a choice between fire and water in making your exit from the world."

In the book *Peoria!* author Jerry Klein tells the story of Eliza W. Farnham, an articulate Easterner who in 1846 took a ride up the Illinois River in a small packet boat named *Banner.* "What she wanted in size...was amply compensated by filth," Farnham would later write about the boat's condition. The floors would be broken, stairs would be rotted and roofs would spring leaks, she went on to explain. The waste of steam in the still-underdeveloped engines would cause the paddlewheel to move slowly, then lurch with such force that passengers were literally thrown off their feet. "A strange habit," Farnham wrote, "that had to be satisfactorily explained to me by a scientific friend...she might average five of these spasms per day."

But that wasn't all. When the sun went down, another nuisance emerged.

"I've heard of flies, mosquitoes, bed bugs and fleas," wrote J.H. Buckingham, another Easterner from New York who rode on the steamer *Dial* between Peru and St. Louis in 1848, "but never could be brought to believe one-half of what I experienced [on the Illinois River]. The heat of the night and the heat of the boat and the lights brought them upon us. The floors, the stateroom partitions, the mast, the ceiling, the freight, the baggage and the passengers were literally covered." Mosquito nets were used, but to little avail. In fact, wrote Buckingham, "it just seemed to attract more of the creeping things to luxuriate."

"Some people slept!" Buckingham explained sarcastically. "Happy immobility! I took my baggage in hand and went ashore at Peoria, and laid down on the steps of the hotel at the top of the hill to wait for daylight."

SITUATED IN THE MIDDLE of the 256-mile-long Illinois River, Peoria and Pekin were popular stops for the early steamboats. Ayars recounts the story of Mrs. Eliza Steele, a New York socialite, who along with her husband made a journey west in 1840. After spending a day in Chicago, the couple took a stagecoach to Peru where they were scheduled to board a steamboat named the *Frontier* and travel down the Illinois to the Mississippi, passing and stopping in river towns along the way.

Just getting to the river proved to be a difficult task.

During the bumpy stagecoach ride on the underdeveloped roads, Mrs. Steele recalled, the coachman was seen walking about with a lantern in his hand.

"What have you lost?" called out one gentleman passenger.

"Only my road, sir," the driver replied.

They were three miles off course.

Once in Peru and on board the *Frontier*, Mrs. Steele sat down to write a letter to a friend. "Fatigued as we were we could not leave the deck, for the 'night sun,' as the Indians call the moon, was shining brightly down upon the smooth surface of the Illinois

[River], lighting up her forest glades as we passed, and throwing fantastic shadows over the silvery water," she wrote. "However, a night and day in a stage coach has beaten the romance out of us, and we at length retreated to our snug stateroom. The mosquito nets were drawn over us, and we soon bid to nature and to you a fair good-night."

Due to heavy fog, the *Frontier* arrived in Peoria several hours late the next day. Mrs. Steele used the time to jot down her impressions of the passing shore. Although not nearly as stately as her native Europe with "its lordly mansions to embellish the scenery," she thought the forests along the Illinois were "lovely" and noted the "long vistas through which the early morning sun was streaming."

"The silvery barked white maple with its bright green leaves" and the "willows dipping its leaves in the stream" all struck her fancy.

The following day the Steeles boarded the steamboat *Home* and journeyed downriver to Pekin where they stepped off and "walked about the town." Before re-boarding they waited as "barrels of flour, in a seemingly endless procession, rolled from the large storehouse on the bank down to the vessel." In addition to the flour, hundreds of bushels of corn and other merchandise were loaded aboard.

Eventually Mrs. Steele and her husband made it to the Mississippi River, but not without "a last farewell to the fair Illinois," she wrote, "upon whose banks, or on whose water we had traveled for four days and four nights." And the river traffic was heavy. "We were constantly passing steamboats," she noted.

THE NAME PEKIN, it is said, comes from the Chinese city of Peking or 'City of the Sun,' now known as Beijing, the ancient capital city. Ann Eliza Cromwell, wife of Major Nathan Cromwell, one of the area's first landowners, came up with the name, although many still believe her intentions, especially in regards to China, are not clearly defined. The best argument for why Mrs. Cromwell named Pekin after Peking is that the cities were believed to be on the exact opposite sides of the world and that 'Pekin' without the 'g' was a more common spelling in the English language.

Nothing but legend supports this claim about the town's naming, and naysayers are plenty. Why name a town after a Chinese city, they might ask, and then *not* give any of its streets Asian-themed names as well? Many of the streets in Pekin bear the names of its early settlers, mostly women, including Ann Eliza, who prominently named a street after herself.

There is another Pekin in Ohio. It was settled in the early 1800s. Could there be a connection? Many pioneers migrated from areas to the east and headed westward stopping short of venturing into unknown territory. They made their permanent camps along Illinois' river banks, where the land was abundant and the natives were friendly. The town of Pekin, Ohio, is so small and home to so few that it is hardly recognized in periodicals on Ohio history. So there is no record to place people in the region. But it's safe to say that the ties to Pekin, Illinois, would seem to be in name only. The naming of Pekin in Ohio likely had Chinese origins as well, although there is no official documentation. It was not uncommon for settlers to name a new city with an Oriental theme, especially when an Indian name or name of a founding father was not already used.

Chinese culture, specifically its artwork, was popular at the time. 'Chinoiserie' was a French term used to describe an art style produced in Europe but influenced by Chinese design, specifically elaborately painted porcelains vases and delicately decorated lacquered pots. The Asian-infused handiwork had been around for more than a century, but its presence was finally being felt in Western homes.

Perhaps the strongest argument for the Chinese connection in the name Pekin comes from nearby Canton, a modest-sized town but still the largest by land area and population in Fulton County, which borders Peoria County to its east. Canton was founded in 1825 by Isaac Swan, whose descendants claim "received its name... from a notion [Swan] entertained that in its location it was directly the antipodes of its Chinese namesake (Canton)." The timeline is fuzzy, but books describing the history of Canton place the naming of Pekin first, and therefore Swan determined "that the two celestial cities should be represented at precisely their opposite pole on the earth's surface."

Even the Canton in Ohio, which interestingly is about the same distance from Pekin, Ohio, as the proximity of Canton and Pekin in Illinois, has East Asian origins. Bezaeel Wells founded Canton, Ohio, in 1805, naming the city in honor of one of its original traders, John O'Donnell. O'Donnell owned a Maryland plantation that he had named Canton after the Chinese city. Wells liked the name too.

Coincidences aside, the naming of Pekin's streets, like the naming of the town itself, also generates spirited debate. The Pekin City Directory of 1870 states that the town's street names may well have been given by Major Cromwell instead of Mrs. Cromwell, although "assisted, doubtless, by his wife." Mrs. Cromwell is listed properly in some early records as Elizabeth Ann Barker, the daughter of Lewis Barker, a wealthy public official who represented Pope County in the Illinois Senate. Is the shortened, juxtaposed and snappier four-syllable name that appears on the city's street sign, Ann Eliza, her husband's way of paying tribute to his wife? Was it perhaps a nickname that he used lovingly in her company and correspondence? Major Nathan Cromwell will later be remembered as being the former owner of the first female slave to be emancipated in Illinois, 'Black Nance,' whose full name was Nancy Legins Costley, who would have been just 16 years old when Cromwell arrived to claim Pekin in 1828.

Most historical accounts, however, always refer back to the Chinese association when it comes to Mrs. Cromwell's intentions in naming the new town. "Why she thus named it the legendary history of the days gone by fail to record, and we can only surmise that in the plentitude of her imagination she looked forward to the time when it would equal in size that other Pekin–the Chinese City of the Sun," was the descriptive but still ambiguous message given by the Pekin City Directory of 1870.

Maybe it was a whimsical novel about the ancient city she was reading or the appreciation of the culture and its people that drew Mrs. Cromwell's imagination into such comparisons enough to inspire naming a city after Peking. The matter of "digging far enough below earth to reach China" may have been discovered after the fact. One early settler remarked that the Illinois' earth "is fertile and black and loamy down to the bottom of China." Was this remark made after the town was named or before? Regardless, the name stuck and the Chinese motif was embraced, even carried to extremes in some instances.

Already a bustling community settled by German immigrants who fled the oppressive policies of their homeland, early Pekin was "crude and boisterous and known for its business failures and reputation as a pest-hole of disease," according to the *Pekin Centenary*, a book published in 1949 to celebrate the centennial of Pekin's City Charter. But Pekin had "one priceless quality" it shared with the rest of America at the time—freedom. "And because of that one quality," the *Centenary* reported, "the muddy, sprawling, disease-ridden Pekin was a finer place than the neat, clean villages of Germany."

In 1829, a general merchandise store opened followed by a grocery and dry goods store. The town's first school was built in 1831 and the Pekin Post Office opened a year later. A church and two taverns followed.

It wasn't until 1849, with a population of 1,500, that Pekin officially became a chartered city. A mayor and four aldermen were elected to make important civic decisions and enact laws. Industries came too. They included a wagon maker, a reaper maker, a distillery and packing plant. Before long, Pekin had grown to be the largest city in Tazewell County and its political and judicial hub. A new 'Grecian-style' courthouse was built and lawyers came, including two future politicians named Stephen Douglass and Abraham Lincoln.

The bitter political rivals and philosophical opposites would eventually become famous for their 1858 series of statewide senatorial debates, and Lincoln's speech denouncing slavery—his first recorded statements on the matter—from a downtown street corner in Peoria would be a crucial step in the top-hatted statesman's rise to the White House. But it was in Pekin that a young Abe Lincoln cut his teeth in the matters of the law. In one instance, as legend has it, Lincoln used his tall, slender frame and a broomstick to get rid of an unwanted bat that was loose inside the Tazewell County Courthouse.

Lincoln sightings and stories in Central Illinois were popular after he became nationally recognized. Once, when he was strolling down a dusty road in the Pekin area, a horse-drawn carriage passed alongside. "Will you have the goodness to take my overcoat to town for me?" Lincoln asked the driver.

"With pleasure," the driver responded, "but how will you get it again?"

"Oh, very readily," Lincoln replied. "I intend to remain in it."

Despite his resourceful ways of traveling throughout the state, the former president's legacy is more associated with trains than steamboats. Not only did a train take him to Washington, D.C., from Springfield, Illinois, to begin his presidency (known as the 'whistle-stop' tour), but a train returned his body in 1865. The funeral train's closest stop to Pekin was in Bloomington.

The young Lincoln never lived near the Illinois River, so his stories came from deeper inland where he cut down trees and built log-cabin homes. Interestingly though, his first stop in Pekin, said to be around the time of the Blackhawk War, was an unexpected one while traveling downriver in a wooden canoe. When Lincoln was nominated for Congress, Tazewell County and the town of Pekin were in his district.

STEAMBOATS PLAYED A BIG ROLE in the growth of the city, and as elsewhere, the ships delivered their share of local tragedies as well. In 1852, the river steamer *Prairie State* was docked in Pekin when her boilers blew to pieces. According to the *Centenary,* "Many passengers were killed or maimed in the explosion and others were scalded and drowned.

"The people opened their doors to the injured, and almost every house in Pekin was occupied by some victims of the *Prairie State* explosion." Since many of the passengers were immigrant transients on the move, many of them remained in Pekin after they recovered.

Among the important deliveries that arrived by steamboat, one of the most amusing involved new fire equipment and a comical contest for primacy between 'native' residents and German immigrants. In March of 1860, a fire broke out in a grocery store on Court Street and quickly spread through downtown, taking out an entire block from Third to Capital Street. The townspeople could only watch in horror as the flames danced "unchecked from one building to another." Soon after, a call went out—more like a desperate plea—that a fire company was needed. A battle of wills emerged between the two sides of town, or as the *Centenary* put it, "a clash between its new and old citizens."

Not one but two fire-fighting companies were organized, one from the 'native' side of town, and the other from the German-speaking side. Both applied to the city council to purchase a fire engine, and both asked to be designated as Fire Engine Company Number One.

When the engines arrived by steamboat, the townspeople packed the shore to see which company would get the Number One distinction. The anticipation was infectious. They watched and waited as the boat arrived with its precious cargo: two shiny new fire engines. When the boat was close enough to read the number on the side, the Germans cheered madly. Their engine had won the honor of being Company Number One. The other fire company members walked off in disgust, leaving the Number Two fire engine behind.

Eventually *three* fire companies were formed, the *Independent*, the *Rescue* and *Defiance*, with more than 200 volunteer members in all. The problem was there weren't that many fires to fight—and when they did break out, it would be cause for celebration rather than alarm. The city didn't help matters when it offered a $10 bonus to the first company to reach a fire and douse it. Suddenly, there were lots of fires in town, a record-breaking number, all very suspicious. Back then 'ten bucks' could buy enough booze for the whole company to enjoy. The city council promptly cancelled the bonus and the number of fires—perhaps unsurprisingly—dropped.

PEKIN CONTINUED TO THRIVE as a community rooted in its German heritage until the turn of the century, especially after war broke out between the European nations. Most of Pekin's early settlers had been living in the 'new country' for more than 50 years, and many residents were now American-born citizens. The devotion to the 'Fatherland' was waning—or simply dying off. Loyalty to the United States was said to be "unquestionable." Signs that read GERMAN SPOKEN HERE where taken down from store windows. This was not out of spite. They just weren't needed anymore. The German-American Bank became the American Bank. The German-Methodist Church changed its name to the Grace Methodist Church, and Pekin's German-language newspaper, the *Freie Presse*, became the *Free Press*, now published only in English. The war against Germany seemed to ignite prejudices in Americans and in Pekin—despite its German heritage—change was imminent. .

As with inland-waterway freight traffic all over the East, the grand era of steamboating on the Illinois was eclipsed by the railroads. When the railroad tracks were built in the mid-1800s, the early packet boats that carried freight between LaSalle and St. Louis began to disappear. The steamboats were still used to ferry passengers and small freight, but many were modified for excursions, or short day or overnight trips, like 'party boats' on the river that were filled with music, drinking and dancing.

By the early 20th century, several family dynasties, such as the Swains and Sivleys, controlled most of the steamboat excursion business on the Illinois River. They owned and operated many of the boats that were docked along Peoria's downtown riverfront and made frequent trips south to Pekin and beyond. One of those boats, one of the largest on the river and one of the last, was the *Columbia*.

WALTER BLAIR
A RAFT PILOTS LIFE

4

MOVERS

THE STORY OF THE COLUMBIA begins in Clinton, Iowa, around 1898, thanks to the family of a lumber tycoon and an old steamer named the *Douglas Boardman*. This was around the time massive rafts made of corded logs were rolling down the rivers. *Columbia*'s roots are found in the once-giant logging industry of the upper Mississippi.

By the middle of the 19th century, milled wood was a precious commodity used to build houses and just about every other thing imaginable, including furniture, barrels, wagons, railroad ties and caskets. The original timber barons imported the logs from the Wisconsin forests to their expanding mill operations along the Mississippi River. The trees were cut down, dragged to the river and tossed in. They floated downstream to an area called a 'chute,' which resembled a funnel, where the logs were corded together to make a raft. Two men, called 'sweeps,' stood on each end with long oars called 'blades' and steered the rafts—some as big as a football field—through the winding river.

The logging industry actually began in the Northeast, but eventually the forests (pineres) were tapped out. So loggers moved inland to the Midwest where the majestic white pine was dense in the forests of Wisconsin and Minnesota. In Wisconsin, the slim, tall trees lined the riverbanks like stalks in a cornfield. Known for its shingled cones and prickly needles (grouped in five, one for each letter of its name W-H-I-T-E), the hearty tree could live nearly 500 years if conditions allowed. But it was building materials that were sorely needed at the time, and vast fortunes were to be made from the trees. So the trees came down.

The idea of transporting freshly-cut timber down the river was simple and logical. Anyone who ever threw a stick in the water and watched it float down the river could claim its inception. On a much larger scale, however, the idea of building a huge raft made of the cut and corded logs was ingenious. But the rivers, they soon discovered, were obstacle courses, narrow and bendy, and the rafts were hampered by sand bars, rocks, even fallen trees.

For the men who endured the task, it was hard, dangerous work that was usually for little pay (about $1 a day plus board). "I recollect that one day we were having a game of ball," recalls Simon Augustus Sherman in the book *Lumber Rafting on the Wisconsin River,* "when the pilot called us to the oars. The raft was sagging into a bend, and into the bend it went in spite of us, one corner striking the bank and taking two or three loads of dirt upon it." It's no wonder that when the rafts were safely secured at the mills, the exhausted men would take a few days just to decompress, usually drinking themselves into a silly stupor before going back upriver and starting the whole process over again. This was either viewed as an economic boom or sinful curse to the mill towns. The burly "muscled" crew was said to have an "insatiable appetite and penchant for booze, brawls and babes."

Despite its hardships and constant delays, the logs would come in droves down rivers like the Chippewa and St. Croix in Wisconsin to the Mississippi, but the rafting process itself was in dire need of an overhaul.

A solution was devised by William J. Young Sr., one of the original timber barons. He came to America in 1846 from Ireland and worked as a freight agent for the emerging railroad lines before settling in Clinton, Iowa and opening a lumber mill in 1860. It didn't take long for Young to become a very rich man. In just six years, he owned and operated the largest mill operation in the country. His success was for a good reason.

In 1865, Young came up with a plan that revolutionized the logging industry. He suggested using a steamboat's power to push and guide the "moving lumber yards" down river. This would eliminate the need for 'sweepers' and the time-consuming job of roping each log together, since a large number of logs could quickly be gathered and made ready for tow. It took some practice, but eventually it worked. Young's plan was more efficient and productive. Soon larger rafts, more logs and bigger profits were moving down the mighty river to the expanding mills. It also meant more steamboats were needed. So the large lumber companies, like the William J. Young Co., became boat builders, too.

In 1893, his health failing, Young bequeathed the family business to his two sons, Charles and William Jr. The Young brothers shut down the lumber mills but continued several other successful financial interests, such as the Clinton Bank. They also kept the steamboats running–including the *Douglas Boardman*.

The *Boardman* was the largest boat the Youngs owned and was used exclusively by the family for personal business, much like a private jet might be today. When the reliable old cruiser's hull was finally used up, the *Boardman* was retired, and the *Columbia* was born.

It was the practice for boat owners and builders to use parts from discarded boats to build new ones. It made good economic sense. The old steamer's hull would eventually rot or become damaged from wear, but the rest of the boat would be salvageable, especially its steam engine. As long as it hadn't been damaged by fire– a common occurrence at the time–it could be used again. Good boat builders would make the wooden hulls from scratch, usually from scotch pine that they had at the ready, and reassemble the other parts, like the rails, decks and pilothouse for the upper works. Then they would name the refurbished boat and put it back in service. The *Douglas Boardman*'s two steam engines and most of its upper works, including the pilothouse, were used in building the *Columbia*.

Like most of the Youngs' other boats, the *Columbia* served the family well by carrying passengers and hauling cargo out of larger ports to the south like St. Louis. In 1905, while stalled by an ice flow in Paducah, Kentucky, the *Columbia* caught the eye of Mississippi River veteran Walter A. Blair, owner of the Carnival Packet Company of Davenport, Iowa.

Born in Galena, Illinois, Walter Atcheson Blair would sit along the hilly banks of the Favre River and watch the packet boats float by until they disappeared around the bend, on their way to the Mississippi River to the west. As a young boy, Blair dreamed of seeing the great river for himself someday. In 1869, at the age of 13, he got his wish. Pursuing better prospects and profits, Walter's father Andrew uprooted the family and relocated his lumberyard business from Galena to Princeton, Iowa, on the west side shore of the Mississippi. From that day forward, Walter Blair would never be far from its muddy waters.

Book-smart and savvy, Blair taught school in Princeton and worked as a scheduler on a small packet boat until he got his pilot's license in 1882. He quit teaching and made the river his full-time job. He bought his first boat the next year and started making a living in the rafting business. By 1892, Blair could sense the rafting business coming to an end and organized the Carnival Packet Company to run freight and passenger boats up and down the Mississippi. His venture was successful, and he soon found that he needed more boats. That's when he discovered the *Columbia* stuck in the ice. Blair bought the boat from the Youngs, removed ten forward staterooms, and transformed the *Columbia* into an excursion boat specializing in day-long or shorter chartered trips along the Mississippi, an expanding business at the time. "She fitted the plan excellently," Blair would later write about his new purchase.

In 1907, the *Columbia* had the honor of escorting President Theodore Roosevelt down the Mississippi River. The president asked for a fleet of attractive steamboats to accompany him on a public relations jaunt for the newly-formed Inland Waterways Commission. The trip was designed to drum up grassroots support for a proposed six-feet-deep channel to be dredged along the Mississippi, which was often too shallow for travel.

It worked. Led by the steamer *Mississippi,* which carried the president, and seven other steamboats including the *Columbia,* the caravan kicked off in Keokuk, Iowa, before hundreds of well-wishers and in a drenching rainstorm. In typical Roosevelt fashion, before boarding the *Mississippi,* the 26th president walked up to the podium, removed his hat and said, "Ladies and gentleman, I sincerely hope my speech will not be dry, for I assure you that nothing else about me is." The crowd went wild. "Drama was his forte," writes author Candace Millar, describing Roosevelt's showy style.

One after another, the steamboats paraded behind the president and the *Mississippi,* smoke billowing and whistles blaring at every boisterous stop at cities along the way. In a show of support, the heads of all states that lined the mighty river were aboard the boats, including Illinois governor Charles S. Deneen, who later described the trip as "favorable" and "decisive." Deneen praised the president for what he said had "a marked effect upon waterway sentiment in Illinois."

The parade of boats ended up in Memphis, Tennessee, where Roosevelt spoke to a gathering of the Deep Water Association. Not everyone was on board with the idea of such an ambitious project. The question was the cost. Specifically, who would pay for the work and how much? Roosevelt's presence and impassioned speech struck a nerve. "Whatever the cost," Deneen wrote, "the country, perforce, I believe must undertake the improvement and extension of our domestic waterways."

"When we consider what an enormous traffic has been developed upon our lakes," Deneen added, "we may appreciate the effect of an extension on these magnificent bodies of water through the construction and improvement of navigable channels, communicating with them at one terminus and with the ocean at the other, and traversing the rich mining, agriculture, and manufacturing regions of the interior."

Walter Blair did not accompany his boat on the entire journey down the Mississippi. Rather he went as far as St. Louis before turning it over to a Captain William Dipple who steamed the rest of the way to Memphis. The *Columbia* played host to Minnesota Governor Samuel Van Sant. A Civil War veteran who grew up in Rock Island, Illinois, Van Sant was a riverboat builder on the Upper Mississippi and like Roosevelt, a Republican. Sharing a concern for the river's natural resources, the two men were good friends. Once while the president was visiting Saint Paul, Minnesota's capital, Van Sant accidentally grabbed Roosevelt's overcoat by mistake. He reached into the president's coat pocket and discovered a loaded pistol. Roosevelt was not shy about carrying a gun for protection, one time telling a reporter after the McKinley assassination that "if it had been [me] instead of McKinley, I would have shot back." Realizing his mistake, Van Sant returned the coat, gun and apparent security breach back to the president. Later Roosevelt would return the favor. When the president asked his friend to participate in the steamboat parade down the river, Van Sant wholeheartedly accepted.

Blair also had ties to Van Sant. He worked for the governor for a time, piloting his raft boats before he launched the Carnival Packet Company, of which Van Sant was a partner. So it was of no coincidence that the *Columbia* would accompany Van Sant and his minions on the trip with Roosevelt down the Mississippi. Before the caravan left, Blair wrote: "Van Sant insisted on presenting me to President Roosevelt (in Keokuk), and since then I have been very glad that I had the opportunity."

Blair had a feisty reputation as captain and pilot. "A little man in stature," wrote the *Davenport Daily Republican* after reporting an altercation involving a landing site in which Blair sternly held his ground, "but he will die game." Blair also had a flair for the dramatic. Piloting the *W.J. Young Jr.* in 1898 on a trip to Muscatine, Iowa, Blair "took along a flattering list of passengers," the paper reported, "and one of the features of the trip was an interesting race, between her and the steamer *J.W. Van Sant.*"

Steamboat racing was not uncommon at the time. In fact it

enthralled both passengers on the boat and those shouting in delight from the shore. "The boats came alongside as they passed under the high bridge," went the *Daily Republican's* play-by-play account, "from that moment on the race was on in earnest."

> The *Van Sant* was caught by the suction of the *Young* and the two boats drew together, their guards touching. Neither could get away from the other. The excitement was intense. For five miles they held together, then by shrewd maneuver on the part of Capt. Blair, who was at the wheel himself, he succeeded in getting clear and distanced his plucky adversary.

The *Young* and pilot Blair were victorious. The crowd cheered wildly. "If Capt. Blair will promise a treat of this kind every week," the papers exalted, "these trips will be wonderfully popular."

Blair's success in the excursion business peaked in 1909 when he boasted that his "little company"—which consisted of five boats at the time—"carried 114,857 passengers and 16,896 tons of freight." But the business of steamboating was volatile. "The next year was different," Blair wrote. "It was a year of extremely low water." One of his boats, the *Helen Blair*, snagged a rock near Rockingham, Iowa and sank. "The rock had been missed by the engineers who marked out a new channel for us," Blair said. He spent $5,000 to raise and repair the *Helen Blair* and put her back in service.

Discouraged by delays and similar unfortunate accidents, Blair started to phase out the business and went back to piloting full time for other companies. He started to sell rather than buy boats. In 1912 he sold the *Columbia* to Herman Frederick Mehl, an Illinois businessman, for $14,500, "which was nearly what she had cost us seven years before," Blair wrote.

Blair kept one steamer, the *Keokuk*, the smallest of his fleet but also the one dearest to his heart. It had been used as a rafting boat to tow logs down the river to mills. He held on to the *Musser*, a name Blair christened her after the Musser Lumber Company, until 1926, when the steamer described as "one of the oldest on the river" was destroyed by fire on August 17 in the middle of the night.

"When fire companies arrived on the scene at 12:10 o'clock this morning," the *Davenport Democrat and Leader* reported, "the steamer was a mass of flames."

The fire's origin was as difficult to figure out as it was to extinguish. "One of the pumps became mired in the soft ground at the edge of the harbor and was extricated with difficulty," the *Democrat and Leader* reported. The fire chief was suspicious. "The steamer had not been in service for several years," he told the paper. "There were no fires in the boilers and no way that I know for it to catch afire unless someone set it afire." No one was ever charged or blamed. It was an unfortunate accident, and Blair had lost his last boat. That day he officially closed the books on the Carnival Packet Company.

In his later years while sharing stories of his life on the river, Blair playfully recounted the time he met another famous steamboat pilot and author. "He was lecturing in Davenport in 1885," Blair told a reporter for *Coronet Magazine*. "I made it a point to meet with him."

Blair was piloting the *J.W. Mills* at the time. "It was my lucky chance that my boat was in port that night when he lectured here." After the lecture, Blair was invited backstage. "Go on and speak to him," he was told, "He's right over there and he will be glad to talk to a river man."

Blair recalls the meeting: "Mark was sitting in an undertaker's chair. He looked dog tired. His big mustache was drooping. 'Hello,' he said, 'who are you?'

"'My name's of no importance, Captain,' I told him. 'But maybe you will recognize the handwriting on this letter.'" Blair handed him a letter written by Mark Twain's wife. The letter had been sent to Blair after Blair wrote Twain saying what a fine "authentic" book *Life on the Mississippi* was. The return letter politely explained that Mr. Twain was on a speaking tour.

"That's my wife's handwriting!" Twain said surprised. "Now where the devil did you get that?"

"After he read it," Blair explained, "he made me sit down beside him and asked questions. I never saw a man so interested in boats and the river. He wanted to know everything. He asked about the way we piloted on the Upper River (he was a Lower River man, you know); about changes in the channel around St. Louis where the Upper and Lower Rivers meet, and about a lot of the old-time pilots who were still at the wheel. Any river man could tell he knew his business.

"When I left," Blair continued, "'My boy,' he said and clapped me on the shoulder, and he was mighty wistful, 'nothing I ever did in my life was as pleasing as piloting a steamboat. Goodbye and good luck.'"

When Mehl bought the *Columbia* from Blair in 1912, he came up with a nickname, one only he used enduringly to describe the boat's longevity. He called it 'the old tub.' It was as much out of respect as it was a term of endearment. As proud river men like Twain often do, Blair must have told Mehl all the stories about the *Columbia*. Mehl excitedly brought 'the old tub' to Peoria and started an excursion business.

THE COLUMBIA WAS A STRIKING figure on the Illinois River. Three decks tall and built mostly of wood, from top to bottom, her style was typical of most stern wheelers at the time with her gothic-like architecture along the rails and a striking white paint job, offset by the black twin stacks and the red bucket planks on the paddle-wheel. "The *Columbia* was about 125 feet in length and of the usual broad beam of river boats," is how the *Chicago Tribune* described her. "The hull deck contained the barroom and chairs and tables amidships. Aft on this deck were the boilers and engine of a typical stern wheeler. The hull, like all riverboats, was flat of bottom and regarded as incapable of being capsized."

At the bow was the stage deck where passengers entered and exited. The swinging stage or gangplank was lowered and raised as needed and held aloft by a boom attached to a thin, straight pole called the stage mast, or jack staff, that almost reached as high as the smokestacks. Several other jack staffs, or 'braces,' lined both sides of the ship and held up the hog chains—a single, wrought-iron rod used to pull up both ends of the hull. The braces jutted at an angle, and the hog chain line always ran in a tight straight line from back to front. This prevented the hull, which support-ed the weight of both the boilers near the bow and the engines in the stern, from 'hogging,' or drooping, on the ends and rising in the center.

The first deck, or main deck, housed the boilers, engine room, snack counter, a few scattered tables and the bar. This deck was always filled with men who would socialize, play cards, have a smoke or generally be as close as possible to their next drink.

The dance floor, or 'dancing pavilion,' took up the second level. The large, open space had a wooden floor from end to end and was lined with windows, called skylights, along the upper sides. Wood-en folding chairs hugged the walls, and a bandstand was in the corner. The most popular spot on the ship, it was always crowded and loud. The promenade, or deck rail, that ran along both sides of the dance floor, had been removed to create more space. There was an exit door on both ends of the deck that led to narrow stairways.

The upper, or hurricane, deck was mostly an open walkway with a deck rail along both sides. The deck at the bow just aft of the stacks was unprotected from above and provided the best view of the river ahead. In the middle were several cabins, or 'staterooms,' for the crew, plus steps to the pilothouse directly above.

The pilothouse stood alone on the roof. The ornate, square struc-ture—the highest point of the ship other than the stacks—was sur-rounded on three sides by glass sectioned windows and heavy cur-tains to keep the sun out. In front, instead of glass was a wooden, hinged breast board. Most pilots preferred the open-air view so that they could "sense the wind and hear the sounds of the river." They didn't have much of a choice. A glass windshield was useless because of frost. The breast board hinges would pivot on the top and bottom and detach at the middle. The pilot could use the top section as a visor on sunny days. A bench was in the back for invit-ed guests, and a stove directly behind the pilot provided warmth on chilly nights. The roof of *Columbia*'s pilothouse was adorned with an open-aired, gilt cupola shaped like an acorn cap, its one very distinctive feature.

IN 1918, 'THE OLD TUB' was said to be worth anywhere between $3,000 and $35,000, which was "not a typographical error," a newspaper reporter pointed out. The staggering discrepancy was based on Herman Mehl's tax assessment the year before. Mehl listed the boat at $2,502 and said the value would only go up after necessary improvements and repairs were made, which demanded thousands of dollars out of his own pocket. The Tax Board of Review revised the estimate and raised it to $4,200, and Mehl paid his 1917 tax bill of $104.61. Still not satisfied, in 1918 the tax assessor asked Mehl to appear before the board for a review, which he agreed to do, but only after the Fourth of July holiday was over. He was busy with excursions all week. The meeting never took place.

Mehl also decided not to insure the *Columbia* that year. It was reported that "underwriters had offered to insure the boat for $35,000," which Mehl refused.

"What do I want insurance for?" he said. "It's impossible for a serious accident to happen in that muddy creek." Mehl was likely referring to the river's depth, no more than 20 feet at its deepest point. Even if the boat sank, he must have thought, how far down could it go? Besides, the ship was the safest on the river, Mehl boasted—and he had the inspection report to prove it.

FROM THE SHORELINE, an excursion steamer like the *Columbia* sounded like a floating music box. The first thing you might hear would be bouncy orchestra music followed faintly by the sound of laughter and cheers. Then the slapping and splash of water interrupted. The volume was always turned up a bit by the nighttime air's natural acoustics.

On the evening of July 5, 1918, John Chance had just returned home from a day's work in the grimy coal mines. He heard the faint music in the distance and went to the window of his small one-room cabin in Wesley City to watch the boat pass by. The *Columbia* was especially striking that night with its "brilliantly lighted" twinkling bulbs stretching from stem to stern and dozens of American flags flapping in the breeze. Two stationary lighted electric American flag displays glowed red, white and blue. Chance watched as the *Columbia* floated serenely downstream. He had viewed this scene many times before, but on this night, something was different.

"The boat was going slow as it passed by my cabin," Chance would later recall. "The searchlight was playing from one shore to the other."

Chance would normally go right to sleep after watching the boat float downriver. The twinkling lights, the swooshing water, and the faint sounds of laughter and music would be like a warm glass of milk on an unseasonably cool summer evening. Even for a hardened coal miner like Chance it was a calming site. A good night's rest would usually come easily after that.

But on this night, sleep would have to wait.

TOP: DOUGLAS BOARDMAN "UPPER WORKS USED TO BUILD COLUMBIA"
BOTTOM: EARLY COLUMBIA
MURPHY LIBRARY UNIVERSITY OF WISCONSIN-LA CROSSE

5

HIT BOTTOM

ENGINEER ALLAN DAVIDSON'S curiosity was peaked. First, a slow bell order from the pilot, and now the lights in the engine room were dimmed. He mumbled under his breath and headed for the door. Outside, the brisk night air tagged Davidson's sweaty skin like a cool fan, a welcome relief from the heat of the boilers inside. He could also light a cigarette here, safely away from the coal dust. He looked toward the bow. The searchlight was still burning. He followed the beam of light as it moved across the mist above the river. Once on shore, the beam jumped up and down in a hurried, dizzying way, then moved quickly back across again. As if it was dancing, Davidson thought.

On top of the boat, Pilot Tom Williams kept the searchlight active, moving it from side to side, always with an eye on the distance to shore. Williams knew the river well. A steamboat pilot for 25 years, Williams was from Meredosia, a small river town in Illinois known for its muskrat trapping and button factory. He was a veteran of the river with a reputation as a good pilot, a soft-spoken guy who did his job with few curse words.

They were drifting a bit, Williams thought, to starboard. He knew it—he could sense it like he could sense the humidity in the air. The willows appeared much closer. The current had picked up, and the boat was front-heavy with its full load of coal. The Wesley City sand bar was close, but how close? Williams pulled hard to port, but the river had other ideas for the boat.

Walter Fluegel, a grocery clerk standing on the first deck, noticed the pilot "playing with the searchlight," as he later testified.

"My God," he said to a friend, "the captain's lost in the fog."

The first scrape was noticeable. Some said it felt more like a "jar." Like the ship had hit bottom.

Guy McIntyre, a pipe fitter from Pekin, had gone to the lower deck to have a cigar. He didn't feel a bump but heard the sound of willows scraping against the boat. Being a machinist, he stopped by the engine room and looked in. He thought the piston rods were moving very slowly. McIntyre started for the front stairs and narrowly missed getting hit by a tree branch. William Tunney, another passenger, said he could reach out and grab a handful of leaves.

Bertha Neff was enjoying the view from a second-deck window. She had been dancing but wanted a break. The boat seemed to be going back into the stream. "Then it struck something hard," she recalled, "like the shore."

The orchestra was wrapping up for the night and had just started into the first notes of *Home, Sweet Home,* the final song.

The dance floor deck was crowded. William Newman was prancing happily when he heard someone yell that the boat was so close to shore "you could touch the willows with a fishing pole."

"Then a smash," he said, "like something had hit bottom."

The music came to a sudden stop when a window crashed in.

Joseph Rupp, enjoying an outing on the river with his three sisters, took a break from the dance floor and went below to play cards and have a drink. "The jolt slid the tables," he said. "A tree broke through a window and brushed the coat from my chair."

Rudolph Lohmann saw a willow branch "twelve inches in diameter" scrape the side of the boat. "Geez, we're on shore," he said to a fellow next to him.

"Well, anybody was able to run her ashore," the fellow said. "Just look at that fog."

"Looks more like white smoke to me," Lohmann replied.

THE WESLEY CITY SAND BAR was dead ahead. Tom Williams grabbed the spokes and turned the wheel, his desperate shift to starboard barely avoiding the bar. But the boat was drifting. He sent a stop bell signal below. The boat slowed, but the weight of coal up front caused the stern to swing sharply back to the right. The back end of the ship was loose and headed straight for shore. Williams felt a "blow," but it was very light. Then he heard a window break.

Captain Mehl stood by. He could only watch. The pilot had full control of the boat's movement. *No danger,* the captain kept telling himself. Then he felt a "slight jar" and heard the sound of glass breaking below. Mehl looked over starboard and could see the dead tree limbs and jutted stumps scraping against the hull. The freshly-cut timber had been washed over by recent rains. He assumed that the reinforced steel he put over the wooden hull during winter could withstand such blows. "Henry!" he shouted to his watchman. "Get downstairs and turn the lights on in the hold." Then he added, ominously, "Check for water!"

Henry ran like the wind.

The *Columbia* had come to a rolling stop. For a moment, everyone froze. Then as the passengers concluded that nothing serious had happened, life returned to normal on the boat. "On with the music!" yelled William Newman to the stunned musicians, who had stopped in mid-song. Bud Ray was standing near the bandstand and noticed everyone had "paused in their figures." Some were picking themselves up off the floor. There were more shouts from across the room for the musicians to continue. The danger appeared to be over. "Go ahead and play," said Bud to the drummer. "It's nothing."

In the engine room, Allen Davidson thought he felt something scrape against the bottom of the boat, but the sound of the steam and pistons prevented him from hearing anything unusual. Then came the stop bell signal from up above. At that moment Henry

Trippler, the watchman, came bursting through the door.

"Mr. Mehl wants you to turn the lights on in the hold, pronto!" Henry shouted.

Davidson looked at him, puzzled at first. *Check the hull?* "For what?" Davidson shot back.

"Water!" said Henry.

FREDA SNYDER AND an escort had gone downstairs to get a sandwich and were standing near the rail when they heard a horrible noise. "Like something rotten had given way," she said. The boat lurched, and they started for the stairs back to the dance hall. Above her Captain Mehl couldn't wait. He left the pilothouse and ran down the back stairs to the main deck. He met Freda Snyder there. She confronted the captain about the noise. "Go sit down," he told her, "don't be foolish. We hit a sand bar in the fog." Freda was admittedly too "nosey-like." She looked around and spotted three men standing near the forward hatchway.

Henry Trippler and first mate W.C. Edwards had been in the engine room with orders from the captain to open the hold and check the hull. Allen Davidson couldn't understand why. The engineer never had a problem with leaks before. He did routine, mostly mundane, checks on the boat all the time. When he had looked in the hull earlier that evening, a curious passenger had asked, "How is she?" To which Davidson had replied, "Oh, I guess she's the same."

Still, a captain's orders are a captain's orders.

Davidson grabbed a flashlight and snapped the latch back. He lifted the wooden hatchway off the floor and poked his head in. He shined a light at the bottom of the hull and raised his head up quickly. His face turned a ghostly white. Without a word, he handed the flashlight to Edwards. He motioned for the first mate to take a look. "When I threw the light into the hull," Edwards recalled, "I saw the water." Trippler snatched the flashlight from Edwards and went in. The water was up to his knees. Trippler and Edwards made a beeline for the top deck. Davidson ran back to the engine room. He had heard the signal of the back-up bell.

Freda Snyder watched the men go about their business. They looked in the hull with a flashlight, and then one went in. He reappeared looking worried. Then two of them ran toward the front stairway. The other one went back into the engine room where bells were going off. In their haste, they had left the hatchway door wide open. Being "nosey," Freda couldn't help herself—she looked in. It was too dark to see, but she could hear it.

"The water rushing in sounded like Niagara Falls," she said.

THE MUSIC AND THE DANCING started up again. The danger of a calamity had seemingly passed. The *Columbia* had skidded against the shoreline and was now backing out. That was all. "It felt just like a landing," was one observer's matter-of-fact assessment. William Freeman wasn't so sure, even though he was one of the first to call for the band to keep playing. The musicians obliged. They gathered their composure and broke into the patriotic war tune, *Where Do We Go From Here?*

"I grabbed my girl and danced twice around the room," Freeman said. "I wanted to get her near the door."

In one corner, there was a woman with a baby carriage, eyewitnesses would later describe—the baby was fast asleep. In a folding chair against the side wall, an "old woman" was knitting with "olive and drab yarn," without a care in the world.

"They went on playing," recalled Lawrence Richmond of Pekin, "and I went on dancing."

As the piano player hit the punchy notes, a "jovial" young boy was said to be delighting the revelers by singing the words to the catchy song:

> *Oh joy, oh boy, where do we go from here, boys.*
> *Oh, where do we go from here?*

Back in the engine room, Allen Davidson received the back-up bell from the pilothouse and set the wheels in motion. The boat had been grounded momentarily and stopped. Now the paddlewheel groaned and turned again, and the *Columbia* slipped off the jutted shore. Outside the engine room gangway, Freda Snyder

went back to the dance floor deck, startled by the sound of rushing water under her feet. "A man in a gray shirt passed me," she
recalls. "He said, 'My God, we never had anything like this happen to us before.'"

Captain Mehl stood outside the dance hall awaiting word from
his crew. He had sent them down into the hull to check for leaks.
He was confident his boat would hold. The worst was over, he
thought; the boat had skidded along the shore. Now his pilot was
backing her out. Soon she would be back in the channel and would
ride the current out—and away from that troublesome Sand Bar 11.
A broken window could be fixed.

Until that evening, Captain Herman Frederick Mehl had been
enjoying a good run. The German-born immigrant had come to
Peoria with his brothers August and Fred just before the turn of
the century. The three siblings were business partners who sold fish
in a market along the Illinois River and cigars at a small tobacco
shop in downtown Peoria.

Then, in 1901, Mehl married into a family steamboat business
and found a life on the river. Like several other family dynasties at
the time, Garland Sivley and his wife Josie were successfully running excursion boats out of the Peoria area. Ethel was the oldest
of their four daughters, a 17-year-old sweetheart when she met and
married Mehl, who was in his early 30s. Mehl began to work for his
in-laws, operating one of their steamboat barges, and soon enough,
he and Ethel started a family. Years later, Ethel's niece, who would
author a book about her grandmother Josie Sivley, remembered
'Uncle Herman' from her childhood. The wet cigar stub he always
seemed to have in his mouth and the thick German accent that
made it difficult to understand him. Of course, the cigar clenched
between his teeth didn't help. Nonetheless, it was a cheery home,
the relative recalled, and Ethel was a "saint." By the summer of
1918, Mehl had his own boat, the *Columbia,* and his own business,
the H.F. Mehl Excursion Co.

Mehl's stature as a captain was in the title only. He fit the uniform, but not the part. He was a bulldog of a man, short and stocky
with a small thin face and a full head of hair that he parted straight

down the middle. It gave him a look of someone much younger than his 40-plus years. He certainly did not meet the stereotypical description of a captain, culled from legends and mythical tales, who would stand at the pointed bow with one knee protruding and spitting out commands with fearful puffs of conviction. Melville described Captain Ahab as someone "made of solid bronze." By comparison, Mehl looked like a mere mouse. But appearances deceive. Mehl's ornery, bullish demeanor, while anything but "Ahab evil," may have been off-putting to some of his workers, but his authority was never questioned. He was the boss, the captain of the *Columbia,* despite his rather diminutive appearance.

He and his wife were a mismatch too. She was a larger woman with a physically commanding presence, although her smooth skin and sweet smile brought out the innocence of her youthful years. As a couple and as business partners there is nothing to suggest that their marriage was anything but loving and successful, despite their age difference. They had two daughters together, Naomi and Ruth.

Ethel was born into a steamboat family and spent most of her life living on and for the river. The oldest of four sisters, she was responsible for taking care of her siblings, even at an early age, when her parents were busy with the excursion business. The boats were their playground. One time while stepping between a docked barge and a steamboat, Ethel's sister Pearl fell into the water. Ethel and the other girls watched in horror as the two boats rocked together and Pearl was caught by the undertow. Just as the wake pulled the two boats apart again, Ethel's mother Josie reached in and pulled Pearl to safety. Josie later used a piece of wood to demonstrate to her daughters the danger of being careless around the boats. She put the wood between the boat's swaying bows and let it break into pieces as they knocked into one another. "Let this be a lesson," she told the girls.

Mehl wasn't flippant when it came to including his wife in business matters. Ethel was river savvy and smart about business. She worked on the *Columbia* and often made tough decisions that did not sit well with the men. The company letterhead listed Mehl as proprietor and Ethel as secretary. Their arrangement was a solid success for nearly two decades, but it was all about to change.

"Captain, captain!" came the shout from his first mate W.C. Edwards, bounding up the front stairs. "Run her ashore," he yelled, out of breath. "There's water in the hold."

"Are you sure?" said Mehl.

"Yes, sir, two feet, sir," came the exasperated reply.

Mehl looked up at the pilothouse, cupped his hands around his mouth and shouted until he was hoarse.

"Run her ashore, Tom! Damn her. Run her ashore!"

The South Side Social Club of Pekin

Will give its second annual breezy, delightful

MOONLIGHT EXCURSION
FRIDAY., JULY 5

CN THE ALWAYS POPULAR, COMMODIOUS, CONVENIENT

NEW STEAMER COLUMBIA
AND BARGE SUMMER GIRL

This trip will start at Kingston, affording friends of the club at that point an opportunity also to enjoy the trip.

The Arthur Knapp Jazz Band of eight pieces from the Winter Garden, in Chicago will furnish music for this excursion.

LEAVE KINGSTON 7:00 P. M., PEKIN 8:00 P. M., RETURNS PEKIN 11:15 P M., KINGSTON 11:45 P. M.

Tickets, Gentlemen 50c ladies 25c (War Tax Included)   H. F. MEHL, Master

COLUMBIA POSTER

6

MIDNIGHT CRUISE

EARLIER THAT EVENING, the *Columbia* had passed by the town of Pekin for the first time with little fanfare. The steamer had left its dock in Peoria and was headed downriver to Kingston Mines, a small mining community four miles south of Pekin, to take on a fresh load of coal and pick up her first passengers.

The weather was "unsettled," with mostly cloudy skies and "fair and cooler" temperatures predicted. "Ideal for boating!" the *Peoria Journal-Transcript* reported. "A pleasant beginning to the summer weekend ahead, an interlude from the worries about the war overseas."

After the Kingston Mines stop, the *Columbia* turned back upstream, and at about 8 o'clock stopped in Pekin where almost 400 passengers came onboard. The ritual was always the same. Enthusiastic crowds waiting on shore would cheer as the boat arrived. The pilot would pull the rope and toll the bell two times to signify a landing. The boat would ease into shore just close enough for the deckhands to lower the boom and stretch the seven-foot gangplank stage into position.

The crowds gathered at the end of Court Street where Pekin's main road met the sandy shore. Men would arrive in their standard seersucker or sack suits and almost always wearing something on their heads, either a derby or straw boater. The women wore light sheath dresses that didn't sweep the floor.

Now that the Gilded Age was over and the Progressive Era had begun, the everyday lifestyle change was most evident in clothing, especially for young women who suddenly found themselves in the workplace while the men were off to war. The transformation to more practical, comfortable clothes was as much out of necessity as it was a fashion statement. Day clothes were looser, jackets belted, skirts rose above the ankle. When going out women wouldn't fuss as much with their looks, especially their hair, and wore wavy brimmed hats without the frilly decorations. The shorter bob-style haircut was gaining popularity and would later become a symbol of independence and free-spirit in the Roaring Twenties.

The electrical revolution also helped women get out of the confines of the home. Motor-driven vacuum cleaners, sewing and washing machines powered by electricity were now readily available on the market, greatly reducing the amount of labor involved with everyday household chores.

Unfortunately, the new machines weren't made for every budget. The cost of electricity was still relatively low, but the appliances were pricey. Many working class families chose to stick with the old-fashioned washboard, wringers and carpet beaters as tools of housework even up until the end of World War II. And in some cases, electricity just wasn't available. It wouldn't be until mid-1940 that some 80 percent of American homes were wired. In 1918, that number was still around 35 percent.

For most middle class women, the electric iron was the one new appliance they couldn't do without. It was far lighter than the heavy cast iron press and eliminated the need to constantly reheat the flat iron surface on a hot stove or range. A thermostat kept the heat a near-constant level. The vacuum cleaner was also popular. In 1915, Hoover introduced the first upright, which would change little in appearance or design for the next 20 years. By 1917, due to supply and demand, Montgomery Ward offered a cheaper portable model in its catalog for only $19.95! The new electric appliances were heaven-sent time- and labor-savers. This allowed women to step outside their domestic cage and enjoy some of the pleasures in life, like a stroll in the park or an evening cruise down the river on a steamboat.

"Laughter and gaiety reigned over the joyous, lighthearted throng that jostled up the gangplank and aboard the vessel," wrote H.W. Humphrey and George W. Barrette, two newspapermen from the *Peoria Journal-Transcript* who just days after the wreck put out a descriptive but sensationalist blow-by-blow account of the accident titled *The Columbia Disaster.* "The bell sounded the signal for the start of the engines, and the big steamer majestically swept out into midstream. The decks were packed with excursionists shouting goodbyes and fluttering handkerchiefs to loved ones as they left the dock."

THE COLUMBIA, NOW WITH a full load of coal and an estimated 496 passengers, headed upriver past the skyline of Peoria and through the raised spans of the three bascule bridges: the McKinley Street Bridge, the Toledo, Peoria and Western Railroad Bridge and the Franklin Street Bridge. The spans met and split in the middle and were operated manually by a bridge tender with a watchful eye. The two separated spans were supported by counterweights and would pivot on each end, then slowly move upward until they were nearly straight up and down, like two arms reaching for the sky in a joyous gesture. The section of the long bridges that actually raised and lowered was on the west side of the river, closest to Peoria. The bridges were so close together that the spans would be raised in unison, and the boat would quickly pass beneath all three, occasionally bumping or scraping the wooden abutments on either side, a common occurrence in the narrow openings.

"Through the draw of the bridges the steamer bore on her way," Humphrey and Barrette wrote.

The bridges weren't as much of a nuisance for passengers as the smoke, soot and smell of raw alcohol from the hulking factories that lined the river banks. Steel and lumber mills, glass and bottle makers, fuel-production plants, alcohol distilleries, breweries and coal mines were some of the many industries in the region at the time. "The sun never sets on Peoria products," the city proudly touted in a description of its home-styled goods and services. "Products manufactured, produced and trans-shipped from Peoria are consigned to every country on the face of the globe."

The outbreak of war was actually a good thing for American manufacturers, and even more so for farmers. Food production in Europe was at a standstill, and supplies for allied troops were running low. American products were being shipped across the ocean to support the war effort and to offset the alarming crisis that had created a food shortage not just in Europe, but worldwide. Americans were asked to ration—in some cases to fast—to meet the demand, which was exploding overseas. President Wilson feared there would be a nationwide hoarding or worse yet, food riots. This was 1916, when the nation's attitude toward war was still in flux. Except for some doctors and nurses who bravely volunteered their time and efforts to the battlefields in France, Americans were not yet on foreign soil.

Wilson ordered the U.S. Food Administration to study eating habits and convince people to sign pledges to reduce their consumption of meats, butter, sugar and wheat flour. The government also encouraged citizens to grow their own fruits and vegetables. Even restaurants were asked to scale back portions—all in the name of patriotism. Wilson's physical presence was also a selling point; tall and lean, the president stood in stark contrast to the man who had preceded him in the office, William Howard Taft—who tipped the scales at 350 pounds. If you are going to ask a nation to ration food, you might as well look the part. Wilson's plea worked: the volume of food exports to foreign nations tripled and food production increased by 25 percent. But it was a double-edged sword for Americans who were asked not only to ration their supplies, but pay more for the inconvenience. Domestic food prices also soared.

Peoria was in the middle of the prairie, surrounded by fertile land and far from any seaport, but its products rode the rivers to the booming markets. Local business leaders boasted in the 1915 *Blue Book and City Directory,* "[goods from Peoria] could be found in Siberia, Australia, Upper Canada, New Zealand, Cape Horn and Greenland." The list of products was endless and varied:

> Each year tons of wire and nails are shipped, trainload after trainload of farm machinery and implements; cars of stoves, meats, marble, finished and in the rough; tons upon tons of paper of various kinds and weights, trainloads of alcohol, grain and denatured; whisky and blended goods; trainloads of German carp and other fish for Eastern markets; manufactured drugs, grocery supplies, barrels and other cooperage; grain foods, wheat flour, meal, etc.; tons of stock food, starch lard, syrup, hides and pelts, tallow, hay, coal from acres of mines and manufactured and natural ice.

The massive scale of production, however, took its toll on the senses. In his book *Peoria Industry: A Pictorial History,* Jerry Klein wrote that the city of Peoria was a "smoky, soot-filled, sometimes malodorous place, alive with factory whistles, the sounds of steam engines and workers carrying lunch buckets."

"There were more smokestacks than church steeples," Klein noted.

Mark Twain would say of river towns like Peoria, that the people in them "don't dream, they work." The stench from the stacks was a testament to a city that works. "Get used to it," the laborers would often say about the acrid smell. Many who endured the smoky factories day in and day out hardly noticed it. For others it was mostly an inconvenience.

The results, though, were hard to argue with: "One thousand various articles manufactured; more than 12,000 persons employed, and over eight million dollars paid out annually as wages," the city claimed. Peoria was a working town.

In addition to its manufacturing successes, Peoria was also the center of a busy entertainment scene and a bustling transportation hub. Streets were slowly improving, trolley cars were popular and steamboats like the *Columbia* lined the shoreline during the busy excursion season, providing both transportation and entertainment.

Once past the bridges and the forest of smokestacks, the *Columbia* sailed into the widest part of the Illinois River, an area known as Peoria Lake. The broad expanse of river was popular with recreational boaters, mostly sailboats or rowboats, which could float unfettered in the calm waters without the worry of being struck by a passing steamboat or barge. There was plenty of room for all.

It was also a welcome break for pilots who had just endured the dangerous, narrow passages of the river. "In the darkened pilothouse high above the happy crowd," wrote Humphrey and Barrette, "Tom Williams, the pilot, with confidence born of years of river navigation, spun the wheel to port and starboard, governing the movements of the vessel. In the twilight of the long summer day the vessel plowed upstream to Al Fresco Park, Peoria."

For the passengers on the *Columbia* this particular night, the end of the line to the north was the Al Fresco Amusement Park, a popular attraction on the west side of the river in an area known as Peoria Heights, or Peoria's north shore. The park was famous for its 'one-of-a-kind' twisty thrill ride, *The Figure-Eight Roller Coaster.*

The midnight cruise was sponsored by the South Side Social Club in Pekin and was a well-advertised event with ads in the newspaper and posters in storefronts. Tickets could be purchased before boarding: 50¢ FOR GENTS, the poster read, 25¢ FOR LADIES. Most tickets were sold in advance. The ads promised patrons would return "shortly past midnight."

Walter Hatton, at the time a spry teenager from Havana, Illinois, remembers the joy of the steamboat rides in his book *Back in Those Days.* "Riding up the river on a steamboat was pleasant and relaxing," Hatton writes. "There was very little noise after it got underway, just a puffing noise from the steam. You could feel a quiver or trembling of the boat, as you looked out and watched the tree-lined banks gliding by. People would charter the big boats, hire a band, and sing and dance on the decks. Once in a while, the parties would get a little rowdy."

A Peoria newspaper columnist eloquently described a steamboat ride at dusk this way:

Green walls of the shoreline rolled past in an endless pan-
orama, the boat gliding silently and majestically with only
the slap of the paddlewheel and the trembling caused by
the steam engines. On clear summer evenings, the sky and
water turn the shade of saffron, and the wake rolls out astern
in a saintly ripple.

There was nothing particularly unusual about the *Columbia*'s
trip upriver that night. As was usual, the excited crowd settled in,
explored the three decks, socialized and enjoyed an early evening
snack or drink while the band warmed up for an evening of rag-
time music and popular Irish waltzes. "There were stacks of wood-
en camp chairs, a special chair they made in those days," writes
Hatton. "The women and older kids would set up a chair and watch
the little ones scamper around. The upper deck was surrounded
by a four-foot high bulwark with a ledge on top. The little ones
couldn't even see over the top, but they didn't seem to mind. They
were too busy playing tag and other games."

Florence Schreck was a 17-year-old passenger on the *Columbia*
that night. She had boarded in Pekin with her aunt, who provided
the tickets, and was looking forward to an evening of dancing. As
passengers bounded up the gangplank, the captain was there to
greet them and extend a helpful hand for those struggling to make
that final step onto the stage deck.

"I loved to dance and swim," Schreck would later recall in a
newspaper interview, but once standing in the middle of the long,
narrow plank, she looked down at the swirling, muddy river and
remembered telling her aunt, "Gee, wouldn't you hate to swim in
this dirty water?"

"All aboard," the captain shouted.

CARL CORIELL
PEKIN PUBLIC LIBRARY

7

SURPRISE TICKET

FIFTEEN-YEAR-OLD Carl Coriell heard such wonderful stories about the Figure-Eight Roller Coaster. What a thrill it was to ride it, his friends would say. But that was like the other side of the world to young Carl.

Earlier that evening, Carl had stood at rigid attention, held his right hand up, palm out and fingers up. He repeated the oath with the others: *I will do my duty to God and Country. I will do my best to help others, whatever it costs me. I know the scout law and will obey it.* A skinny kid with short, brown hair and thin, straight lips, Carl was hardly distinguishable from the other scouts who looked like younger versions of British Army Lieutenant General Robert Baden-Powell in their khaki choke-collar tunics, knee breeches, canvas leggings and their campaign hats, later to be recognized as 'Smokey the Bear' hats, among other names. Baden-Powell wrote *Principles of Scouting* and founded the Boy Scouts in 1908, a movement that quickly caught on in the United States.

The scout uniform with its wool pants and long-sleeved shirts may have felt like wearing a bulky blanket, but for all its "smartness and equality," it was also very practical. The shirts had thick, strong seams that could be made into a makeshift stretcher, and the hat's leather straps could serve as an emergency tourniquet. The Boy Scout was a walking first aid kit. Carl looked at the clock and realized that he needed to hurry. He gave the other scouts the secret sign and rushed out the door.

It was a Friday, the day after the Fourth of July holiday, and the town of Pekin had put on quite a show. The Gehrig 7th Regiment Band had worked its magic by performing renditions of Sousa marches to appreciative crowds lining the cobblestone streets. The patriotic music coming from the band was a boost for young Carl, whose own brother Vern Coriell, a circus showman and acrobat, known as the 'Toad,' was one of the fighting 'doughboys' overseas. (Vern's most famous act was bouncing up a flight of stairs using only his head—no hands or feet!) "Pekin's man of the circus!" is how Carl affectionately described his big brother. Carl watched as bandleader Charles Gehrig smiled and waved the baton. Glorious multi-colored fireworks blasted off to the rousing music. The crowd had roared in approval.

The Gehrig name and band had been a mainstay in Pekin for many years thanks to a little ingenuity and a town's love of music. In the mid-1800s, Charles' father, Edward Gehrig Sr., a civil war veteran, cigar maker and musician, formed a small musical group in Peoria and traveled downriver to entertain at dances and other functions. The town of Pekin liked Gehrig's music so much they invited him to open a cigar shop and start a community band. Gehrig came and stayed. For nearly four decades, the band played and the crowds showed their enthusiastic support. Then in 1901, Edward died and Charles took over, keeping the band in the family and where it belongs, the city proclaimed, "in the capable hands of a Gehrig."

"There are many other and larger musical organizations in Central Illinois," the *Pekin Daily Times* boasted, "but for real music, the Pekin band takes first rank with the best of them."

Carl ran to the Post Office at the corner of Elizabeth and South Capital. He waved to his dad William, a 40-year veteran of the postal service, grabbed his bicycle leaning against the back door, and pedaled madly toward the courthouse square—to sell popcorn.

Homer Hyers' fancy new Saxon automobile on Court Street was a good indication popcorn was nearby—Hyers was Carl's employer. Carl handed out bags of the salted popcorn and collected cash: 5¢ would get you an 'ample' bagful, 10¢ a 'family-size' bag, and a quarter got you the 'jumbo' bag. Carl was careful to say "thank you" and "come again" while under the watchful eye of his perfectionist boss.

Hyers must have told Carl to buck up for a busy night. The steamboat was coming to town, and the streets would soon be filled with potential customers heading to the landing at the foot of Court Street. They might want a treat before boarding. But young Carl Coriell was in for a surprise. Around dusk, as the crowds were making their way to the riverfront, Hyers told his youthful apprentice to take the rest of the evening off. He had a ticket for the steamer *Columbia,* and Carl could go if he wanted. The boy couldn't believe his luck. The boat was going upriver to the Al Fresco Amusement Park and *the Figure-Eight Roller Coaster!*

Carl grabbed the ticket from Hyer's hand and, still bearing the burden of the heavy scout uniform—one that became even more cumbersome when wet—held onto his hat and ran with the others down Court Street.

He had a boat to catch, a ride to the other side of the world.

FOR A WHOLE WEEK Lisle Burns fought with her mother about taking a ride on the *Columbia.* She begged and begged, but Mom stood her ground. The late-night excursions were too "public" for an innocent teenage girl to go alone, Lisle was told. Her mother was determined. Just as determined, Lisle continued to wheedle and chip away at her mother's defenses. After seven days of relentless effort, she eventually broke through. She got permission to go.

A pretty gal with a flair for the dramatic, Lisle graduated high school with honors and was voted senior class president 1918. Her friends teased her for "having the ability to faint"—or to feign fainting. In her yearbook, Lisle jokingly listed her occupation as "boasting" and said the one thing she hated most was "homely boys." Now the girl who was "not as quiet as outward appearances indicate" was ready for a night of dancing and socializing on a moonlight cruise up the river.

She was also in love, or so she thought, with a guy named Leo who was shipping out soon to join the war effort. This could be their last night together for some time. He would be hanging out with some buddies, but she was sure he would be just as excited to see her as she would be to see him. Lisle reached into her bedroom closet and took out the pretty graduation dress she had worn a month before. It was white with a pleated skirt. This would be perfect, she thought, and ran to the riverfront to meet her beau.

LUCILLE BRUDER NEARLY FAINTED from lack of breath when she and her brother John came running down Court Street, huffing and puffing along the way. She hadn't expected to be so late. Lucille had made arrangements to meet six co-workers at the dirt landing in Pekin and wait for the steamboat *Columbia* to arrive. But there was a snag. Lucille was delayed at home on Caroline Street.

What a disappointment it would be if I didn't show up, she thought. The crowd was expected to be large, and the boarding would take some time. Lucille knew she had to hurry.

This wasn't the way the 18-year-old graduate had planned it. Her father Romey, a cigar maker, and mother Emma didn't want her to go. It was late and, well, her parents were worried. Lucille convinced them it was safe, and they insisted she bring along her younger brother John. Lucille resisted at first but eventually gave in. John could go, too, but they needed to leave—now! John and Lucille made a run for it. In the distance, they could see the black smokestacks above the tree line.

"Run to catch it," Lucille shouted, in full stride.

FARTHER DOWN COURT STREET, in a house blocks away from the crowds, nine-year-old Wilma White was enjoying the company of her two older cousins, Ana and Dorothy. The two sisters were visiting from Iowa and had seen the ad for the *Columbia*. A night out would be perfect, they thought.

They asked Wilma's mother, their Aunt Minnie, if they could take little Wilma along. Minnie hesitated. It would be too late, she told them, for a nine-year-old. The two teenage girls pleaded their case. Wilma wanted to go!

"I'll make you a pan of fudge candy, your favorite," Minnie told her daughter.

It was settled.

Aunt Minnie had won the battle.

Wilma stayed home. Ana and Dorothy would go on the *Columbia* that night without their young cousin.

LEO MACDONALD MAY HAVE driven his vehicle to the landing like many others or just hoofed it. The Dixon, Illinois, native had spent the summer working in Pekin and was looking forward to a little "batching it up" with his three buddies, the Lohmann brothers, Hermann, Rudolph and Paul.

Hermann Lohmann may have given Leo a playful punch to the gut when they met that night. That was his thing. He was a professional boxer by trade and loved to tease his buddy. 'Weenie' was his nickname because of his diminutive stature (only four feet nine) but he was built like a tank, stocky and strong. Like most fighters, because of the high number of bouts fought, his record was an even mix of wins and losses. But 'Weenie' was no slouch when it came to fighting top competitors. Introduced at each bout as 'The Pekin Kid,' he challenged three times for the bantamweight crown, ending up with two 'no decisions.' The 'Kid' was all business in the ring, but tonight, the compact dynamo was looking to cut it up in a different way.

Hermann's brother Rudolph, whom his pals called 'Curly,' wanted nothing to do with his sibling's kidding around that night. He wanted a drink! Curly was having second thoughts about going on the trip after his buddy Leo told him the story about how the *Columbia* hit rough weather and ran into an island. The pilot was able to ease off and safely make it back to shore. A little "back-and-forth" is the way Leo described it. Nothing to it, he told his buddy. But Curly wasn't so sure. He wanted a closer look. He leaned over the bank and looked downriver to see if the grand steamer was on its way.

Meanwhile, Leo was looking around for someone else. He glanced over the crowd and spotted his young lady friend running toward him with open arms. She was as pretty as ever in her new dress—a white graduation dress with a pleated skirt. Leo smiled. Lisle Burns had a big smile on her face too.

NEARBY, LUCILLE AND JOHN Bruder had reached the landing after a final sprint. Panting and winded, they just made it up the gangplank before the stage was raised. "Now I need to find my friends," Lucille said to her brother.

AS THE PASSENGERS finished boarding, Aunt Minnie was turning in for the night and reprimanding herself for worrying so much about Ana and Dorothy. Her nieces were capable and old enough to be out. Minnie went to bed hoping for a peaceful night's rest and knowing at least one thing wouldn't weigh heavy on her mind as she drifted off. Down the hall, tucked safely under the covers, was a satisfied nine-year-old girl soundly sleeping off a belly full of fudge.

FRANKIE FOLSOM
MURPHY LIBRARY UNIVERSITY OF WISCONSIN-LA CROSSE

8

FRANKIE FOLSOM

A MASTERPIECE!

Russian-born artist Karl Briullov had finally made it. His painting *The Last Days of Pompeii* was getting rave reviews. The massive work–183 inches tall and 236 inches wide–had just been unveiled at the artist's studio in Rome. It was 1833. Briullov was praised for translating to canvas what Pliny the Younger had transcribed when he witnessed the destruction of Pompeii by Mount Vesuvius in 79 AD:

> You could hear women lamenting, children crying, men shouting. There were some so afraid of death that they prayed for death. Many raised their hands to the gods, and even more believed that there were no gods any longer and that this was one unending night for the world.

The poet Sir Walter Scott stared at Briullov's masterwork for more than an hour before describing it as "not just a painting, but an epic in colours."

Next year, the writer Edward Bulwer-Lytton, also inspired by

Briullov's painting, wrote a fictionalized version of the tragedy. *The Last Days of Pompeii* became a popular novel. In 1877, a stage version of the book was performed in London's Queen Theater. The adaptation featured a volcanic eruption, an earthquake and lavish Roman banquet scene complete with "all the naughty parts." It was an expensive, colossal flop. The volcano wouldn't erupt, the earthquake never shook and an acrobat on a tight rope—said to have the suppleness of an elephant—fell into the frightened cast like a "stricken buffalo."

Gee, would it play in Peoria?

William and Emma Capoot wanted to find out. The Pekin couple had tickets to a performance of the *The Last Days of Pompeii* for July 12, 1892. The small packet boat *Frankie Folsom* was offering rides from Pekin to Peoria for patrons who wanted to see the play and take in a fireworks display at Lakeview Park. The *Frankie Folsom* headed out that evening with a passenger load of 40, including the crew.

The ten-mile cruise upriver was uneventful. The play, considerably less ostentatious than the London production, went off without a hitch. The fireworks were impressive. "Prof. Paine has been giving a pyrotechnic display [in Peoria] for the past two weeks," the *Decatur Daily Republican* noted. "A good view of the exhibition can be obtained from the lake in the northern part of the city, and large numbers on excursion and small rowboats took advantage of the free exhibition."

The patrons returned to the *Frankie Folsom* around 10 PM, and Captain Edward Loesch backed the ship out and headed downriver for the trip home to Pekin. It was a warm night, but the air seemed unsettled. The darkening clouds were scarcely visible in the night sky.

Then with hardly any warning to the captain, crew or passengers, a wind storm struck the boat. "The storm burst with a suddenness that was remarkable," the *New York Times* reported. "It blew up with rapidity little short of marvelous. Every gust of the squall would sweep some poor unfortunate into the waves." Captain Loesch attempted to ground the boat, but it was too late. It capsized, trapping those still onboard. "A window was smashed in, and a woman pulled out," the *Times* reporter wrote. "She was breathing but died in a few seconds."

"As the volume of water rushed into the cabin," the *Times* continued, "frantic efforts were made to escape. One man clambered through a window, only to fall into the lake. Furniture was shifted about and many were injured by it, [knowing] they were unable to make any efforts at escape."

"The cruel waves of the Illinois tonight bore down to death a score of persons who were enjoying themselves on the *Frankie Folsom*," the *Daily Republican* reported. "Owing to the howling tempest, the cries of the passengers could not be heard."

IN ALL, TWELVE PERISHED. William and Emma Capoot barely escaped with their lives. "News of the terrible disaster went through the town like a charge of electricity over a copper wire," the *Peoria Star* reported the next day.

Now nearly 26 years later to the day, the Capoots were headed back to the foot of Court Street in Pekin to the same spot where the *Frankie Folsom* boarded that tragic July night. They were going on the *Columbia* for a midnight cruise.

The Capoots could thank their neighbors on Washington Street for the dubious honor. The 60-year-old printer and his 55-year-old wife had vowed never to go on the water again, especially on a steamboat and certainly not on the Illinois River. Their neighbors persisted. William resisted at first. "No more boats for me," he often said, stubbornly. But there was something about this night and this boat that changed his mind.

In the fall of 1917, after another busy excursion season, the *Columbia* was steered down to Mounds City, Illinois, where it spent the better part of September and October receiving an overhaul at the Howard Ship Company. Captain Mehl planned to have new timbers and stringers installed, and he intended to repair or replace about two-thirds to three-fourths of the planking. The hull was rebuilt with a new three-quarter-inch steel plate. With a new paint job the boat was ready for its annual inspection. Mehl reportedly spent $17,000 on repairs and was rewarded with a glowing report from federal inspectors. In fact, they were so impressed by the boat's condition that they dubbed her "the safest boat on Western waters." Mehl couldn't have been happier. In ads that summer the boat was touted as the NEW STEAMER *COLUMBIA* and the words SAFETY FIRST were painted on its side.

"We expect a big year in the excursion trade," Mehl said.

Mehl had good reason to be confident in 1918. The excursion business was booming. The *Columbia* was booked in advance with all sorts of chartered picnic trips and organizations and clubs hosting their annual meetings and gatherings, sometimes two or more a year. Just a year earlier, in 1917, Mehl ended the *Columbia*'s excursion season in style by hosting a "big cabaret show" blowout. And a few days before that, the boat was packed with "Pekin baseball fans" as the traveling American Baseball League held its reception on the *Columbia* in route to Havana for a big game with the Distiller team of the new Central League. "Both teams and their backers will go on this excursion and most of Central Illinois is going to the game," the ads crowed. "Meet and shake hands with Ty Cobb and other crack players." The *Columbia* left Pekin at 11 AM and didn't return until 8:30 that night. The round-trip ticket for the event cost 50¢.

In a gesture of good will, before the start of the new season, Mehl offered the new and improved *Columbia* to the war effort. "She is the only river steamer so far offered," he boasted. "She has not yet been called and until she is, the present contracts and services will be carried out."

Mehl's assertion that he offered the *Columbia* to the government for use in the war was likely correct, but very few steamboats were called to serve. Railroads played a bigger role in the war effort at home than riverboats. The rails carried the heavy goods, mostly coal, to the Eastern ports. When transport needs could not be met by trainloads, river transportation took over, but it was scarce, and usually involved less crucial if still necessary goods.

In Madison, Indiana, several women formed 'the shirt club,' making cotton undershirts, bedsacks and other items to be used by the troops. The women worked from home and received a certain amount of money for each article they sewed. In time, more than 2,000 women joined up to make garments and sheets by the box loads. The question was how to get the boxes to the cargo and military ships on the coast. The trains were full. Since Madison was conveniently located on the Ohio River and just north of the busy steamboat town of Jeffersonville, Indiana (across from Louisville), paddlewheel boats and trucks were used to transport the goods upstream.

Mehl must have figured his boat could handle both passengers and whatever trade demands the government had, perhaps transporting goods down the river to St. Louis and the mouth of the Mississippi or upriver to LaSalle, Illinois, where a barge could take the supplies to Chicago and the big steamers that could carry the load across the Great Lakes. But the *Columbia* was never called to serve in any government capacity, and Mehl likely was relieved, since he already had the season fully booked with excursions.

NOW CONVINCED THAT steamboats were structurally stronger and safer than they were two decades earlier, William Capoot took his wife by the arm as they strolled down to the dirt landing. Maybe it was safety in numbers. Maybe it was the stable weather. Maybe it was just the ribbing from friends and neighbors for all those years. Whatever changed their minds that night, it was a decision they made together and a journey they would take together—just as they had 26 years earlier on a boat to Peoria to see a play. "Lightning doesn't strike twice in the same place," William reassured his wife as they boarded the *Columbia,* together—arm in arm.

TOP: AL FRESCO AMUSEMENT PARK
BOTTOM: FAMOUS FIGURE-EIGHT ROLLER COASTER
PEORIA HISTORICAL SOCIETY (PHS)

9

AL FRESCO

LOOK UP! THERE ATOP *the circle swing! Keep your eye on the man attached to the wire! He's on fire!*

A gasp from the crowd and then—whoosh!—the flaming man bent his knees, leaped forward and slid down the wire and into the river with a splash.

He's okay, folks! The crowd went wild.

Thanks for watching the Slide For Life!

And welcome to the Al Fresco Amusement Park!

Thanks to a visionary Chicago 'capitalist' named Vernon Seaver, the Al Fresco Amusement Park opened its castle-like gates in June 1904 and became an instant success. Seaver was president of the Trans-Continental Amusement Company at the time, and with true entrepreneurial fortitude decided to build several amusement parks similar to the popular White City Amusement Park in Chicago. The amusement parks with the White City label would eventually appear in several U.S. cities along with foreign countries, like the United Kingdom and Australia. They were scaled-down versions of Chicago's World Columbian Exposition in 1893, famously known as the 'White City' for its striking, all-white, elaborately designed structures. Crowds were mesmerized by the beauty of the gleaming buildings, especially at night when thousands of electric lights lit up the elegantly designed facades. But the buildings themselves, built mostly of white stucco instead of stone due to time and budgetary constraints, were not meant to last. When the Exposition was over, most of the structures were either torn down or destroyed by fire (in time, only one building survived and later was rebuilt to become today's Museum of Science and Industry). The memories of the Exposition however could continue, at least, on a much smaller scale. The White City Amusement Parks were not exact replicas of the 'White City,' only a representation of some of its most popular attractions, like the Midway and the Ferris Wheel. When Seaver was looking for a new location to build a park, Peoria was on his list. He took a boat ride down the Illinois River to take a look.

It's easy to see how Seaver was attracted to the second-largest city in the state and the biggest metropolitan area on the Illinois River. Like Marquette some 200 years before, he was drawn by the high bluffs and breathtaking vistas coming around the bend. "The city is a delight to the eye," its town leaders later boasted. "The great river which lends its name to the state, here broadened into a lake, sweeps by in a gentle, outward curve seven miles long, from the narrows above to the converging and wood-crowned heights below. There are few more charming landscapes on earth than that which greets the eye from the brow of these high bluffs."

Even the town's name was considered sacred to its roots. "It would be difficult to find among all the names of cities, American or European," the city touted, "a more euphonious combination of letters than go to form the names Peoria, Illinois." Both Peoria and Illinois were names of pure Indian origin, although their original pronunciations and meanings have been debated since as far back as 1673. That's when Marquette first recorded the word *Peouarea* in his notes with a different sounding [oo] or [w] in the middle than is used today. The Peorias were part of a pack of Indian tribes that made up the Illini Confederacy.

The meaning of the word 'Peoria' has never been officially determined. There are many translations. They include: 'runaways or seeders,' 'carriers or packers,' 'he who comes with carrying a back on his back,' 'a place where there are fat beasts,' 'prairie fire,' and 'turkey.' The most commonly used translation is a variation of perhaps the most engaging of the group and shortened to mean 'land of fat beast.' But there was no menacing creature lurking in the woods. The 'fat beast' likely referred to the wide part of the river known as Peoria Lake.

The name 'Illini' is rooted from the word *Ionca*, which according to *Place Names of Illinois* has an unknown name and origin. In 1666, it was pronounced 'illnoowek,' again with an [oo] sound in the middle. The name was translated into French where the 'wek' was replaced by 'ois' or race. Its meaning too is interpreted in several ways but always with a common theme: 'people' or 'man.' 'Excellent people', 'superior people,' or 'perfect and accomplished people' were all derived from Marquette's original observation when he wrote: "When one speaks of 'Illinois' it is as if one said in their language 'the men'—as if the other Savages were looked upon by them merely as animals." The Indians in the Confederacy were physically well-built specimens, so Marquette was on to something. The most commonly used meaning is ramped up a bit by a more descriptive variation, 'the perfect manly man.'

But it wasn't just the name or the view that was attractive. "Below is the busy city with its stores and shops and public buildings... broad streets...shaded homes all stirring life...its street cars gliding like a weaving shuttle in and out...its steamboats at the landing, the silent expanse at the lake...and moving railroad trains."

And yet "look back at the bluff from the city below," promoters challenged the unmoved, and behold "its magnificent fronts now crowned with noble residences with all their appointments of shade and golden plats.

"All these take offer to him who takes delights in the works of nature and of man and especially to the one who first emerges upon the scene from the level prairie land behind, a landscape of quiet beauty that can never be forgotten."

Arriving by yacht and inspecting Peoria's shoreline for the first time, Vernon Seaver must have felt like an unidentified famous traveler "familiar with many cities and lands" who beheld the scene some years ago and exclaimed, "It is the finest site for a city I ever saw."

The idealist from Chicago found a perfect spot for his new venture, and he promptly leased the land from a prominent jeweler in town named Thomas Webb. Seaver's new amusement park was located just below the north bluff of Peoria in an area known as Peoria Heights. While the name 'Al Fresco' means 'to enjoy the outdoors,' the park would later become known as a 'trolley park' because it was funded in part by the streetcar companies in Peoria, who saw a good opportunity to increase their business and profits.

"The street car line was expanded," wrote the *Peoria Journal-Transcript*, "from the end of Adams Street to a point just above the amusement park." The new streetcar line would end at the top of Grandview Drive, a tree-lined road on the top of the bluff with breathtaking, panoramic views of the river. There the passengers would step off and walk the rest of the way down the Gibson Path to the park. Even the path was lined with "electric lights, a water fountain and comfort stations." The demand was so great that the Old Central Streetcar Company had to put two or three more cars behind the first motorized one just to accommodate the crowds.

The park's north shore location, known as a tranquil place to enjoy views of the river, was transformed overnight. The peaceful setting was now filled with glowing lights and constant music, footsteps and chatter. "The north shore became more accessible and soon teemed with humanity seeking excitement," the papers reported shortly after the park's opening, "but not the sweet relaxation that we know and grew to love for a brief while."

Once inside the park, patrons could brave the Figure-Eight Roller Coaster, a twisting, turning thrill ride said to be the first of its kind anywhere in the world, or the impressive Ferris Wheel that stood 65 feet from the axle to the ground and could hold eight people per gondola.

The Ferris Wheel was a treat. The large circular structure had become popular just a decade earlier at the Columbian Exposition in Chicago when an engineer named George Washington Ferris was commissioned (actually his spinning wheel design beat several others) to build a monument that would match or rival the Eiffel Tower—which was featured with great fanfare at the previous World Exposition in Paris.

In Chicago, the Ferris Wheel was a major success and to many a pleasant surprise. Even before the wheel was built, critics denounced it. It was unstable, they said, prone to breakdowns and downright dangerous. It looked like it would fall right over due to weight or resistance. Ferris proved them all wrong. Even with gusty winds whipping off the lake, the 265-foot-tall wheel with an 825-foot circumference and 36 'bus-sized' passenger cars was as sturdy as a brick, and despite a construction delay that consumed several weeks, it worked flawlessly on every turn, just as Ferris had told them it would. Ferris's own wife Margaret was one of the first to proudly ride it. Due to its popularity at the Exposition, scaled-down versions were built in theme parks throughout the country.

While the Ferris Wheel was perfect for sitting back, relaxing and enjoying the sweeping views, the roller coaster was a fast-paced 'thrill' ride that gave some riders goose bumps and others downright panic attacks. "I never was so frightful in my life," wrote Agatha Wales of her first—and presumably last—experience on a coaster in 1914. "If the dear Lord will forgive me this time [for riding], I will never do so again." But others were ecstatic. "Before you can remember what comes after 'Thy kingdom come,'" one patron cheerfully described the twisty ride, "it shoots you to the stars again." The figure-eight design was said to be a new feature of the ever-changing, twisting world of roller coasters, and Seaver got on board, opening one of the first at his newly named Al Fresco Amusement Park in Peoria.

Many of the park's features were recycled from other theme parks, including the benches, lights and statues that were previously used at the 1904 World's Fair in St. Louis. It cost 10¢ to enter the park— "a bargain"—and extra for the rides and shows. "A summer resort free from vulgarity," is how the *Peoria Journal-Transcript* described the new park, "where families can go and have innocent fun."

The crowds ate it up.

There were daredevil, high-wire and diving acts, a Wild West show, music and dancing, and even a swimming beach with bathhouses where patrons could change clothes and rent bathing suits for 25¢. One man calling himself 'Rollo the Limit' roller skated down a 75-foot incline, turned a backflip and landed on a platform where eight men waited to catch him. When 'Rollo' missed, which was said to have been often, he had to be cut out of the platform. The Cherry Sisters, a singing act, were said to have been so bad that people threw "things" at them, forcing the frightened girls to exit behind a screen. 'Master Tommy,' who dove 75 feet into four feet of water, was one of the high-diving acts. A horse was listed as the other.

The amusement features were endless. There were hypnotists, palm readers, a house of mirrors, a thrill swing, a tunnel of love, camel rides, motorcycle-jump acts, balloon ascensions, costume photograph booths, escape artists, and that impossible Slide for Life, with the flaming man zipping down the wire into the river.

The most popular attraction by attendance was the Japanese Garden. The large, two-story pavilion overlooked the river and was always packed with patrons who could "enjoy schooners of beer and other refreshments while watching free entertainment." Big-time vaudeville acts and dance troupes were often on the bill, including a trick artist named Harry Houdini. In another pavilion, patrons could "dance to the music of a piano or fiddle" for 5¢ a dance. There were free 'big band' concerts at night.

The Fourth of July was always busy at the park. A 'fort' was built on the boat dock, and a barge was decorated to look like a warship. Men would set off fireworks in a spectacle that was described as "the most realistic battle to be seen."

The steamboats would come, too. The park was a perfect stop for excursion trips on the river, especially for those who lived outside of Peoria and far from the convenience of a streetcar line. A long pier was built to accommodate several boats at a time. The steamers would be tied to the capstans along the pier, the stage lowered, and passengers could step off and enjoy a stroll down the park's colorfully-lit midway or brave a thrill ride before heading back to the boat for the trip home. Usually the stay was brief but memorable. The *Columbia* docked there on July 5 as scheduled but only for a half-hour.

GEORGE HYME HAD STEPPED off the boat that night at the Al Fresco Amusement Park, fidgety and frustrated. A Navy veteran and experienced sailor, Hyme had noticed the *Columbia* looked low in the water when he boarded in Pekin.

"The boat's not safe," he told his wife at the time. "That could mean water in the hull." On the trip upriver, he approached a deckhand with his concerns, but he later claimed he was shrugged off.

A whistle sounded to signal *Columbia* passengers to return to the boat for the trip home. The shrill blast of air would sometimes take patrons by complete surprise. They were so caught up in the excitement of the park that they lost track of time and had to make a mad dash, just reaching the boat before the stage was lifted. George Hyme and his wife were in no hurry. In fact, they weren't going back on the boat at all. They stood on the shore and watched as the large steamer pulled away from the pier and disappeared back downriver. The old sailor trusted his instinct. He and his wife took a train home instead—perhaps saving their lives, certainly avoiding a catastrophe.

TOP: STEAMER COLUMBIA AS IT LOOKED ON JULY 5, 1918
MURPHY LIBRARY UNIVERSITY OF WISCONSIN-LA CROSSE
BOTTOM: THREE UNIDENTIFIED WOMEN ON THE RAIL DECK
OF THE COLUMBIA; PEORIA HISTORICAL SOCIETY (PHS)

10

FULL AHEAD

"EVERYBODY UPSTAIRS!" shouted Captain Mehl, as the dancers stopped in their shoes.

They were understandably confused. It had been a chaotic few minutes. The boat had unexpectedly run ashore, and a branch had broken through a window. The ship came to a brief stop and was backing up. There were no warning bells or emergency signals. Now the band was playing again, and everything seemed to be back to normal. The gaiety and laughter from earlier in the evening had returned.

They were just minutes from home.

"Everybody upstairs!" shouted the captain again. The urgency in his voice seemed to rise as he repeated the order. Mehl knew what the others did not. There was water in the hull, a full two feet, and the boat was slowly losing buoyancy.

Twenty-year-old Carl Aiken was making ice cream at the concession stand when he heard the captain's voice across the room. "I was talking to a girl," he recalled. "Addie was her name. I knew her well. We had run into a bank, I think I told her. She asked me if it hurt anything. I said, no, it didn't hurt anything that I know of."

"Get upstairs, everybody, quick!" Mehl bellowed over the music. The captain's next words got everyone's attention: "She's going down!"

This time the band stopped for good.

Tom Williams in the pilothouse heard the captain's orders to run the ship ashore. He had to make a quick decision. Send the ship back into the jagged shoreline, or try for the shallower water and softer landing on the other side of the river. The middle of the Illinois River at that point was the dividing line between two counties, Peoria and Tazewell. Peoria County was on the west side of the river, or the starboard side of the boat when heading downstream. The shoreline on the Peoria side was underdeveloped and overgrown, all hanging tree branches, submerged stumps and pointed rocks. The east, or Tazewell County side of the river was lined mostly with hanging willows and bushes. But between the brush was a clearing dotted with a few residences, then known as Wesley City. A dirt road and railroad tracks were also on the Tazewell side. The town of Pekin was on that side of the river, too, just a mile or so downstream.

Williams had moved stern-first away from the Peoria County shoreline, taking some broken branches along. Now the bow was pointing toward the Tazewell County side. It would be impossible, Williams thought, to turn the boat around and ram the Peoria shore again. He had no other choice. The boat would have to go ashore on the Tazewell County side. He ordered full ahead and started to turn the wheel to port.

Mark Twain once wrote that a pure steamboat pilot "cares nothing about anything on earth except the river." A good pilot must rely on his memory to understand the "shape of the bend and the shape of the river perfectly."

"A pilot can't stop with merely thinking a thing is so and so; he must know it," Twain wrote.

Pilot Williams must have *known* it that night. Several years before, while steering a steamer named *Peoria,* he ran into a bank in a narrow channel near LaSalle, Illinois. The boat struck just above the water line. "I could not feel a jar in the pilothouse," he later recalled. "Neither I nor the master thought anything of it." Williams backed the boat off the bank and landed a mile-and-a-half away. The hull was examined and found to be carrying three feet of water. "I did not have a thought of danger," Williams said later of that night, adding that he also knew nothing about the water in the hull. Now Williams had struck the shore again, and with a pilot's instinct and memory that Mark Twain says "must incessantly cultivate until he has brought it to absolute perfection," he made another fateful decision. Williams moved the *Columbia* back to midstream and steered the boat to the safety of the Tazewell County side of the river.

In the dance hall, the boat seemed to shake again.

BELOW DECK, IN THE engine room, Allen Davidson watched the lights flicker, then go out. The water hit the dynamos, he thought. The ship was thrown into an "inky darkness."

If the urgency of the captain's orders or the earlier brush with the shore—including a shattered window—wasn't enough cause for alarm, now there were several new and profoundly more serious issues at hand: The boat had shaken again; the lights were out; and dancers were literally being swept across the room by an upending floor—the boat was listing!

Alta Cook jumped from her seat and tried to grab her friend's mother who had fallen and was sliding along the smooth dance floor. "People fell down to their knees," she said. "Then halfway across the dance floor it seemed to fly up into our faces." The water was over the rails.

Roy Jones, a crew member who was working in the engine room, could hear the thud of panicked footsteps above. "I saw water rushing in over the bow," he said.

"Water quickly poured over the decks," the *Chicago Tribune* reported, "and scores were trapped as they vainly tried to breast the torrents of water that poured down companionways and blocked the exits to the upper decks." The next few moments were radically different, as the *Tribune* describes:

All in the briefest space of time there were a million emotions put into action. At first there was no shouting, no calling aloud. Each person silently and grimly tugged to save the thing which seemed most important at the moment. Feet thudded with ridiculous celerity across the slippery decks as the list to starboard sent men, women and children into a furious race downhill.

Chairs and tables, parts of the ship's gear and metal buckets clattered abeam as the decks went awash. Men, women and children clutched and gripped and held fast to each other and to fixed objects and to movable things. An indescribable chaos of things and persons swept down against the wall of the dancing salon and stuck there. All movable things in the hull deck went with a swift slide into the river. Then the silence broke and a wild chorus of screams and shouts for help burst out.

The *Washington Times* put it this way: "The entire scene was turned from gaiety and pleasure into a hideous nightmare of horror."

AUGUST MEHL, THE SHIP'S purser, heard his brother shout for everyone to get up top. "The crowd rushed for the upper decks, and I ran for the engine room," he said. He saw his wife running ahead of him on the companionway and ran after her. When they reached the second deck, the boat listed. "I saw my wife thrown overboard," August said. "I grabbed at her skirt, but it slipped from my fingers."

At this point, passengers in the dance hall describe an eerily similar perception. Thrown into sudden darkness and struggling to gain their footing on a slippery, tilted dance floor, there was a moment just before the ceiling came crashing down when they all heard it—or thought they heard it—the horrific sound of timbers cracking.

COLUMBIA'S FALLEN SMOKESTACK
MURPHY LIBRARY UNIVERSITY OF WISCONSIN-LA CROSSE

11

FALLEN BEAMS

IT WAS ALL OVER in an instant. The blackness, the rushing water and the dance hall ceiling that dropped like a "house of eggshells… crashing down into kindling," as a reporter from the *Chicago Tribune* described it.

The speculation of how it happened would vary considerably and eventually would be the task of investigators to figure out. The "hull broke into two halves" was one reasonable explanation. Another was that the hog chains, the thick iron cables that supported and balanced the weight of the hull, had snapped. Some believed that the old boat had simply rotted and cracked. All was conjecture.

Only a few facts were clearly known: The boat had struck the shore, a window had broken, and the hull was leaking. Why it "crumpled like a match stick box" before sinking was anyone's guess, at least initially. Over the next few days rumors even circulated that the crew, including the pilot, had been drinking—and who was that pretty woman seen coming in and out of the pilothouse?

Spirited discussions, speculative assumptions and hyperbolic allegations all erupted to explain a terrifying reality: The boat had collapsed and pancaked on top of itself with only a portion of its roof, the pilothouse and half the stern paddlewheel sticking out of the murky water. The rest of the boat, for the most part, was in long, tattered pieces. Several jack staffs poked through the wreckage at odd angles like needles in a pin cushion. The gangplank boom was still hanging and leaning forward off the sunken bow, and the twin stacks had toppled over, one to the starboard and the other directly on top of the boat. The *Columbia* settled on the muddy river bottom in about 20 feet of water.

Unlike the stories of the *Titanic,* where anticipation and fear would fester in the cold night air before the huge ship went to the bottom of the Atlantic, for the partygoers on the *Columbia* there was be no time for reasoning or any sort of preparation. No orchestra played *Nearer, My God, to Thee.* No shivering matrons in lifeboats watched their loved ones perish before their eyes. For many on the *Columbia,* the arrival at death's door came swiftly and without warning. The boat collapsed and sank almost instantaneously.

"The ceiling of the dancing pavilion thundered down with a mighty weight," newspapermen Humphrey and Barrette wrote in their booklet *The Columbia Disaster.* "Huge I-beams which supported the upper deck fell prone across the polished floor, pinning beneath them scores of those entrapped."

Down in the wreckage, in a dance hall that was "crushed like an eggshell," hundreds of passengers were either trying to escape or were trapped by fallen beams, shredded timbers, broken shards and rising river water. Many were not moving at all. "Fate played kindly with some," was the phrase used by Humphrey and Barrette.

"I grabbed my girl and got a big gulp of water," said William Newman, who had danced around the room to be closer to the exit. "It was black, and I knew I was near dead."

"We could feel pipes and things fall on us," recalled Florence Schreck.

Guy McIntyre, the machinist who almost got whacked by a tree branch on the lower deck, this time narrowly avoided the falling debris. "The black water appeared, and I stuck my hand out and caught hold of a pillar," he said. "I pulled myself up and hung on to a cross beam." The beam was the same one he had admired earlier stretching across the upper part of the ceiling.

Esther Bellville was with her friend Verah Flowers. The two teens were teasing each other about nearly missing the ride back home after stepping off at the Al Fresco Amusement Park. "The whistle of the boat blew," Esther recalled, "and we made it just before the gangplank went up." They were enjoying a soda near the orchestra when the lights went out and the boat listed. "Dancers slid across the floor and towards us," she said. "Then the roof fell in. We grabbed a column, but it cracked in two, and I was thrown into dark waters, down and down."

"I couldn't swim," she added, "so I grabbed someone's hand and another person's foot." The hand didn't struggle, but the foot did. "I knew I had grabbed on to the leg of a swimmer." She held on for dear life.

Guy McIntyre clutched the cross beam and banged on the ceiling now resting just inches above the deck floor. "Men struggled about me," he said. "I got my lip cut and struck on the head." The spark from a match gave McIntyre a better view. He banged on the ceiling until it cracked. "Suddenly, I saw a light and yelled for help. Hands came through, and I pulled several women out."

Florence Schreck remembers the jolt, the ceiling falling and someone swooping her up. Then she hit the water and passed out. "I was in heaven," she said. "There was white and gold everywhere. It was beautiful."

Esther Belville held on to the "swimmer's" foot and made it through the window. The man who pulled her through thought the hands clinging to his leg belonged to someone else. When he turned and saw Esther, there was a look of shock and dread on his face. "He thought I was his wife!" Esther remembers. "He turned and went back to look for her." Another man asked Esther to help with his injured girlfriend. "He wanted me to give her artificial respiration," Esther recalls, "but someone else told me she was dead and pulled me away."

Alta Cook, who had reached for the hand of her friend's mother when the boat started to tilt, was now desperately trying to stay above water. "I held my breath, took a gulp of river water and held my breath again," she said. "It slammed me and others against the walls and ceilings."

John Reuling was struggling. He had become tangled in the wreckage and couldn't move. His wife Lottie, who John described as an "expert swimmer," made it to the shore first, but when she realized John wasn't behind her, she went back. She was hit in the head by falling debris and went under. John freed himself and swam to shore. Lottie never returned.

Arthur Knapp, the drummer in the orchestra, could see a sky-light window that was now close to ground level. He crawled through it to safety. Eugene Bailey, a piano player, was close by. He was standing near the orchestra with his brother Ben. "That's when the tremor was felt," Ben remembers. The deck began to tilt. "She's going down," Bailey told his brother. "Beat it!" Ben fled. He never saw his brother alive again.

Seventeen-year-old Emma Ropp heard someone crying, then "the lights went out and people went crazy," she said. "A man smashed a window and I crawled out." A woman rose up beside her and asked, "Can you swim?"

"No," said Emma.

"Hold on to my shoulders then," said the stranger. "Keep cool and don't choke me, or you will drown us both."

John Brooking and his wife Lydia were on the lower deck when the boat shivered. He recalled, "My wife said 'something awful has happened,' and I reassured her that we were just backing out. There was pandemonium—shrieks—people struggling and jumping overboard. Then the water came up around my feet and legs.

"I couldn't see anything so I jumped and caught a stanchion overhead with both hands and told my wife to hang on to me. She got her arms around my neck. The water came up over my shoulders. I heard my wife gurgle when the water reached her face.

"I couldn't let go with either hand for the current, chairs, things floating against us and the others struggling in the water. It took every bit of my strength to hang on. To let go meant certain death to us both. I managed to work my shoulder under her chin and 'hump' it up so her face was above the water."

Alice Masen was near the door on the dance floor when someone screamed, "The boat is sinking!" Just then the lights went out. "I groped for the door," Alice said, "and clung on to something. The deck was as steep as a roof and the boat lay over partly on its side. I couldn't crawl up, so I just held on."

Earnest Langston was in front of the candy counter when the panic began. "It passed like an electric shock through everyone," he remembered. "I got on a barrel to get out of the way. It fell with me and pinned me under it. The water began pouring in, but I didn't give up hope for a minute. Women began sobbing and gasping for breath and the cries were just terrible. I was thrown from the water and afterward was picked up."

"I can still see those people yet crying and wringing their hands," Langston would later tell a reporter. "They go back in forth across my eyes and I just can't brush the thoughts of them away."

Charles Grover was on board with his wife and two nieces. They were sitting near the dance floor deck when the crash came. Grover desperately beat out a window then reached for his wife's hand. With "great difficulty" he pulled her through. Then he turned to his nieces, Blanche and Mabel. He pulled Blanche through the hole and looked for Mabel who was "nowhere in sight." They found Mabel later on shore. She had jumped into the river when the boat went down and swam away–to safety. She was only ten years old.

Walter Fluegel got up to the top deck. "It was dark as pitch," he says. "I swam along the side where I believed my wife to be and dived down. When I came up again, she was there...only a foot from me!"

"The force of water was so strong," he added, "that it took a string of beads from one woman's neck and tore off one of my wife's stockings."

Outside in the still night air, the sound of muffled cries and screams carried across the river. In Wesley City, lamplights began to go on in the shacks beyond the brush. The peace of the evening had been violated.

Coal miner John Chance had been in his cabin lying on a cot

when the "brilliantly lighted" steamer passed by. He could hear the music and laughter as the boat drifted to the Peoria side and then back into the middle of the river. The lights went out, and he lost sight of the ship in the blackness. Chance turned to his work partner, Ben Wilson, and started to say something about how the boat didn't seem quite right to him, but before the words left his lips, "the shrieks of the dying" had reached his ears. He grabbed his miner's hat and headed out the door.

BACK IN THE CHAOS of the broken boat, a young girl felt the hand of another—a boy's hand—in the darkness. He pulled her up, and they held on to the gangplank boom for what seemed like forever. At least they were safe, she thought. "I'm going to marry you some day," she said, rewarding the young man's heroism.

Carl Coriell tipped his scout's hat and smiled.

ETHEL MEHL
COURTESY NANCY CLOUD LOESCHNER

12

STRAIGHT DOWN

AUGUST MEHL COULD ONLY watch and pray. His wife had been thrown overboard and was somewhere in the churning water. The fact that she could swim was of some comfort to him and her only hope. The sound of his brother's voice could still be heard up top. "Everybody upstairs," the captain kept shouting. August Mehl followed his brother's orders. He ran for the stairs and away from the surge of the rising waters, now rushing in like a wave. "The water was coming up to the staterooms on the top deck and immediately below the pilothouse on the listed side," August recalled.

As the purser of the *Columbia*, August Mehl was responsible for all things involving money, including the food, drinks, concessions and ticket sales. It was a thankless task with few rewards. The pilot and captain got all the glory, while the purser did all the brain work—like counting. When boarding, Mehl would set up a podium at the front of the ship and collect the tickets and cash. The job was well suited for a man whose brothers ran a tobacco shop—the empty cigar boxes made perfect money holders. If it was a hot and sunny day, he would use an umbrella on a long pole for shade. A head count would be based on tickets sold. There was no list of passengers by name.

August's wife Emma helped on the boat, too, usually in the kitchen or café on the lower deck. Both were running to the upper decks when the boat began to lean, then Emma went barreling over the rails. August reached for her trailing skirt but had to let go of it. He heard a splash but could see nothing else in the darkness. The lights were completely out.

CAPTAIN MEHL, SHOUTING orders the whole way, safely made it to the top deck. "I told everyone to get up just as quickly as possible," he recalled. "I could see that we were sinking fast." It was then that the ship croaked, groaned and fell. "I felt it go down, straight down," he added.

On the top deck, Captain Mehl found his wife injured and bleeding from a wound on the forehead. Ethel Mehl had been on the dance floor deck when the boat listed. "Something must have struck me in the head," she told her husband. "I came to in the water and grabbed a handrail. I reached for a life preserver. With one hand, I held on to the boat and with the other, the life preserver. I kept afloat until someone pulled me out."

"Keep cool, don't lose your head," the captain told his wife.

"I won't," she replied.

Mehl started handing out lifebelts that were packed about the netting in the hurricane deck rafters. One by one he threw them to rescuers below. "Is that you, McIntyre?" Mehl shouted. Guy McIntyre had crawled out of a small hole in the dance floor ceiling and was trying to keep his footing on the broken boards. "Take charge down there," Mehl said, "and do what you can to get these people to shore alive." Every able-bodied man was now a hand to help.

The two lifeboats—standard rowboats called 'skiffs'—were on the side of the boat just below the pilothouse. They were quickly lowered and filled by those who were the first to make it out of the death trap below. "Women and children first!" the men were heard shouting.

Engineer Davidson, first mate Edwards and deckhand Trippler were able to make it to the top deck. They had been the first to see the water in the hull and sense a problem. They quickly ran up the stairs. Captain Mehl would later marvel at the resiliency of his crew. "They all worked like heroes," he said.

Tom Williams was tossed around in the pilothouse but not seriously hurt. When the boat settled, he was able to tap on the bell rope. The bell—just aft of the pilothouse and between the now fallen stacks—tolled in distress.

"George is missing," one of the crew members must have told Mehl. George Stewart, a deckhand, was the only crew member of the *Columbia* not accounted for.

Harry Crall managed to climb up from the second deck. "I was talking to a woman who looked lost," he said. "I told her to stand where she was and wait for a boat." She looked at him with shallow, empty eyes. Crall turned around, then turned back again. The unfortunate woman was gone. "I think she fainted and drowned," he said. Crall's fears about the woman later were confirmed.

IN THE DISTANCE, on the Tazewell County side of the river, lights dotted the shoreline like fireflies that stayed lit. If there was a mist in the air before, now a cloud of dust and steam settled about the ship like a veil. It was tough to see past the broken rails, but the lights flickering along the shoreline were a sign that someone had heard the tolling bell and cries for help. Some of the beams seemed to be getting closer. Then through the smoky haze, several rowboats appeared with men ready for work. Some had their illuminated miner hats on.

Just minutes earlier in Wesley City, John Chance and Ben Wilson put on their mining hats and ran outside. Chance was half-asleep when he heard laughter and music outside the window of his moored cabin boat. He saw the *Columbia* drift toward the Peoria County shore and suddenly jerk back again. Then the lights went out, the music stopped, and so did the laughter. There was a brief silence, and then the sound of screams and cries could be heard in the distance. He roused Ben from sleep and went out into the night. They needed rowboats and extra hands.

In shanties along the shoreline, gas lamps popped on. Partially dressed men with sleep still in their eyes emerged from the shacks. Mostly fishermen of 'modest means,' these men knew the river well, and they knew what the tolling of a boat's bell meant. Chance rounded them up, and together they pushed the skiffs off the landing and rowed into the darkness like a brigade of soldiers.

"The screaming and calls for help rose into a soul-wrenching medley of appeal," is how a writer for the *Chicago Tribune* described it. "The river was suddenly and mysteriously dotted with boats. The oarsmen fought with their crazy oars against a swift current almost beyond their strength. But they reached the side of the 'broken beauty of the river.'"

On the "broken beauty," Captain Mehl and his crew were busy handing out life preservers and helping passengers who had escaped through the dance hall skylights. The two lifeboats were quickly filled and dispatched to shore. That's when they noticed several boats coming toward them. It was a reassuring sight. The beams of light from the miner hats helped too. They cut like thin swords through the misty air, but they provided something, anything, to help on this dark night. For the first time, the captain and crew could make out bodies in the river. Some were struggling, some were not.

As the makeshift band of brothers reached the sunken ship, their boats were besieged by frightened passengers struggling to tread water. Many had fallen in or jumped overboard when the *Columbia* listed and sank. Those who knew how to swim made it to shore. It wasn't far. The others were fighting for their lives. Pauline Binzuel was in the water. "When I came to the surface, people were swimming about me," she recounted. "I saw women in the water, and some of them had children. I can't say how many drowned, but those that I saw in the water seemed to be nearly exhausted." Pauline swam until a man came to her aid. "Some of the men were holding the women in their arms," she said, "and others were attempting to keep their heads above the river by clinging to clothing."

The men in the rowboats went to work. They grabbed at outstretched arms and pulled. The weight of wet clothes made the task immeasurably more difficult. Although women had begun to shed the floor-sweeping garments that were popular before the war, the heavy cotton fabric was still like a drag anchor when wet. The men doubled up, each grasping an arm and pulling with all their might. After being heaved onto the boat, the drenched and frightened passengers were taken to shore and into homes where they could "dry off and have a cup of coffee or a drink of whiskey."

Back on the boat, hearing the cries from below, rescuers began ripping back boards to reach the trapped and suffering. It wasn't long before they realized the grisly truth. The body of a woman with her hands clinging to a baby carriage was found through a small opening in the second deck. It was impossible to pull the woman and the baby carriage out together, so a man reached down and pried her fingers from the buggy's handle. He lifted the lifeless body through the opening and reached back down again, but the carriage was too big. It wouldn't fit. The buggy, with its gruesome cargo, would have to be removed later.

The men in the boats briefly stopped their rescue efforts when they heard a man shouting. A short, stocky man in a blue suit and hat had climbed to the highest part of the wrecked ship.

"She's all busted in!" Captain Mehl cried to the oarsmen. "For God's sake, go up and have Peoria keep any of the big boats from coming down here. They'd knock us all to pieces." Just then a familiar sound in the distance grew louder and closer.

The wail of approaching police sirens told them help was on its way.

LISLE BURNS
TAZEWELL COUNTY GENEALOGICAL AND HISTORICAL SOCIETY (TCGHS)

13

BLACKING OUT

JET BLACK AND SLICK—it was a cultivated look. Leo MacDonald greased back the sides of his hair with pomade and pulled his bangs over the top, combing it into a high mound in front. Call it a pompadour now—call it whatever back then. It was some head of hair. The pompadour would become a popular style for men in the 1950s and 1960s when rockabilly artists and actors who liked fast, hip-swiveling music, hot rods on the strip and cruise-in diners gave the look a new hipness. James Dean, Little Richard and Elvis Presley all had killer pompadours. But long before that wave hit, Leo McDonald's mash of hair must have turned some heads that night on the *Columbia*.

That's because most men at the time wore their hair short with a high part on the side, tight around the ears with thin sideburns. Then they plastered it down with waxy pomade. Always pomade. A 'military neatness' it was called, due to the fact that most 'young bucks' had anticipated losing their hair to Uncle Sam anyway.

Leo was different. He liked the flair in front.

Lisle Burns, his girl, liked it too.

Lisle was having a grand time on the *Columbia*. She had fought with her mother for a whole week to go on the boat that night and be with her beau Leo before he shipped out. She even wore her pretty graduation dress with the pleated skirt. It was soft and airy and waved about when she twisted, perfect for dancing.

Leo wasn't much for dancing, but he liked to watch. He had lost track of his pals the Lohmann brothers. His buddy Rudolph, a.k.a. Curly, was probably up top somewhere, he thought, hanging on to a railing and having a stiff drink. Leo's story about the *Columbia* ramming an island on an earlier excursion trip had rattled Curly to the bone. Curly told Leo he was going to stay close to the top deck, just in case.

Leo was standing by the soda fountain near the dance hall entrance when the boat shook. He was chatting with a young lady named McCune who had boarded with several dozen other passengers at Kingston Mines.

"Hey, Mac, what would you do if the boat sank?" she asked Leo.

Leo never got a chance to answer. Just then, it did.

The ceiling came down, the floor collapsed, and the last thing Leo remembered before "blacking out" was a marble soda fountain coming straight for his face. Then nothing.

Lisle remembered being on the dance floor when she felt a thud. "The boat struck the bank, and it was enough to knock some dancers off their feet," she said. Then the water came–quickly. "Next thing I knew, it was up to my neck." Then the ceiling hit the floor. Lisle struggled in the darkness. "I couldn't swim a peg," she said. She spotted a skylight window now lying low to the ground and crawled through it, but she lost her footing and slipped. "There were awnings on the windows. Every time I stepped on them, they gave way. All the way, I was praying every minute that my mother wouldn't hear about the wreck until I got home." She somehow managed to find her way to the top deck and waited for help. A friend named Jimmy Burton soon found her. There was a man directly behind Jimmy whose face was a "solid sheet of blood." Lisle recalled, "I didn't recognize him at first." Then she took a closer look. "Leo!" she cried and nearly fainted.

Leo had a "fearful gash" on his forehead from a direct hit from the soda fountain. "I had on a white shirt, and there wasn't a spot left that was white," he said. After Leo "came to," Jimmy Burton found him struggling to get his bearings. Burton grabbed him and together they crawled through a window and reached the safety of the upper deck where they found Lisle. That's where they stayed until a rescue boat arrived.

Leo insisted on escorting Lisle home before going to the hospital. He recovered from his head wound and soon shipped off to the war, returning a year later. Leo and Lisle were married in 1922.

Later, recalling that "horrific night" in a 1968 newspaper article commemorating the 50th anniversary of the wreck, Lisle claimed that high mound of hair on her husband's forehead may have cushioned the blow and spared his life.

"It was the pompadour that probably saved him from more serious damage," Lisle Burns MacDonald told the reporter.

At least, that's the story she told her seven grandchildren.

ROWBOATS AT WRECK SITE
MURPHY LIBRARY UNIVERSITY OF WISCONSIN-LA CROSSE

14

CLEAR ALL TRACKS

IN A SMALL ROOM on the third floor of the Peoria Union depot, a man wearing a white shirt, black sleevelets and a green visor reached for a pad of writing paper and a lead pencil. It was just past midnight. The room was dry, hot and lighted only by a single lamp. It had been a quiet evening, almost sleepy quiet, but a telegraph operator was always on call. Now with pencil and paper in hand the man listened intently. The telegraph sounder had sprung to life.

The telegraph was a great communication tool for rail companies that saved time and money by transmitting 'hold order' or 'proceed messages' between depots by Morse code, instead of the old-fashioned way of meeting face-to-face.

A railroad telegraph operator would relay stop calls and 'hold' certain trains while others were allowed to pass through. It was an unending task, and one that carried great risks. The altering, or 'drooping,' of a single word during transmissions could bring trains together and cause serious delays or injuries. That's why a telegraph operator was said to be "a man of varied pursuits and great responsibility." And in the middle of the night, when it wasn't as busy, that responsibility often required trying to keep eyelids from drooping, too. The loud clacking of the telegraph sounder would help. The operator would open his eyes, shake off the brief rest and swing his feet from off the top of the desk. Then he would alertly listen. A series of clacks and clucks—clack for short dash, cluck for long—would spell out the message.

For the operator in Peoria that night the message was short and direct: CLEAR...ALL...TRACKS.

More clacks and clucks, long and short and short and long, came through the sounder. A boat had gone down in the Illinois River. A special train was requested between Peoria and Pekin.

The operator went to work. Tapping on the keys, he sent the information to the manager in the rail yards of the Peoria and Pekin Union Railway roundhouse across the river. The sounder clacked on in the manager's office. A special train was needed, the message read.

A special train? At this hour? The manager tapped a question back to the operator.

WHAT DO WE CALL IT? he asked.

He waited for the sounder to clack again. In time it did, and he wrote it all down.

The COLUMBIA WRECK SPECIAL was the response.

THE PEORIA AND PEKIN Union Railway, based in East Peoria on the east side of the river, acted as a towing service for regional train companies like the Chicago, Peoria and St. Louis Railroad that operated track lines ending at points south and north of Pekin and Peoria. The P&PU trains shuttled cars between the two cities using a ten-mile stretch of track that ran along both sides of the Illinois River and crossed over using a private trussed bridge north of Wesley City. The P&PU engines hitched up the cars and transported them to the main yard and the roundhouse, where they were sorted and stacked and sent back to the base track starting point.

Unlike train engineers and conductors on other rail companies that stretched across state lines, employees of the P&PU would work a full shift and go home each day to their own beds. The sacrifices would be working late, odd-hour shifts and the occasional Sabbath or holiday away from family.

The yard manager on this particular night shift had his orders. Within ten minutes, the eight-car train was ready to move south to Wesley City, pick up passengers—presumably from the wrecked boat—and move them to Pekin. There wasn't much more information known or needed. A team of engineers and conductors were quickly assembled.

Chester Stringer, a conductor, volunteered. He had drawn the short end of the straw and was working late that night, but there was another more important reason why he asked to be part of this special assignment.

His wife and young son were on the *Columbia*.

WILLIAM EAGAN, a restaurant owner from Peoria, was one of the first rescuers to reach the sunken boat. Eagan was near Wesley City when he heard the tolling bell and came running to the shore. He asked a fisherman if he could borrow his rowboat and pushed off. The current was strong, making rowing difficult.

"The boat was in complete darkness," he said, "except for a red and green lantern at the bow. You could scarcely see the hand in front of you."

As he neared the wreck, woman and children began grabbing at the gunwales trying to pull themselves aboard. Each time the boat would tip and take on water.

"I would make it back to shore and have to drain the skiff," he remembered.

But he kept going back for more.

On his first trip, Eagan picked up four women and three children. The second trip yielded five more women. One woman fainted in the boat, he recalls, but others maintained their "coolness."

"Then they realized the great danger they had passed through and would appear half-dead," he said.

Eagan saw two women jump from the steamer.

"One came up and made a grab for the *Columbia*'s wheel, but the other never appeared on the surface."

Several men on the top of the ship were handing out life preservers and shouting "women and children first." Not one of them attempted to board the skiffs, Eagan recalled.

One man, Eagan noticed, had his head split open but was still lending a hand. A couple of miners with head lamps provided the only light.

A man swimming about the boat picked up a child that had been wearing a life preserver and put him in Eagan's boat.

"That's mine!" a frantic voice came from another boat.

The woman said she had tied the life preserver around her baby and threw it overboard. "The mother and child reunion," said Eagan, "was the most pathetic and appealing sight" he had ever witnessed.

The shoreline was getting crowded with women and children calling for their "husbands, fathers, brothers, sisters or sweethearts." Each time a boat returned to the banks, they ran for it, splashing wildly through the shallow water in a desperate search for loved ones.

The sound of sirens and vehicle engines now filled the night air. The police arrived and immediately sent out a call for anyone with a motor vehicle to help in the rescue effort. There just weren't enough ambulances available. A special train was on the way, they were told.

Fritz Pugh, a taxi driver, put his vehicle into service as ordered by police. He had arrived early and helped in the rescue effort on shore. Now he was directed to shuttle passengers to Pekin. Pugh listened as the awful news of the wreck emerged from the backseat of his cab. Each time he returned to the shore, there were more people, more grieving family members and more victims with stories to tell.

Before taking another carload back to Pekin, Pugh noticed a small boy sitting on a life preserver. He was wet and shivering. The boy said he had run away from his parents at the Amusement Park and stolen a ride on the boat. "I had a dandy bath and got my hair washed and drank lots of water," he told Pugh, with glee.

A boy his age, Pugh thought, couldn't possibly comprehend what just happened to him—could he?

Pugh played along.

The boy continued: "I drank an awful lot of dat water, but I wasn't full," he said, as Pugh chuckled. "I could a drank a lot more!"

Pugh told the story to a reporter who ran with it. It looked good in print.

Shocker: A 'STOWAWAY' HITCHES AN UNSUSPECTING RIDE.

But it wasn't true.

The young boy was not a stowaway. Four-year-old Elmer Modenhauer had run off briefly and became separated from his family when the boat sank. Now he was alone on the shore shivering, with thoughts only a small child could imagine.

His mother, sister, aunt and cousin were still missing.

Elmer never saw them again.

ON THE COLUMBIA, men with grappling hooks removed broken boards and uncovered a horrifying sight in the debris. A woman and two small children were clinging to one another in a loving embrace.

They had all perished together.

"That's the Witchers!" one of the rescuers must have shouted, recognizing Amy Witcher and her boys, seven-year-old Donald and one-year-old Richard.

The word reached shore. The family found huddled together had died together, so went the story as it was passed along. The four Witchers, including Clyde, a refrigeration man in town, were all on the boat, and now they were all gone.

That's the news that made the papers the next day: ENTIRE FAMILY WIPED OUT! ANNIHILATED! The story was right on one count. All four Witchers—mother, father, two kids—*were* on board the *Columbia* that night. But Clyde was away from his family when the boat suddenly went down. He survived.

Now the grief was exponentially greater. Somewhere, a husband and father would have to be told the dreadful news about his wife and sons.

ONE OF THE RESCUE WORKERS must have recognized the grave circumstances of the moment and gruesome task that lay ahead and
told someone to make a call. One man was needed now. The phone
lines were busy, but finally a connection was reached. The operator rang the requested line.

Back in Pekin, on the corner of Bacon and McLean streets,
inside the home of a well-respected doctor, the telephone's ringing
box started to go off. In the dark, a hand fumbled for the receiver.
A call was waiting.

"Put them through," a man's voice told the operator.

The line clicked.

There was background noise on the other end and static.

"This is Coroner Clary," the man said, clearing the sleep from
his throat. "How can I help you?"

TAZEWELL COUNTY CORONER LAWRENCE R. CLARY
PEKIN PUBLIC LIBRARY

15

MORE HELP

THE MAN SET THE PHONE receiver back on the hook and took a deep breath. The message was almost unbelievably grim. He looked at the time. It was 1 AM. He got out of bed, threw on a white shirt and a blazer and prepared to go to work.

By all indications, Lawrence R. Clary was one of Pekin's most popular citizens. Besides being the county coroner, Clary was a well-respected physician who ran a busy private practice. Every day he would greet loyal patients lined up outside his Fifth Street office with a cheerful 'good morning.'

A burly man whose loose-fitting clothes always seemed wrinkled from work, Clary had a round face with wisps of hair on the sides and no hair on top, something he preferred, like most balding men at the time, to cover up when going out. A solid Democrat, if asked, Clary had a Republican to thank for his choice of hats. In 1906, President Theodore Roosevelt was on an inspection tour of the Panama Canal excavation site when the jovial commander posed for photographers while perched in the driver's seat of a huge Bucyrus steam shovel. The massive piece of machinery couldn't hide the president, who wore a white suit and a white straw fedora with a black band. The press immediately dubbed it Teddy's "Panama hat."

Clary liked the look too.

Born on April 1, 1883 in Paola, Kansas, Clary moved with his family to central Illinois as a young boy. He graduated from Pekin High School in 1902 and not long after left for Chicago to study at the Chicago College of Medicine and Surgery, a private institution conveniently located next to the new 656-bed Cook County Hospital. In 1913, he earned his medical degree.

Chicago was where the action was, but Clary missed home. The small-town life missed him too. He served only a year at Chicago's Columbus Memorial Hospital before returning to Pekin and opening a 'large' and successful practice.

In 1916, at the age of 33, he was appointed coroner of Tazewell County. The coroner's work was arduous. It involved issuing death certificates, determining cause of death and calling for a jury's inquest to fix responsibility for accidental or unexplained deaths. Scalding deaths in children were common. A pot of boiling water used to wash dishes or clothes would be left unattended and a curious child would tip it over or fall in. Motor vehicles or train accidents were also becoming more prominent. Just weeks before the *Columbia* accident, Clary had investigated the death of a boy who was playing on the railroad tracks and was crushed to death under a freight train. After a sensational inquiry and trial, the jury found no fault with the railroad.

Now in his third year as county coroner, Dr. Clary was about to face his most difficult and emotionally challenging task yet. The early morning phone call was brutally honest, if it was accurate. He was facing multiple fatalities, possibly hundreds.

Clary kissed his wife Bertha goodbye and looked in on his young daughter Helen Marie, who was still sleeping. He reached for his Panama hat, opened the front door and quietly left.

WHEN THE ALARM reached Peoria, five police patrolmen named Horn, Huff, Schemel, Feinhotz and Schnebly hopped in an emergency car and headed across the bridge to the dirt road that headed south along the shoreline to Wesley City on the Tazewell County side of the river. The vehicle hit every rut along the way. The siren horns on the side of the car wailed as fast as the men could crank them. When the officers arrived, they found "a scene of chaos."

There was little light, and their flashlights made only "ghostly shafts." The shoreline was crowded with passengers huddled in blankets and rescuers launching boats and returning with more desperate souls. Some were hurt, some were scared, some were lost, and others were just wet. The officers ran to the water and helped the victims to shore. "Children and girls were frantically screaming for aid to find their parents or friends," the papers reported. "They threw their arms around the police officers' necks and begged to be taken home."

It was apparent more help was needed.

A taxi was parked nearby. They found the driver and told him to put his vehicle in service. Take the uninjured back to Pekin, they told the driver, and send word for more volunteer vehicles. Anyone with a motor car should get there quick. Fritz Pugh obliged and was on his way.

The skiffs returning from the *Columbia* were barely able to stay afloat. Loaded with passengers and filled with water by the time they reached the banks, the oarsmen would waste precious time bailing out their boats before heading back.

The officers figured another steamer could help. If anything, the powerful searchlight could illuminate the dark night.

A frantic call was put out, answered by the *Julia Belle Swain*.

AT THE FOOT OF PEORIA'S Main Street, the *Julia Belle Swain* had returned from a cruise and was moored for the night. The three-decker steamer with its 'wedding-cake' tiered design and gingerbread trim looked similar to the *Columbia*, but it was slightly smaller, with a side-wheeler design and no decorative cupola above the pilothouse. The Swains were another steamboat family that built boats and steam engines after the Civil War and ran an excursion business on the Mississippi and Illinois Rivers. The *Julia Belle*

Swain was their largest boat to run out of Peoria. The family had several boats on the rivers, as opposed to Mehl's single steamer, but the rivalry was friendly.

There was enough business to go around.

The steamboat trips were popular almost around the clock. Day and evening trips were advertised in the local papers, and daytime shopping excursions were always crowded—busy homemakers who lived in towns along the river would hop on the boat like they were boarding a city bus, cruise upriver to downtown Peoria, and shop at one of the department stores. The boat would then return them home before their husbands got off work. Civic groups and union organizations chartered the larger boats for outings and picnics. There would be food, drinks, music and dancing.

The boat trips were praised by patrons who wrote to the newspapers and described the "card contests and vocal and instrumental music," along with "wet and dry sandwiches and refreshments." A "peppery boat ride" read one pronouncement. "The best trip up the Illinois River ever pulled off," boasted another free advertisement.

In later years, a popular show-biz couple—and Peoria natives—named Fibber McGee and Molly would reminisce about the "good ol' excursion boats" on their weekly radio program.

Several days before the Fourth of July, four steamboats including the *Columbia, David Swain, Percy Swain* (the former named for the patriarch of the Swain family, the latter for one of his sons) and *Saint Paul* made an excursion trip to the same location—Henry, Illinois, a small town on the north leg of the river between Peoria and LaSalle. A rare photograph was taken showing all four boats docked together, one right next to the other. Considering the history of steamboats and the petty feuds and jealousies that would sometimes erupt between rival captains and pilots, this show of unity was an encouraging sign.

Enthusiasm, it was said, was overflowing.

"We were letting her cool down," said Captain E.G. Geiger of the *Julia Belle Swain.* "That's when we got a call for help." It took some time to work up a good head of steam, but soon the *Julia Belle Swain* was on her way.

A YOUNG MACHINIST in East Peoria, Melvin 'Pat' Patterson, was working the late shift when a call went out for rescue workers. He volunteered. In the darkness, Patterson and others probed the wreck with their bare hands until they felt something, anything, between the boards. "I think I got something," someone would say, and other men rushed to their aid.

One man was trapped for more than an hour, according to a newspaper report. "The prisoner talked coolly during the work of rescue and asked them only to 'hurry.'" He was eventually freed.

But time was no one's friend. The cries from below were fading. No more escapees emerged from the skylights. The bodies in the water that were moving had all been picked up and brought to shore. Even the hand searches were proving fruitless, hampered by darkness and heavy planks manpower alone couldn't budge. "All I could do," said Patterson, "was grope in the black water for arms, legs and feet—when we freed a corpse, it was lifted through the window and skylight."

The realization that few survivors would be found alive was reaching the throng along the shoreline. The rowboats were no longer returning to the boat. The sound of splashing water and cries for help could no longer be heard in the distance.

Reality was setting in like a dark cloud, yet rescuers desperately clung to an elusive sense of hope. The men who scrambled over the wreck—already exhausted from a day's work in the factory or mines—struggled on. From the shore, their shadowy figures could be seen searching for an outstretched hand or listening for the sound of rustling water. The crowd watched in horror as they pulled another body from below, arms and legs limp.

By degrees, the mood changed from hope to despair. "There goes another body!" someone would cry out.

On shore, police officers were asking everyone to go home. There was nothing they could do until morning. The cars were lining up now—nearly a hundred or so were said to have heeded the call. They would take the helpless back to Pekin.

Yet one arrival's work was just beginning. The car door flew open before the vehicle even stopped. A burly man stepped out. He was neatly dressed and looked ready to take charge. A Panama hat rested on his head.

A WHISTLE BLEW.

Captain Mehl swore he heard it. The commander of the *Columbia* had been handing out life preservers until they were nearly gone. Now he was waiting on the top of his crumpled boat, pondering what had just happened. This much he knew: his boat had listed, sank and collapsed; his wife was injured, but alive; lifeless bodies were being pulled from the wreckage; strangers were coming to help; and policemen were directing traffic. Whatever else may have been going through the mind of the captain as he watched and waited one can only imagine. His thoughts, however, were interrupted by the sound of the whistle again—a steam whistle!

Mehl climbed to the top of the pilothouse and strained to see. The fog and steam and dust were still blinding, but he could make out the outline of an approaching boat, a boat with smokestacks.

The *Julia Belle Swain* bore down on him.

"No, no, no!" Mehl shouted.

Captain E.G. Geiger had made it downriver in record time. A boat was in distress, he was told, but where? The air was thick with fog...or was it steam?

The Wesley City sand bar was up ahead.

This would be no time to put another boat in peril, Geiger thought, even an empty one. He sent a stop bell signal to the engine room below and the *Julia Belle Swain* held fast.

In the distance, the sound of man's voice drifted through the haze.

"Keep away! For God's sake, keep away!"

TOP: JULIA BELLE SWAIN
CHILLICOTHE HISTORICAL SOCIETY & MUSEUM
BOTTOM: COLUMBIA WITH THE SWAIN BOATS IN HENRY, ILLINOIS
S&D REFLECTOR

16

ON THAT TRAIN

KATE STOVER CAN'T RECALL how she reached shore, but she remembers running. "Like a wild thing, I ran, through the mud and sand and past the underbrush."

She ran and ran.

"I just wanted to get away from the river and its horrors," she remembered.

She scrambled up the railroad embankment and fell on the tracks.

A train whistle blew.

Then she was out.

The engineer saw her clearly in the glare of the train's headlight: a woman stood on the tracks, wildly waving her arms. He blew the horn, but she wouldn't budge. A vision in white, she kept screaming and waving, he recalled. The engineer slowed the train to a stop. He had no choice. The '*Columbia* Wreck Special' had reached Wesley City.

The train's crew found Kate Stover unconscious beside the track. Her torn skirt was soaked through. Physically she recovered, but when retelling her story she had no recollection of signaling for the train. She remembered only hearing the sound of the whistle, and then nothing. But the engineer and crew remembered seeing the woman in white, like an "apparition," they said, screaming and waving for the train to stop.

It saved her life, they told her.

SEVEN-YEAR-OLD Everett Stringer had been having the time of his life. He and his mother Jesse were enjoying the view on the hurricane deck when the trouble began. They could hear the music coming from the deck below, then confused sounds. The boat went dark. The bell started ringing, and then came the "cries of the injured" and "yells for help."

Jesse Stringer acted quickly. She put Everett on the railing, took off her straw hat, and threw it in the water like a life preserver. "She pulled up her dress and tucked it in her pantaloons," Everett remembered, "and told me to jump in the water and paddle like a dog."

Jesse jumped in, too.

Up until that moment, young Everett couldn't have asked for anything more. The trip was everything a seven-year-old boy could want or dream about. There was the cruise on the big boat, a visit to the Amusement Park and a ride on that fancy Figure-Eight Roller Coaster. Then on the way home—a surprise!

"I can't remember how I got into the pilothouse, but somehow I did," Everett said. "My father and Captain Mehl were best of friends."

A visit to the pilothouse was a thrill for a kid of any age. "There was a radiance and splendor about the place which seemed related to the pulpit of a church or inside the private office of a bank president," wrote Fred Way Jr., in his book, *Pilotin' Comes Natural.* "When a youngster comes aboard a steamboat for the first time, his normal impulse is to rush upward as high as he can go."

But the excitement wouldn't last. Unless invited, a wide-eyed boy could only make it up to the pilothouse steps before being stopped in his tracks by a painted sign that read: NOTICE—NO PASSENGERS BEYOND THIS POINT.

"I was on fire to ascend those heights," wrote Way about his own exploits.

Young Everett Stringer was lucky. He got inside. "I sat on somebody's lap with my hands on the spokes of the wheel," he said. "I couldn't see over the wheel, but I felt real big. The captain let me steer the *Columbia.*"

EVERETT AND JESSE reached shore by hanging onto her straw hat and paddling through the water. They walked to the railroad tracks on the hill and sat down.

In the distance, a train whistle blew again and again.

Everett stood up and pointed. "My dad's on that train!" he proudly shouted.

Chester Stringer, a conductor, was sticking his head out the window of a passenger car. He strained to see—what? Hope. He knew his wife and young son were on board the sunken ship.

Jesse spotted him and started waving.

Everett waved, too.

Then the train came to a stuttering stop, brakes screeching and steam panting.

Chester was his own moving train. He hopped off from between cars and ran down the track. Faster and faster he ran until he swept up his wife in his arms and only let her go to do the same to his son. "I remember them hugging," Everett said, "and then Dad gave me a hug."

The rest of the crew ran to help a young lady in white who had fallen near the tracks.

A MAN WALKED ALONG the bank searching for someone he knew. He wasn't like the others who were waiting for news about loved ones they suspected were still on the boat.

He was looking for someone on shore.

He was also wearing a uniform.

August Mehl had done his part on the sunken boat. He had handed out life preservers and helped his brother get the woman and children in boats. Now he was told to wait. The rescue was over.

The recovery would begin at daybreak.

His wife Emma never left his thoughts. When he last saw her, she was running in front of him. The boat tipped, and she fell in the water. His heart had been heavy ever since.

But Emma was safe, picked up by a boat. Mehl must have felt awash in relief, at least briefly, before the full weight of the catastrophe descended onto his mind.

AT 2 AM, CORONER CLARY took command of operations. A man of his stature was needed among the confused passengers and the rescue crew waiting for someone to tell them what to do next.

The first order of business was settled: The rescue operation would be halted due to darkness. The work of recovering the bodies would resume in the morning. Everyone on the boat, crew members and rescue workers alike, was ordered to wait in a skiff until daybreak. The 20 or so bodies that had been recovered in the first hours were put on a small launch, a makeshift floating hearse, which would be sent to Pekin at first light. Clary was in the process of securing a vacant building to send the bodies. So far, only about a half dozen had been identified, including the three members of the Witcher family. The corpses were wrapped in white sheets and laid side-by-side on the flat-bed boat. A derrick, or boat with a crane, was summoned to help with removing the planks that covered the dance hall deck, where most of the remaining bodies were expected to be found. No other boats would be allowed near the wreckage unless directed. The *Julia Belle Swain* was ordered to stay clear.

The current was strong, and someone suggested that precautions be taken to prevent any bodies in the wreckage from drifting away. A fishing net was reportedly placed around the prow of the boat, but it didn't hold. Another idea thrown about, most likely by a fisherman, involved using a cable that stretched across the river that had grappling hooks tied to it. Whether or not the cable-hook contraption was actually used—or even attempted—isn't known. A human lookout, however, was stationed downriver later the next day, but that was because of an entirely new and different problem—

one that no one saw coming. The weather had been unsettled. The river was already running high. An all-out storm would be disastrous. For now the skies were still and work continued in earnest.

Clary had questions, and he sought answers. He summoned the captain for an estimate of the number of bodies he thought were still in the wreckage. "There are at least a hundred bodies below," Mehl told him, although he really didn't know. In fact, Mehl would later tell a reporter, "There are probably not a hundred down there, more like forty."

No one really knew for sure how many passengers had made it to shore. There was no head count, only an estimate. By morning, newspapers across the country, rushing to meet early edition deadlines, reported "up to 300 or more bodies" may be found in the wreckage. They were wrong. Mercifully, Mehl's first guess was more accurate.

Clary ordered Mehl to stay put. He would be needed to direct recovery workers, specifically to spots in the buried dance hall deck and the narrow exits where many of the bodies still might be. No one knew the boat better than the captain, was Clary's thinking. Mehl agreed.

Clary had seen and heard enough. He returned to his office in downtown Pekin and immediately sent a telegram to the Chief of Police in Chicago. It read:

> PLEASE SEND AT ONCE A PROFESSIONAL DIVER WITH COM-
> PLETE OUTFIT TO RECOVER SUNKEN STEAMER A LARGE
> NUMBER OF BODIES.
> ANSWER AT PEKIN.

The response was prompt. A diver would be on his way by train in the morning. He was expected to arrive by noon.

In the meantime, Clary sought out a local man named Earl Barnewolt. He had a diving suit and could get operations started first thing in the morning, Clary thought.

The coroner had another call to make, this time to a colleague. A phone rang in the home of Peoria County Coroner W.B. Elliott.

"The matter probably is as much yours as mine," Clary told

Elliott. "As far as I can see, the boat is in the middle of the river, although river men tell me it's closer to the Tazewell side. Most of the people are from Pekin, so I suppose most of the burden of the investigation will fall on me."

Regardless, Elliott offered his assistance. He would be there the next day.

There were more phones ringing that morning all the way from the state capital in Springfield to Washington, D.C., and the office of William C. Redfield, Secretary of the Department of Commerce. By law any commercial boat on an inland waterway was under federal jurisdiction. The captain and pilot licenses were issued through the Department of Commerce. A steamboat wreck was their business.

A thorough investigation by that department was expected.

VERAH FLOWERS
TAZEWELL COUNTY GENEALOGICAL AND HISTORICAL SOCIETY (TCGHS)

17

IN
SHOCK

COAL MINERS JOHN CHANCE, Ben Wilson and several fishermen who ran for their rowboats when the first cries of help were heard were told to go home, or to wait in a skiff until daybreak. They had done yeoman's work and were exhausted. For many who went home, the shoreline was markedly different from what they had seen hours earlier when they ran half-asleep and half-dressed from their shacks.

Hundreds of automobiles now lined the lone dirt road, one behind another. It was a clanging, smoking, rumbling mass. The parade of slow-moving or stopped vehicles prompted a newspaper reporter to write this description of a relativity new concept in motorized travel: "The motorists kept in the tumbledown road until they could proceed no further. Then the vast herd of dead machines stood like some jangle gathering under the drooping willows of the cozy bank." Another writer called it a "traffic tangle."

On the embankment just above the road, a train was still puffing steam. Many of the women and children, huddled in blankets or comforted by a donated wool jacket around their shoulders, made their way up the hill and boarded one of the seven coach cars. Some didn't wait. They walked the mile or so back home.

But other survivors, like Carl Aiken, found an efficient—yet seemingly much more dangerous—way to travel that night. His story is almost unbelievable. As noted earlier, Aiken was working the ice cream stand on the dance hall deck of the *Columbia* and talking to several girls when the boat gave way. He ran to the high side of the boat, but the "huge crowd pushed me to the low side, and that's where I stayed," Aiken recounted. "All you could see and feel was the dark water—all you could hear was glass breaking and terrified screams."

Aiken grabbed an I-beam that was closer to the dance room floor. He crawled along the beam until he reached a skylight. "I saw the crew working best they could. I went in the pilothouse and grabbed a life preserver for my own safety."

Aiken said there was a man with a life tank (presumably a cylinder or storage tank of some sort, likely a hollow one, that could have easily been found on a steamboat—especially one that was in pieces—and used as a floating device).

"'Buddy, help me get this thing off [the wall?],' he said to me and so I helped him. We picked up two women on the way over and drifted downriver about a mile before we could head to shore."

Was it true? Did Carl Aiken and several other stragglers really float away from the wreckage clinging onto some type of floating device as he claimed, and end up a mile or so downriver? Aiken never mentioned anything about commandeering a boat, which would seem to make more practical sense. But the probability of an unmanned free-standing rowboat ready for the taking in the middle of all the unfolding chaos seems low. There were only two lifeboats on the *Columbia*, and both were quickly filled. The rest of the boats came from the shore, manned by experienced oarsman who probably never left them unattended. There was never any report of a boat missing or one found so far away from the wreck.

"We went to the house by the 'White House Crossing' and notified Pekin and Peoria. In a few minutes, a bunch of cars came from Pekin...and I took one," Aiken said.

The story seemed improbable, but not impossible.

The 'White House Crossing' is an area along the river located on the north edge of Pekin that was famed for its shallow depth. From time to time, when conditions were right, the water level would dip so low that a person could simply walk across. The first settlers knew about it. They would use that point to get their horses, carts and families from one side of the river to the other. Eventually, when the early bridges were built, the locals would take advantage of its easy accessibility, despite the risks, and cross the river on foot to avoid paying bridge tolls. The area was distinctly marked by a white house—hence the name—that has since been torn down.

So according to Aiken, he and three others—two men and two women together—floated downriver to the 'White House Crossing,' gained their footing and trudged along the muddy bottom to reach the shoreline. It was the wildest escape story of the night, and Aiken knew one place he could go to tell it.

The day after the wreck, Aiken made a special trip to the offices of the *Peoria Journal-Transcript*. In the bustling newsroom, the editors and reporters listened to his harrowing tale with dropped jaws. The story floored them. But there was one more matter to correct. In the papers the day before, the name Carl Aiken was listed as one of the missing in the *Columbia* wreck. "Anything else you want to add?" the stunned newspapermen asked him before he left.

"Yes," Aiken said, "tell everyone, I'm not dead."

BACK ON SHORE, law and order were being restored, and tough decisions were being made. The police were directing the "traffic tangle" and helping the "lucky ones" to a volunteer vehicle or the special coach train on the hill. Soon the hundreds on shore would be returning home to their families and sharing the harrowing stories of the grand steamer that hit the shore, plunged into darkness and collapsed. Many would surprise their loved ones with the astonishing news, while others would find a house filled with friends and relatives waiting in shock.

In Pekin, crowds gathered at the railroad station. Many had no idea who would be returning and who would not. "The scenes of grief and mourning are expected to be greatly increased," wrote a reporter. "It will be Pekin's saddest day."

Esther Bellville was one of the lucky ones. She and her friend Verah Flowers were on the dance floor when it started to tilt. They slid down into the dark water and reached for a column, but it snapped in two. Esther managed to grab a foot and hold on. She made it to shore. Now she was in a car headed back to Pekin, alone and confused. She had lost sight of her friend Verah in the darkness and chaos.

Verah is a good swimmer, Esther thought, trying to stifle her worst fears, *but what if that column had struck Verah in the head?*

"I was dazed as I stumbled into the hallway of Verah's home," Esther recalled. "I called out, 'the boat sank!'" The house was full of people. Esther remembered looking around for Verah. Then she fainted.

"I found out about Verah the next day," Esther said. Her friend's body was found with a big bruise on her forehead, she was told.

A few days later, a letter was published in the *Pekin Daily Times.* It was signed from "a person who had spent considerable time at the Flowers home." It was a tribute to Verah. "She was jolly with her friends, but modest in demeanor at all times," the letter read. "She built character as she grew to a budding womanhood...her life...a model for young girls to follow." The letter continued with a sense of sentiment, regret and vulnerability: "Though the mother has lost a loving daughter, the brother a kind sister, the church an earnest worker and society a brilliant gem, we feel that Verah has not lived in vain."

That Sunday in Verah's church, a piano bench would sit empty on the altar, as the congregation mourned the loss of its young organist.

ALL AROUND VERAH'S HOME, throughout the Pekin community, similar scenes of panic and grief were playing out. The word of the wreck was spreading. "The whole town was aroused," is how a newspaper writer put it. Residents were interrupted from their sleep by the news of the tragedy. Many didn't have family members on the board the *Columbia* that night, but virtually everyone knew someone who was—a friend, a co-worker, a church member, a neighbor—the entire town was enveloped by its sadness. They would share this loss together.

On one street in particular, Washington Street, the porch lamps were flickering on one right after another. The block lit up in its glow. Neighbors ran from house to house. But one house remained quiet and dark. The couple who lived there had stepped out for the night. They were last seen walking arm-in-arm to the landing. William and Emily Capoot had planned to take their first boat trip since surviving the *Frankie Folsom* disaster 26 years before. Now they were among the missing.

IN A HOUSE on Court Street, Minnie White woke up in a rush. It was late, around midnight, and her nieces Ana and Dorothy hadn't yet returned from the *Columbia*.

Minnie's daughter Wilma was sleeping in the room down the hall. Now awake, Minnie walked to the top of the upstairs hall landing and froze. A white, cloudy apparition floated by. Family member Carole Starrett recalls the story as it was passed down by her mother and grandfather. "Frightened by this [ghostly vision]," Starrett says, "she went back to the bed, woke my grandfather up and told him about it." They discussed it briefly. The boat was landing, and the girls would be home soon enough, they agreed. The apparition on the stairs they could not explain.

At 2 AM, they were awakened again. This time, church bells were ringing, a signal something was wrong. Ana was back, Minnie soon discovered, but not Dorothy.

Dorothy White died on the *Columbia* that night. She was a member of the Church of Christ, Scientist, Starrett recalls, who believes "that a person who 'seems to die' does not go anywhere; they simply adjust to another level of consciousness which is inaccessible to those they have left behind."

"Dorothy's family," says Starrett, "never came to claim her body."

"My mother Wilma was only nine years old," Starrett explains. "She did not know how to swim and would have never survived the wreck."

Wilma married in 1929, and Starrett grew up in the same house on Court Street. "I still think about that cloudy, white apparition on the stairway," she says.

AS THE REALITY of the night was unfolding, details of the wreck began to trickle into newsrooms across the river and around the country. The papers scrambled. They needed to change the morning headlines. They also needed someone to get the story.

In Peoria, one man in particular was about to get a call.

EARNEST EAST
PEORIA PUBLIC LIBRARY

18

HE'S TALKING

EARNEST EAST WAS accustomed to the telephone ringing at all hours. So he wasn't surprised when it happened again that night. The clanging bells shook the newspaper reporter from a deep slumber. East gathered himself and picked up the receiver. The crackling voice on the other end said there was an urgent Western Union message from the *Chicago American,* the newspaper that employed East as a correspondent. Locally, East wrote for the *Peoria Star.*

"Let's hear it," he said.

The operator read the message about a steamboat wreck on the Illinois River.

East never removed the phone from his hand. Another click and he was connected to the Peoria Police Department.

The police confirmed the news: an excursion boat had gone down near Wesley City.

The next call East made was to a taxicab service.

Peoria had two daily newspapers, the *Peoria Star* and the *Peoria Journal-Transcript,* which actually consisted of two editions, the *Transcript* in the morning and the *Journal* in the afternoon. The

Peoria Star was an afternoon-only edition sometimes called the *Evening Star.* Pekin also had its own daily newspaper, the *Pekin Daily Times.*

Thanks to the telegraph and the telephone, the addition of 'wire services' meant news could move faster and travel farther than ever before. Soon, printed news, both in newspapers and periodicals, expanded at a blistering pace. By 1910, the industry reached its peak, with 2,600 daily newspapers in circulation. But just because news was easier to obtain, that didn't mean it was always accurate. For the printed papers of that era, it was the trust of its readers that suffered the most.

Before the start of the 20th century, New York newspaper magnates and bitter rivals William Randolph Hearst and Joseph Pulitzer perfected the 'yellow journalism' style of news reporting, with 'scare headlines' and 'fake interviews,' among other journalistic travesties. Hearst and Pulitzer unapologetically used their newspapers to influence–even propagandizing shamelessly–public opinion on issues like labor disputes and foreign affairs, including Hearst's admittedly biased support of the Spanish-American War.

When Theodore Roosevelt became president and spearheaded the progressive movement, the popular magazines such as *Atlantic Monthly* and *Harper's Weekly* followed the president's lead by featuring detailed stories on reform issues like labor, government corruption and corporate greed. The 'investigative reporters' pleased Roosevelt at first. The magazines helped promote part of his political agenda. Social issues gained national attention. In a world without radio, television or internet, printed journalism had the greatest and most immediate impact.

In 1906, the relationship changed. Roosevelt grew frustrated with what he described as the "excessively negative tone" in American magazines and newspapers and coined the name "muckrakers" to describe the reporters that he thought focused excessively on exposing problems and scandals, or in some extreme cases, creating the scandals themselves. Some writers–including one of the most famous muckrakers, Lincoln Steffens–even suggested that the corruption reached all the way to the White House and dared to target some of Roosevelt's closest allies, friends and supporters who the president had counted on to help him win re-election. Roosevelt's view of the press turned sour.

"There are in body politic, economic, and social, many and grave evils, and there is an urgent necessity for the sternest war on them," Roosevelt proclaimed in a speech, and then went on to praise the "writer or speaker, every man who, on a platform or in a book or magazine, or newspaper, with merciless severity makes such attack, provided always that he in his turn remembers that the attack is of use only if it is absolutely truthful." But Roosevelt was resolute in his attack against excessive "mud-slinging."

"Any excess almost sure to invite a reaction; and, unfortunately, the reactions instead of taking form of punishment of those guilty of the excess, is apt to take the form of punishment of the unoffending or of giving immunity, and even strength to offenders."

Roosevelt never backed down from a good fight, but this was clearly one-sided. "Hysterical sensationalism is the poorest weapon wherewith to fight for lasting righteousness," he said.

Hearst and Pulitzer's 'sensational' newspapers were some of the biggest culprits, and the publishing titans didn't seem to mind as long as people were buying their newspapers. They became almost absurdly rich and powerful. Hearst would even run for political office himself, although he was never elected.

But times were changing.

By 1918, with America at war, the country was more determined than ever not to be duped by the malevolent and devious editors. Most urban newspapers were presenting the news of the day, or at least giving it a good try, without the sensationalism and rabble-rousing of the past. "Muckraking was plainly going out of style," noted authors John Tebbel and Mary Ellen Zuckerman in the book *The Magazine in America 1741-1990*. "For nearly a decade they had delivered successive hammer blows on the public skull, creating a colossal national headache, and now people were beginning to sense how good they would feel when it stopped."

But one problem just precipitates another. While the stories now presented mostly adhered to the facts, they were also expressive pieces written with a novelist's flair and filled with colorful descriptions, comparisons, anecdotes and—more often than not—wild exaggerations.

The coverage of the *Columbia* wreck was no exception.

For example, one eager reporter for the *Peoria Evening Star* couldn't help himself when describing the story of Mrs. Henry Heinken, "a young matron of Pekin," who was in the hospital suffering from exposure and bruises. "She was in the water struggling and sinking when one of the rescue skiffs scraped her up and pulled her in," the reporter wrote. "She was absolutely naked! Every bit of clothing except her hose and shoes were torn off. Even her corset was gone!"

A portion of the writer's story was good journalism. Mrs. Heinken *was* in the hospital for cuts and bruises, and she did have a harrowing tale to tell about being trapped in the water. "My body was submerged, but my head was above water," she recalled from her hospital bed. "The only thing that kept me from being drowned were the bodies beneath me."

But that thrillingly salacious part about her being nude? There wasn't an ounce of truth to it.

"There was not a stitch of my clothes missing!" she scolded another reporter from the same newspaper, and then turned to the night nurse, who nodded wildly in approval like she had been asked by a judge under oath.

The correction was printed the next day.

LIKE MANY REPORTERS at the time, Earnest East rarely had his name listed in the paper. Bylines were not used much. But his work on the *Columbia,* despite being unaccredited, would be influential in newspapers across the country. East's work and name would eventually find new life thanks to a popular newspaper column he wrote called *The Parade of History.*

East once said that "autobiographies should be brief to avoid dullness." So, with that admonition in mind, he was born in Millmine, Illinois, in 1885 and came as a young writer to Peoria where he met his wife Georgia. He started at the *Peoria Star* in 1906.

Now 33, East was about to cover his biggest story yet. A half-hour after receiving a call that a steamboat had gone down, East took a taxi across the bridge from Peoria and was on the Tazewell County side of the river in Wesley City.

"The night was dark, and objects could be made out with difficulty," he later recalled. "A few automobiles were parked nearby, but most of those saved had gone elsewhere." East picked up a few details from stragglers on the riverbank, mostly gawkers who lived nearby and had been awakened by the cries for help.

East found a man on shore who had a rowboat and urged the stranger to take him on the river. There wasn't much of the *Columbia* still visible, but East determined that what was sticking out of the water wasn't very far from the shore. The man obliged, and East hopped aboard.

Even for such a short distance, the trip was laborious, hampered by darkness, debris and the hanging willows that, according to East, "made progress slow." East could hear voices and told the oarsman to steer the boat in that direction. They found three or four other men in a rowboat similar to the one East was in.

"That man there," another journalist motioned to East as his finger pointed to a short, stocky figure, slumped over with elbows on his knees and hands cupped over his face, "is the skipper of the boat."

"And he's talking," East was told.

East got out his pad and pencil and couldn't write fast enough.

"I'm a pauper," were the first words he heard the captain say.

THE FIRST INTERVIEW with Captain Mehl took place right there, in a rowboat next to the battered remains of the *Columbia*.

"I shouted to the passengers to get on the upper deck," Mehl said to the reporters. "I told Tom to run her ashore. He started toward the Tazewell side, because he could make it quicker than he could turn and get back to the Peoria side. The water started coming up over the lower deck, and I knew we were gone. I got through to the top. I told everybody to get up as quickly as possible. I could see that we were sinking fast. It was not long before the boat went down, almost straight down. There were two jolts that made the boat quiver. The first one was slight...then the nose of the boat hit the branch of the tree."

The sound of pencil tips scratching on paper could be heard as the captain continued unabated. "Tom didn't jam the boat inshore as he should have done, but he held it back and let it go again in the deep current. Whatever it was we hit...'the old tub' just busted in two."

The reporters wrote down every word of the captain's impromptu press conference—every last word. But the captain wasn't finished.

"Everything I had was tied up in that boat out there," Mehl said, pointing to, as one writer described it, "a dark, enshrouded hull."

"But I don't care so much about that," he continued, "it is the people down there." Mehl looked in the direction of the water. His thoughts were his own now. *How many bodies were still in there?* he must have wondered. How many more would be brought to the surface in the morning? It was almost too much to bear. Mehl turned to a reporter and asked the obvious question, "Pretty tough, eh?"

The reporter agreed and kept on writing.

THERE THEY ALL WAITED patiently in the swaying rowboats: the captain, rescue workers and reporters. It would be a long night, longer than usual it would seem. There was a good reason why. Three months earlier, at the beginning of April, the American people had been asked to do something for the war effort and for each other. It was an order from President Wilson, a proclamation to implement an idea that was invented centuries before and given a name, like its purpose, that put three simple words together and meant: Daylight Saving Time.

Captain Mehl slumped forward and put his head back in his hands.

The rest of the men glanced at their watches.

POSTER PROMOTING DAYLIGHT SAVING TIME
LIBRARY OF CONGRESS

19

DST

IT WAS LATE ON March 31, 1918, a Saturday night soon to be a Sunday morning and the beginning of a new month, when Daylight Saving Time officially became a household phrase in America. It started with a crowd of gawkers lining the streets surrounding the Metropolitan Building in Manhattan. At exactly midnight, the crowd strained their necks and looked up at the huge lighted clocks, each 26 feet in diameter, one on each side of the building. A signal was given and the lights shut down—the largest four-dial clock tower in the world went dark.

A hush came over the crowd.

Time was literally at a standstill.

Then there was a cheer!

The crowd was festive despite the late hour and the start of Easter Sunday. A community chorus sang the *Star Spangled Banner*, and the New York Police band and Borough of Manhattan bands took turns playing *Over There*. The excited throng kept staring at the clock dials frozen in time. It just couldn't be, they thought.

It was deep in the tower's belly where all the work was taking place. Hired mechanics had made their way up to the tower's inner workings and begun the arduous task of advancing the 13-foot hour hands manually. They had two hours to get the job done. Then promptly at 2 AM, the lights flickered on again. Like magic, the clock tower was once again illuminated. Hundreds of late-night souls strained their necks again to see the clock dials' hour hands in the glowing beams. The hands were pointing to the number...three.

Three! It was 3 o'clock! For the first time in history, the nation had moved itself ahead one hour. The crowd shouted and cheered. Daylight Saving Time had officially begun.

"Blasé New Yorkers for whom New Year's Eve celebrations have lost their thrill," wrote a reporter for the *New York Times,* "rubbed their eyes and marveled at the novelty of an Easter Sunday of only 23 hours."

The idea for daylight saving is most often attributed to Benjamin Franklin during his years as an American delegate in Paris in the late 1700s. Thanks to the oil lamp, Franklin would stay up late, usually playing chess, and sleep until noon the next day. One morning, quite early, he was awakened by a sudden noise. He threw open the tight window shutters and was even more startled by the amount of daylight coming into his room. "I looked at my watch," Franklin later wrote in an article that appeared in the *Journal De Paris* on April 26, 1784, "which goes very well, and found that it was but six o'clock; and still thinking it something extraordinary that the sun should rise so early, I looked at the almanac, where I found it to be the hour given for his rising on the day." Perhaps with a mix of astonishment and dry humor, Franklin wrote "that having repeated this observation the three following mornings, I found precisely the same result."

Ever resourceful, Franklin had an intriguing thought. If he had slept six hours until noon through daylight and 'lived' six hours the night before in candlelight, then wasn't that just a waste of precious light and expense? "This event has given rise in my mind to several serious and important reflections," he wrote. Franklin went to work figuring out the math. Assuming that 100,000 Parisians burned half a pound of candles per hour for an average of

seven hours a day, and calculating the average time during summer months between dusk and the time Parisians went to bed,
Franklin concluded that the amount saved, as he put it, would be
an "immense sum." Franklin proposed that all Parisians rise with
him, when the sun rises, and to compel the naysayers, he proposed
"a tax [be laid] per window, on every window that is provided with
shutters to keep the light out."

"Let guards posted after sunset to stop all the coaches that would
pass the streets," he bravely declared. "Let the church bells ring
every time the sun rises. Let cannon(s) be fired in every street, to
wake the sluggards effectually, and make them open their eyes to
see their true interest."

Franklin's dry wit and humor notwithstanding, his scheme
alarmed Parisians who weren't ready for change. They thought
Franklin's idea was madness, and a surprising one at that, coming from an American intellectual and a figure that was so well-
liked in France. After he left Paris, Franklin mulled over the idea
and marveled at "inhabitants," this time Londoners, who continued "to live much by candlelight and sleep by sunshine." Franklin
used the economy as an example, saying residents had little regard
to the costs of candlewax and tallow. "For I love economy exceed-
ingly," he explained.

Eventually the idea of extending the day during the summer
months was proposed. Instead of getting up by daylight, usually
too early, then why not just move daylight later in the day and pro-
long the evening sun?

"Everyone appreciates the long, light evenings," wrote William Willett, a London builder who is credited with the idea of
extending daylight. "Everyone laments their shortage as Autumn
approaches; and everyone has given utterance to regret that the
clear, bright light of an early morning during Spring and Summer
months is so seldom seen or used."

Like Franklin, Willett was struck by the amount of people who
kept their blinds shut in the morning hours even though the sun
was fully out. If getting up too early was the crutch, thought Willett, then why not just stretch the light of the evening hours. Euro-

pean countries would adopt the idea first. On April 1, Easter Sunday of 1918, Americans did as well.

Across the country, at some point during that day, U.S. citizens in every state, every big city and every rural community reached for their pocket watches and mantle clocks and moved the minute hand ahead one revolution. It was an order from the president to extend an hour of daylight and conserve energy in a time of war. The longer days, it was said, would save on rationed war materials like gas and coal, while indirectly stimulating production of food products.

And it was good for you and your neighbor, too! The extra sunlight would "increase the health of communities by offering an additional hour in the summer months for recreation through baseball, tennis and other daylight sports," the government exulted. At least that was the concept. It worked in Europe, was the thinking, so why not here?

The audacity of moving time forward one hour was not lost on zealous newspaper editors, who used their influential editorials to satirize the occasion. The *Washington Times* offered up this helpful tip:

> If perchance you are prone to stay out late Saturday night,
> be sure and tell wifey the time you come in, before the clocks
> are turned up, otherwise you will be an hour worse off.

The same newspaper also cooked up this fictionalized exchange:

> "I'll meet you at 2:30 o'clock in the morning," said one man
> to another in front of the Times building this morning.
> "Yes—no you won't either."
> "Why, you poor fish. You can certainly be there at 2:30."
> "Wrong, Archie. Follow me closely. There will be no 2:30
> in the morning. When the savings law goes into effect at
> 2 o'clock, the hands on the clock will be moved around one
> hour to 3 o'clock. So there will be no half-past two."
> "Well, I'll be——!"

In New York, the crowds sauntered home bearing witness to

history, but also realizing that a full hour of sleep would be lost to the strange new time configuration. Even more important, considering it was Easter Sunday, many needed to get up early for church services. "There were late-comers [to church]," reported the newspapers the next day.

For many, getting to church on time was the least of their worries. The newfangled time change proved difficult to get used to. Many factory workers who got up at the crack of dawn or worked staggered shifts had a difficult time adjusting to the new schedule. The war angle worked for widespread support, but there were already grumblings that after the war came to an end, so would this silly thing called Daylight Saving Time. It was a one-time event, many concluded.

They were right.

1918 would be the first and last time every state would abide by the new law. The war would end, and all 48 states, and even individual cities, could decide whether they wanted to make the time switch the following year or not. Most did not.

The law would be revised and re-enacted again during World War II where it remained in effect until that war came to an end. Finally, in 1966 the Uniform Time Act was passed and a nationwide Daylight Saving Time was mandated. But it wasn't required. Any state that wanted to opt out could do so by passing a state law, provided that it exempted the entire state. In 1972, the law was amended to allow states that straddled a time zone boundary to exempt only a portion of the state. Indiana was one such state, and it was split until 2006. Now the entire state observes the annual time change.

But in July 1918, just three months after Daylight Saving Time went into effect for the first time, rescuers in rowboats in the middle of the Illinois River were waiting for daybreak so they could resume the task of searching for bodies in the wreckage of a sunken steamboat. They checked their timepieces and calculated how long the darkness would last. Of course, the sun would rise as always, but the seeming disconnect with time shown on their watches ratcheted up their anxiety.

"The moon shone brightly," the *Chicago Tribune* reported. "The bosom of the river became smooth again and ripped laughingly about the ragged and broken timbers which were thrust ludicrously into the stream. It was considered too dark for exploration. The cries for help died away.

"Then everything was quiet," the paper noted.

CARL CORIELL HAD A LOT to think about as he rode in the back of a packed funeral car. The ticket he received from his boss to go on the *Columbia* that night was as unexpected and thrilling as the ride he took on the Figure-Eight Roller Coaster. Now he was heading home with his Boy Scout uniform heavily soaked with river water and the sounds of "awful screams and cries" ringing in his ears.

What a strange thing to be in a funeral car, Carl must have thought. The funeral car had been put into service as transport for the living. Back in Pekin, he stepped out and found his bicycle right where he had left it, near the downtown square by the popcorn stand. Carl rode his bicycle the rest of the way home and found his worried parents and sister-in-law waiting for him.

They were relieved to see he was safe. Carl told them about all the people who were still by the shore, searching for loved ones. His father, the postmaster, wasted no time and headed out the door to see if he could help others.

"I was sitting at the top deck bench on the port side," Carl told his mother and sister-in-law, Edna, whose husband Verne, Carl's brother, was serving overseas. "We felt a severe thud and within seconds were sliding across the deck into the river."

He went under the water, Carl told them, and nearly lost his Boy Scout hat.

"When I came up, I rescued it and clamped it on my head. The moonlight showed the boat's cables just above my reach, but by buoying myself up I was able to grasp them and pull myself and one of the girls I had been talking to onto the gangplank boom."

They hung on for nearly two hours before being rescued, he explained. "[The girl] said she would reward my heroism by marrying me when we were old enough."

The marriage proposal was soon forgotten, but Carl felt brave enough that night. "My training in scouting," he later recalled, "had taught me to 'keep my cool' in emergencies."

After telling the story, Carl sat at the dining room table and tried to straighten out the brim of his water-logged hat. He was still wearing the heavy clothes. "Take off that wet scout uniform and take a bath," Carl's mother ordered. "Then go to bed," she said sternly.

"Go to bed?" asked Carl, noticing the light through the window shade. Why, the sun was just coming up, he thought.

COLUMBIA WRECK AT DAYBREAK
MURPHY LIBRARY UNIVERSITY OF WISCONSIN-LA CROSSE

20

WHEELS OF JUSTICE

7 AM DST SATURDAY, JULY 6.

Finally daylight.

It had been a long wait, nearly five hours, in the unseasonably chilly night air.

The rescue workers, mostly volunteers from nearby factories, fisherman or coal miners who lived along the shore, had spent the night doing hand searches in the twisted wreckage before being called off the boat. It was all they could do with just a thin beam of light from a miner's hat or the glow of a rowboat's lantern to lead their way. They were exhausted, but few took the option of going home.

For the coal miners, this was comparatively easy work. These were hardened men who spent their daylight hours underground where the air was damp and filled with the smell of sulfur and coal dust. A death sentence for some, since just breathing in the mines would often induce the fatal black lung disease. Cave-ins were common as well, occurring without warning and often resulting in miners being trapped or crushed to death. A mixture of coal dust and methane could cause explosions that sent fiery gases through the dank tunnels, scorching earth and flesh in a flash.

Mines flourished in the mid-1850s when locomotives began to use coal instead of wood to fire their boilers. Then in 1873, steel plants in Illinois introduced the Bessemer furnaces that burned bituminous coal. By 1917, Illinois was the third-largest coal-producing state in the nation with 810 mines delivering 86 million tons of coal annually.

Most of the open mines in Tazewell County were a series of underground rooms and pillars, a technique for extracting coal that removed coal and other material in stages and used waste to form pillars that supported the room's roof. If the pillars were too small and weak, the roof would push down and collapse the room, which was called a 'squeeze.' One squeeze could create a disastrous chain reaction that would send the weight of one collapsed pillar into the next room, increasing the pressure on the adjacent pillar until it too snapped into a paste of rock dust, and so on. Such mishaps usually cost several miners their lives.

In Pekin, some seven or eight mines operated in the late 1800s with names like Old Hope and Champion. Only two, the Broadway and Lakeside Mines, would still be operational through the mid-1900s. The rest were mined then backfilled, or 'longwalled,' and sealed shut. Safety measures improved over the years, but coal mining accidents still occurred at alarming rates. Yet, for many who lived in Pekin and Wesley City, it was all in a day's work.

The fishermen were also a hearty lot, living off the river and doing their jobs while dangerously perched on unstable boats and at the mercy of the unpredictable river. Too often, they would fall overboard, only to be found later by other fisherman. This occurred frequently enough that an informal rule developed on the river, as one old-timer explained: "[If you] ever come upon a floater, don't put him in your boat. The smell will never come out."

NOW THE MEN HAD waited anxiously for morning to arrive. They checked their watches. At last the sun was cracking over the horizon. A grisly task was ahead.

And the grim-faced, weary men were not alone.

A few reporters had also spent the night on the river. They weren't about to leave and miss the story.

Earnest East was among the die-hards. "The scene at daylight was a strange one," he wrote for the *Peoria Star.* "On either bank were automobiles and clustered about the hulk of the *Columbia* were motor and row boats—curiosity seekers chiefly. Along the Tazewell shore scores of discarded life preservers lay in the mud."

Another reporter described it this way: "Just as dawn broke and the unsettled mist which hung over the boat moved way, the first workers plunged into the work. Diving and wading in knee-deep water, between decks, volunteer workers vigorously prosecuted a search for bodies."

Captain Mehl was ordered by Coroner Clary to stay in sight. Mehl knew the boat better than anyone else and could direct rescue workers where bodies might be buried. With grappling hooks and axes in hand, the workers began to cut holes in the boat. "Here, this is where the exit would be," Mehl would tell them, and they would begin to hack away at the layers of broken boards.

From the shore, the first glimpse of the wreck in the faint morning light was unsettling. The *Columbia,* a once-striking figure on the Illinois River, looked like a broken toy.

Earnest East wrote, "On the port side, toward the Tazewell shore, the hog chains—steel overhead braces running from stem to stern and carrying the load of the boilers in front and engines in stern—hangs loose and sagging under a tremendous strain, carrying the weight of the super cabins and super-structure thrown about them as the boat listed and sank. These bear mute testimony, that the hull beneath the water was buckled under the impact on the sand bar in the dense fog." Debris was everywhere. "Drifting downstream this morning was all manner of wreckage, useless life preservers, life floats, pieces of broken 'gingerbread' ornamental woodwork, hats, handkerchiefs, and the miscellaneous fragments mutely testifying to the way the boat went to pieces as she backed to her doom."

"Shoes, hats, dancing pumps, sweaters, and wraps of all character were hauled from the water-covered checking room in the dance floor lobby," wrote Humphrey and Barrette. "Up from the concession stands, the lunch room, and the café of the lower deck, floated myriads of gum packages, candies, peanuts, popcorn, and even soggy ice cream cones.

"Knitting, on which some industrious matron had been laboring just before the crash, was found floating between the decks of the collapsed boat. The needles hung loose in the wool of the sweater of khaki yarn which she had started, probably during the early portion of the trip."

Knitting had become a popular pastime during the war. When news started coming in from across the Atlantic, one story struck a nerve: troops from the United States were underdressed for the cold French winter, a consequence of a rush into the war without thorough planning or preparation. As the news spread, so did the yarn. Women spent their free time furiously making sweaters for the shivering 'doughboys' overseas. A sweater of khaki yarn was very likely intended for some man in France.

In addition, clothing was being rationed, and many women simply made their own, including footwear. "Lavender slippers made for beautiful boudoir wear, were fished out of the swiftly flowing stream," Humphrey and Barrette wrote, "only one was completed."

Something else was moving up the river. Through the light morning mist, a flatbed barge was seen cutting through the swift current. It had a large crane on it. Then another small barge appeared, this one bearing a portable air pump and a long hose that curled up high into a mound. The arrival of the small boats caught everyone's attention, since no boats had been allowed to come close to the wreck. But these two carefully maneuvered closer to the sunken steamer. Several men stood on their decks. One man in particular caught the eye of onlookers because he was dressed so strangely in an oversized, bulky jumpsuit with a large ring cut in the top through which his head, tiny by comparison, poked. He was holding a helmet that looked like a large fish bowl with a cage in front. The diver's name was Earl Barnewolt.

During the night Barnewolt had received an urgent phone call at his Peoria home. A mechanic who ran a busy auto repair business during the day, Barnewolt wasn't used to late night calls. The caller was even more unexpected.

"This is Tazewell County Coroner Lawrence Clary," the voice said.

Clary had no problem with his motor vehicle, Barnewolt was told.

"You own a diving suit, is that right?" Clary asked.

"Yes," replied Barnewolt.

"Then we need your help," the coroner told him.

THE WHEELS OF JUSTICE started turning as soon as word of the *Columbia* disaster reached government offices in Springfield. In no time, Governor Frank Orren Lowden called an army of investigators to the wreck site.

The 57-year-old Lowden was as sharp as his well-tailored suits. A staunch Republican who became the state's 25th governor in 1917, Lowden never set foot in Illinois until he was in his teens. Born in Sunrise City, Minnesota, the clean-cut and ambitious son of a blacksmith lived on a farm in Iowa from age seven and came to Illinois as a student. He settled in Chicago where he later taught and practiced law. While in the Windy City, Lowden married Florence Pullman, daughter of millionaire George Pullman, the inventor of the railroad sleeping car. They met on a ship bound for Europe and shared a romantic tour of Paris together. Lowden quickly won Florence over, but her father, a formidable man with an explosive temper, was a different story. Fortunately, Lowden was equal to the challenge. Although his childhood was of modest means, Lowden was now a sufficiently successful and prosperous man. It took some convincing, but Florence wooed her doting father for consent.

Lowden's wealth didn't distance him from the people of Illinois, who respected his candor and appreciated his years as a scrappy lawyer. In 1920, his political career peaked when he became a leading candidate for the Republican nomination for president, nearly a shoo-in at the time to be elected. The delegates deadlocked between Lowden and General Leonard Wood, resulting in a compromise candidate, newspaper publisher Warren G. Harding, who was remarkably similar to Lowden in looks and background and went on to win the general election by the largest margin in American history, with 60 percent of the popular vote.

But in the summer of 1918, Lowden had his hands full. He was now a wartime governor with greater responsibilities and concerns. The workforce was depleted, production was down—or devoted exclusively to the war effort—and prices were up on just about everything. Although a steamboat wreck on the Illinois River was not on his agenda for that year, the governor didn't back away.

Like a general barking orders on a battlefield, Lowden ran through a list of state officials he wanted to lead the charge. "Find Sackett and Mansfield," he insisted.

William L. Sackett, the Commissioner of the State Waterways, was reached at his home in Morris, Illinois, a town about halfway between Peoria and Chicago. He would take the first train to Peoria.

Assistant Attorney General C.F. Mansfield wasn't difficult to find either. Conveniently, he was staying in a downtown Peoria hotel attending a murder trial, which had just wrapped up. He was looking forward to a summer break when he received the news about the *Columbia*. The hoped-for respite would have to wait. Mansfield would be Lowden's first state official to arrive on the scene of the tragedy.

But there were others on the way.

C.N. Postgate, of the state's utilities commission, took a train from Springfield to Peoria. A diver named Dunscombe was summoned from St. Louis, arriving aboard a government steamer named the *Comanche* that had been dispatched to the wreck. Dunscombe's job was to inspect the hull and figure out why the *Columbia* sank. Dunscombe came with good credentials, Lowden was told. He was an expert diver who worked many jobs for the state and federal governments.

In Pekin, Coroner Clary was busy organizing disaster efforts with local officials. He and Tazewell County sheriff Jack Wilson spent the early morning going through a list of safety concerns.

Security was a top priority. The wreck site was exposed, and there were still bodies to be removed. The curious were already gathering along the shore. Clary had no idea what to expect, but he took no chances. He called for the Home Guard troops stationed in nearby East Peoria.

The Home Guard was a group of ordinary citizens who took on the role of the National Guardsman during the war. An estimated 40 percent of the U.S. combat forces in France was made up of soldiers from the National Guard, so the ranks on the home front were severely depleted. When the National Guard soldiers shipped off to war, the Home Guard was quickly assembled and trained. In many instances, they received no pay and wore no uniforms. It just depended on how much each individual state or county was willing to spend. The rag-tag group of volunteers—described by one observer as "a cross between a civic club and a sheriff's posse"—may have been the "second team," but they were a useful and effective replacement back home. Clary needed them to help with crowd control and, if necessary, to suppress any disturbances. The Home Guard soldiers arrived in Pekin that morning with "shouldered guns," wrote one reporter.

Clary had seen the first bodies removed the night before. He had no idea how many passengers had been on board, how many had perished or how many had walked away. He asked Captain Mehl and other crew members how many bodies they thought lay in the wreckage. There could be a hundred or more, Clary was told. Clary's job as coroner would be to identify and determine the cause of death in each case. A formal inquest would be required. There was no time to assemble a panel of jurors, so Clary contacted five members on May's jury, the same number of jurors who worked on cases during the last coroner inquest.

From his office, Clary had called upon a local man—Barnewolt—who had a diving suit to begin the search. He also sent a telegram to police in Chicago. "Send a diver," he wrote, one with experience in shipwrecks. There was no question which diver Clary had in mind. The 'Hero of the *Eastland*,' Harry Halvorsen, he was told, would be on the next train out.

A derrick, or crane boat, was ordered to lift the heavy planks from the top of the boat. Eventually, the wreckage would have to be removed. The derrick could help. All other river traffic was blocked.

It was early Saturday morning. Clary had been up since 1 AM, and his work was just beginning. With his wrinkled blazer unbuttoned and Panama hat on his head, Clary left his downtown Pekin office and went back to the wreck site to identify the dead. That would be the first order of business, he told eager reporters on his way out. "There will be no inquiry until all the bodies are removed," Clary announced.

AT THE DEPARTMENT of Commerce office in Washington, D.C., when William C. Redfield read the telegram about the wreck of the *Columbia,* he probably shook his head in disbelief. The last boat wreck with a significant loss of life had been an exhausting event for his office. In 1915, Redfield spent three weeks in Chicago gathering witness testimonies in the case of the sunken steamer *Eastland.* More than 800 people lost their lives in the accident, mostly employees of the Western Electric Co. and their families, who were heading to a picnic in Michigan City, Indiana. The *Eastland* never made it off the dock. The boat was overloaded and unbalanced when it gradually leaned to one side and toppled over into the sewer-laden waters of the Chicago River, trapping hundreds below the waterline.

Redfield's comments and public hearings on the wreck were closely scrutinized by the people and press of Chicago. The hearings led to several indictments and criminal charges against the captain, chief engineer, steamboat inspector and owners. But that wasn't enough to satisfy an angry and despondent community, especially a big, boisterous and politically corrupt one like Chicago. The sentiment—fueled by supportive media reports—was that no real justice had been served, that the government had investigated and ultimately protected itself. The United States Department of Commerce was at the center of it all.

The Department of Commerce and Labor was created under the Roosevelt administration in 1903 to control and regulate big business, but it proved to be too much for one department to handle. A decade later, with President Taft at the helm, the department was split in two. Several of its branches and agencies were transferred to the newly formed and named Department of Labor.

The no-nonsense Redfield, with his distinctive walrus-type mustache, was appointed Secretary of the Department of Commerce—sans the Labor—in 1913. It was a position he relished despite its tribulations. Until then, Redfield's political aspirations and ambitions were usually followed by disappointments. He served two years in Congress and made an unsuccessful run for the nomination of Vice President of the United States. When he declined to be a candidate for re-nomination to Congress in 1912, newly elected President Wilson looked at his fellow Democrat's record in business and labor issues and picked him to be part of his cabinet.

The job proved to be just as challenging as any elected position. The United States Steamboat Inspection Service was under the Department of Commerce umbrella, and in July of 1915—almost immediately after news of the *Eastland* disaster hit the papers—the blame game was on. The federal inspection service was accused of "dereliction of duty" not just concerning the *Eastland,* but in many cases involving steamers under their jurisdiction.

E.N. Nockels, the head of the Chicago Federation of Labor, was the first to recognize a problem and report it. Nockels wrote a scathing letter to the assistant secretary of the Department of Commerce directly attacking the administration for allowing another boat—the *Christopher Columbus* in this case—to run at full capacity of nearly 3,800 passengers "with the excuse that she runs but five miles from shore." The crowded condition, Nockels warned, without "sufficient life boats or able seaman," in the event of an accident "will prove to have sacrificed the lives of thousands of people, even if she were tied to the docks." The letter was dated June 22, 1914, a full year before the *Eastland* disaster.

Nockels' forecast was eerie. "We believe the conditions of the excursion passenger steamers are altogether too unsafe to be permitted to continue without a most vigorous protest from this federation, as a matter of record, in the event of an accident in the future, that we at least had registered a protest."

In the *Eastland* case, the Department's steamboat inspectors were suspected of acting only in the interest of shipowners who had balked at the new La Follette safety law that required boats to carry more life boats, rafts and other heavy equipment to match the size of its passenger load. Robert La Follette was a Republican senator from Wisconsin and one of the first political figures to organize reform and push for a controversial progressive agenda. La Follette supported hot-button social issues at the time, such as the women's suffrage movement, minimum-wage laws and safety regulations, not only in the work place but anywhere a mass of human life prevailed, as was the case on trains and ships. La Follette believed that if institutions were more democratic then "opportunities of its people are more equal."

Inspired by the *Titanic* disaster, the La Follette Seaman's Act of 1915 was designed to increase the safety for passengers and improve working conditions for the crew. The ship owners roundly objected. The new laws regarding weight and space restrictions would greatly reduce the number of passengers per trip, they argued, and thus profits, which in turn meant there would be fewer boats, and so on—the familiar arguments against any new regulations. Even the company that owned the *Eastland* protested directly to Secretary Redfield against compliance with the safety provisions on the grounds that it would be "impossible to operate the boat and make expenses." There were also concerns that the extra weight would make the boats, especially the long steamers that sailed the Great Lakes, too top heavy and vulnerable to dangerously high winds and waves.

La Follette didn't back down. The safety bill passed and was signed by President Wilson in March of 1915. But the law itself was not scheduled to go into effect until the following navigation season. In a show of good faith the *Eastland* owners immediately installed six additional life rafts and three new life boats, but the matter of passenger limits was still not mandated by law. Therefore, critics clamored, the Department of Commerce and its Steamboat Inspection Service were in no hurry to enforce the regulations *and* the owners themselves were under no obligation to comply.

Nearly 2,500 boarded the *Eastland,* which was permissible, but the number of "children under five and others admitted without tickets" raised the total number of passengers considerably. The added life boats and extra weight were mostly on the port side of the ship, the side closest to the water when the *Eastland* was docked. Those who got on the ship either made their way or were forced to stand on the port side and make room for the throng of passengers still waiting to come aboard on the starboard side. The boat started to list, slightly at first and without much notice, but then gradually, slowly, the steamer tipped into the water. It was later determined that a clogged ballast—a hole on the side of ship used to fill the hull with water and keep the ship evenly leveled—also directly contributed to the ship's unbalance. But one fact was undisputable. If the La Follette law had been in place and enforced, only 1,200 passengers, or fewer than half the number of passengers that actually boarded the *Eastland* that day, would have been allowed on the ship. And some 800 souls would not have died.

After the accident, the president of the International Seaman's Union conceded the boat was doomed. "No passenger boat is safe that will not stand up with its maximum load of passengers all on one side without water ballast," he said. "Nothing short of the capsizing of the vessel would have been sufficiently convincing evidence to prove its stability and the fact that it was overloaded."

The remarks did not blame the inspectors directly, and in fact the ballast problem was likely caused by a build-up of silt or dirt from the filthy river and had nothing to do with the Department of Commerce at all. But the question of overloading and enforcing the laws concerning overcrowding was the most obvious explanation as to why the ship capsized, and the easiest to understand.

Redfield had no choice but to come to Chicago and defend the Commerce Department against the charges. His initial comments to the coroner's jury seemed harsh and unsympathetic. "When he left the room," the jury foreman later noted, "the opinion was expressed that his talk was plainly an opening statement of the defense...supplementing his statements with a suggestion that the jury take no action against his men until they are heard...he impressed me as a special pleader for the men in his service, with an infinite capacity for muddling."

Redfield's main objective of course was the accident and why it happened. He held an investigation of his own and called to question the very same men who worked under him. The questioning was "not only leading, but argumentative," in defense of his department, the press noted.

"Now look back and think of the time when you were not a mere government official," Redfield asked one of his embattled inspectors at the hearings. "Think of the time when you were just a man and remember when you were a seaman whose judgment was [solid] and then tell me based upon your judgment as a man, before you lost out to become a government official, tell me whether you really think as a seaman that the *Eastland* was a good sea craft."

Redfield's blatant sarcasm was evident when he questioned one of the indicted inspectors about his son-in-law who just happened to be an engineer on the *Eastland*. "I hear from the watchdogs in the press that you are guilty of having a son-in-law?" Redfield asked. "Did you arrange for him to become your son-in-law and then arrange for him to get a job on the *Eastland* so her passenger-capacity could be increased?"

The people and press of Chicago were not amused.

The aftermath included a blistering rebuttal from the lieutenant governor, who demanded that the scope of the investigation go beyond the *Eastland* wreck and include a thorough examination of the steamboat inspection service's work over the past 15 years. Redfield was forced to make a statement of retribution.

"I am willing and ready to search every corner and cranny for the ultimate truth in regards to the United States inspection service and the *Eastland* disaster," Redfield said. "I came to Chicago for that purpose and my purpose has never wavered. I am sorry. I am hurt and I am willing to admit it at this time."

Redfield was down, but not out. He took one last parting shot at his critics and closed the book on the matter by saying, "I have been mistreated and prejudged by the Chicago press and by Chicago citizens. My record should have protected me, but it did not. My life is an open book—my 30 years of public life—and yet when I come here to make an investigation, I am judged in advance."

So it would have been understandable that July day in 1918, three years after the *Eastland* debacle, if the Secretary's heart skipped a beat when he was informed that another deadly steamboat accident had occurred on his watch. Despite whatever regrets he may have felt, there was work to do—and Redfield got right to it. He called for the two steamboat inspectors in the region, Captain George R. Bower and Rees V. Downs, to go to the wreck site and begin a preliminary inquiry. Both men arrived in Peoria from St. Louis on Saturday.

The acting supervisor of the Steamboat Inspection Service, Fourth District, based in Louisville, Kentucky, was Captain George M. Greene. The wreck was under his regional jurisdiction, and Redfield wanted Greene there too. Bower and Downs would report to Greene, who would report to the Deputy Supervisor Inspector General of the Steamboat Inspection Service, D.N. Hoover, who in turn would report directly to Redfield.

The wheels were in motion. But they were already turning the wrong way for Captain Greene. Greene was in Evansville, Indiana, when he got the call. Although he left by train in the morning, "the only connections I could make required that I stay overnight at Mattoon, Illinois," Greene would later write about his unfortunate delay. And it got worse, as Greene acknowledged: "In boarding the train in Mattoon, the porter directed me to the wrong train, and as there was no one at the steps of the car when I got on board the train, I did not learn of the mistake until we were some 20 miles out from Mattoon.

"This made it necessary for me to wait for another train to back to Mattoon, and then transfer to another train to Peoria."

The irony of a 'steamboat man' held up by a train was not lost on Greene or his superiors. They likely got a good chuckle out of it. But the mistake cost him precious time. He arrived in Peoria Sunday evening, a full day after Bower and Downs. "They immediately went to the wreck," Greene reported to Inspector General

Hoover on the work of his two regional subordinates. "They made considerable progress in their investigation, having taken several depositions, before my arrival."

Two of these early depositions were key, he wrote—the captain's and the boat's pilot. But while the apparatus of officialdom was moving into gear, the tragedy on the Illinois River was still unfolding.

CORONER CLARY AND CAPTAIN MEHL AT WRECK SITE
MURPHY LIBRARY UNIVERSITY OF WISCONSIN-LA CROSSE

21

A PAINFUL GROAN

AUTO MECHANIC Earl Barnewolt not only *had* a diving suit, as Clary was told, he was an expert diver too. Tall and broad-shouldered, Barnewolt arrived at the wreck site early Saturday morning with several other men looking to help. Clary was pleased. Barnewolt's posse included Herbert Fitch, who manned the air pump (a critical role and the only man Barnewolt trusted with the job, it was said) and Ora Barnewolt, Earl's brother, who owned a construction company and had expert knowledge with materials found on the *Columbia*. Ora would help the rescue workers clear the debris. Coroner Clary had asked Earl if he could get the recovery started first thing in the morning. The men quickly assembled their gear and told Clary they were ready.

Barnewolt's diving suit was tight, bulky and drastically restricted his mobility on land. He was like the tin man with no oil. His helpers had to finely tune him up for the dive. Like tailors in a clothing shop, they gathered around him and began readying the suit. The straps were tightened and the weighted boots pulled over his feet. The round metal helmet was carefully placed over his head and the wing nuts were turned to make it airtight. Barnewolt looked through the cage-like portholes in the front and sides of the helmet. He gave the signal for his partner Fitch to turn on the pump. It made a rumbling noise as the air inflated the hose that ran from the pump to the top of Barenwolt's helmet. He took several deep breaths and gave the 'go' sign. Then he grabbed the hose and leaped into the muddy river.

There was an immediate problem. The river had risen a foot overnight due to recent rains. The water under the surface was dark and murky and nearly impossible to see through. Barnewolt would say later that whatever he accomplished the rest of the day was through sense of touch only. He began reaching and touching.

Almost instantly he grabbed onto something.

ON THE SURFACE, rescuers with saws and axes in hand began chopping at the broken boards, and the derrick's crane operator began lifting the heavy planks off the top deck. When enough debris was cleared, the men put pike poles in the water, dragging for bodies. They yielded nothing. They put the poles in again and repeated the process. Again there was nothing. They kept at it. Then one man felt something. The slightly bent pole was carefully pulled up. A nervous anticipation rose as the men stopped to see what might be attached. They all breathed a collective sigh of relief when just a lone life preserver dangled from the end of the pole. The men regrouped. They set the poles down and grabbed their axes again. They cut through more of the debris and the crane lifted more of the loosened boards away. The poles were dragged along again. This time another man felt a substantial tug.

"I've got a body!" he shouted. There would be many more.

UNDER THE WATER and in complete darkness, diver Barnewolt reached out and felt an arm. A woman's arm, he thought. A piece of lumber lay across her chest. Barnewolt tried to lift it, but it was too heavy. He surfaced again and asked for the crane's line. He hitched the line to the board and gave the signal to lift. The board budged just enough. A woman with "badly bloated face and blackened lips" was pulled from the water. Edith Lee was her name, a Pekin woman, the daughter of Moses Lee. She was the first person to be extracted from the wreckage that morning and identified. It may have been one of the rescuers who recognized her.

Barnewolt took a short break, then a deep breath and went under again.

This time *he* almost didn't make it back up.

AFTER EDITH LEE, an unidentified woman, about 25 years old, came next. Then another woman, said to be about 20 years old. A rescuer could only say he thought she was from Kingston Mines, the papers reported. He could not place her name.

"That's Jimmy Blackburn," said another worker as the body of a man was dragged out of the river. It was easy to see how 'Jimmy' was recognized. The men knew his familiar face, usually a cheerful one, beaming from behind a long counter asking, "What can I get ya?" Blackburn owned a "wildy popular" saloon in town.

A woman dressed in a yellow jacket of "mixed silk and cotton" was found near the exit of the dance floor. She wore a locket with the initial 'D' on it.

"I've got another," a worker shouted. He jumped in the water and asked for a rope. "I tied the rope about the foot," he later told reporters. Soon the body of a boy appeared; he seemed to be about twelve years old.

"There is another," the worker shouted again, pointing to a spot several feet away. A heavyset woman was brought out and laid beside the boy.

Another woman was found. In her "tightly clenched" hands were a handkerchief and a pocketbook containing a silver dollar and a stamp. "She had a gold tooth," said a newspaper report, "but there were no other means of identification."

The rescue workers with "calloused hands," a journalist noted, tenderly carried the bodies to the small tugboat where they were laid side by side and covered with a sheet.

CORONER CLARY ARRIVED back at the wreck site and immediately began examining the bodies. He checked for jewelry, necklaces, lockets, watches, bracelets—anything to help with identification. The bodies were difficult to recognize, bloated and bruised. Clary made a difficult decision. The families would have to endure the excruciating, gruesome task of identifying their loved ones by sight. It was the only way. He nodded toward the tug pilot who pulled away and headed downriver. The first victims of the *Columbia* were heading home.

Captain Mehl never left his boat. From the moment it sank until daybreak he stood by its side. Now trying to keep his balance on the unstable boards that used to be his proud 'old tub,' he watched in horror as the bodies were removed one right after the other. There was nothing he could do but watch and wonder. A reporter nearby asked him what he was thinking. "I'm at a complete financial loss," he said. "But I wouldn't care about the boat, the money, or the inconvenience, if I could just bring back the lives of those people."

From a short distance away, another pike pole was removed from the water and a rescuer's voice could be heard.

"I've got another one," the man said.

BELOW THE SURFACE, Barnewolt was struggling. The diver had discovered several more bodies, including that of a mother holding her baby, but the river water was muddy and dark. Suddenly he became tangled in debris and couldn't find his way out. His lifeline, the air house, was snagged by fallen I-beams and pipes. He jerked the hose. Herbert Fitch, who was manning the pump, felt a slight pull, a signal the diver was in distress. He frantically called for several men to jump in. With help, Barnewolt managed to free himself and find his way back to the surface. He sat on top but never removed his helmet. A few minutes passed before he stood up again. The men watched and waited. They weren't sure what the diver was going to do next. Then Barnewolt gave the familiar 'go' signal, grabbed the hose, and pointed toward the water.

He was going back under.

IN PEKIN, GRIEVING FAMILIES who had searched for their missing loved ones the night before nervously gathered outside the police headquarters for more information. "Thread by thread," the newspaper reported, "the reports of the disaster trickled in." Several bodies had been taken from the wreckage, they were told, and would be arriving by tug that morning. "The chaotic throng then surged from the police headquarters to the dock, the same dock from which the steamer had left the evening before." They waited and watched from the shore, "hour after hour in anxiety for the arrival of the tug."

A hush came over the crowd with the first glimpse of the tugboat. "A painful groan arose from the throng," a journalist from the *Chicago Tribune* noted as the boat approached shore. "The horror of the disaster was revealed."

"The bodies were stacked up like cordwood," is how writers Humphrey and Barrrette sensationally described it in their story, *The Columbia Disaster.*

The tug scraped the sandy shoreline, and a rope line was extended. The first body was removed. It was the body of a small boy. "An old woman, her face red, walked by the side of a young man who carried the child," wrote the *Chicago Tribune.*

Volunteers were called to duty. The strong men waited in line to carry the white-sheeted bodies from the shoreline to the Empire Building in downtown Pekin. Coroner Clary had secured a small vacant space in the building as a temporary morgue. The coroner didn't want a scene by the river. The families would have a chance to identify and claim their loved ones at the morgue, they were told. But their grief could not be contained.

The crowds moved away from the river and lined the cobblestone streets like it was parade day. The lamp posts were still adorned by flags and bunting from the Fourth of July celebration. There they stood several persons deep, in front of the downtown shops. On a normal Saturday, the streets would bustle with crowds socializing and frequenting their favorite stores. But today, the crowds were static and most businesses never opened their doors.

"On the sidewalk, quiet groups watched as the shrouded forms were carried in a continual stream throughout the day," the *New York Times* reported, "from wharf to the morgue for identification." The few ambulances in service began to arrive too.

"Conversations were in whispers and necks were stretched to gain a sight of the sheeted stretchers inside," went the report. "Somewhere in the distance a coronet played *Nearer, My God, to Thee*. Women and children were in tears."

The quiet whimpers were broken only by the chatter of voices and clinking of glasses coming from several open doors. The saloons were open as usual. "As each additional body passed," the *Times* reported, "the grumblings in the saloons increased."

Captain Walter Frederick of the Home Guards stepped up patrols. The soldiers were ordered to stand guard at the rear and front of the makeshift morgue. The front of the building got so crowded that the ambulances were diverted to the back entrance. Soon, the unorganized mass of people gave way and a line into the morgue was formed and began to move through.

The bodies were placed in long rows on "hastily constructed slabs," and mothers, fathers, daughters, sons, friends and relatives walked slowly past each body. A sudden shriek indicated that another family member had been found. "Time and time again," wrote Humphrey and Barrette, "the eyes of the guardsmen were dimmed by tears because of some sad episode within the morgue. Strong men broke down and wept like children when they saw the forms of their sons and daughters among the dead. Mothers cried aloud, became hysterical and fainted. There were scenes that would move even the least emotional. But the Home Guards went grimly about their ghastly task, blinding themselves as much as possible to the many horrors they saw."

The Red Cross women were there too. "Angels of mercy, clad in their veils of white," wrote the *Chicago Tribune*. "They ministered to the bleeding hearts of the anguish-stricken relatives of those who had perished in the disaster."

Anna Mogga and her father were at the morgue that morning. Anna and her mother Emma had tickets for the *Columbia*, but at the last minute, Anna felt sick and decided not to go. She told her sister Hilda to take her place. Hilda had been found alive, Anna and her father had soon learned, but Emma was still missing. "My dad heard the victims were taken to the Empire Building," Anna remembered. "We went down there and walked past the rows of dead bodies until we found my mother. As you passed, a man would lift up the sheet to view the body."

For years after that, Anna recalls, there were no white bed sheets at their house. "We simply could not handle white sheets," she said.

Another family tragedy is told through the eyes of 19-year-old Walter Loomis. As several newspapers reported, Loomis was either working at the wreckage or helping carry victims from the tug to the morgue when a white sheet that was covering one of the bodies shifted slightly and a woman's arm fell off to one side.

He recognized the ring on the finger.

"My God," Loomis cried out. "That's my mother."

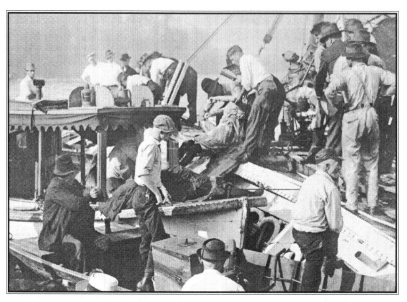

ANOTHER BODY GOES ON THE TUGBOAT
MURPHY LIBRARY UNIVERSITY OF WISCONSIN-LA CROSSE

22

HOT WATER

STATE OFFICIALS SILENT.

The state officials in the paper's headline referred to C.F. Mansfield of the Attorney General's office and Walter Sackett, Commissioner of State Waterways, both sent by the governor to investigate the *Columbia* disaster. They arrived Saturday morning "just in time to see a body brought up," the story read, but made no formal announcement.

The state's most powerful lawyer, Illinois Attorney General Edward Brundage, was conspicuously absent. He was said to be at his summer home and "impossible to communicate with." Fortunately, Brundage's assistant and second-in-command, Mansfield, was in Peoria on official business. He was the first state official to arrive. Sackett had been reached at his home in Morris. As soon as Sackett stepped off the train, both men met with Coroner Clary and Tazewell County state's attorney E.E. Black. Mansfield refused to go on record, so Black, the trusted local official, made a brief comment on his behalf. "Every investigation possible will be made," he said. "We will make every effort to place blame on this catastrophe."

Reluctantly, Superintendent Sackett was forced to make a brief statement. He indicated that should the investigations result in blame being attached to any of the ship's crew, officers, or owners, there would be no hesitation on the part of state officials in seeing action was brought against the suspected persons. Aside from that—which as it turned out was more than reporters had expected—there would be no further comments.

The self-imposed gag order wouldn't last.

The townspeople were desperate for answers, and an angry backlash against the captain and crew was growing.

As noted earlier, in Pekin that Saturday morning most businesses stayed closed or opened their doors late—except the saloons. As the drinks flowed, so did the accusations. In an effort to avoid mob action Black published a lengthy statement in the next day's newspaper. It read:

> This statement is made that relatives and friends of those whose lives were lost in the ill-fated steamer *Columbia* may know that every effort is being made to obtain the facts and circumstances which caused the disaster will be made from every angle, and without regard to whom it may strike. I was at the scene of the disaster shortly after it occurred, and intend to remain on the job until a complete, final investigation is had, and that this investigation will be made through this official with the assistance of the attorney general's office. Upon the result of this investigation depends the course of action that will be taken.
>
> You will readily understand that these facts and circumstances cannot be published at this time. I desire to say further that various organizations such as the Home Guards, Red Cross, sheriff's force, police force, and city officials have given invaluable service as well as many other individuals. Any persons or persons having knowledge of any fact or facts bearing upon the *Columbia* tragedy, will be performing a public service by communicating with the state's attorney's office at once.

(Signed) E.E Black, State's Attorney for Tazewell County.

Clary followed suit. The coroner had no idea who was on the boat when it went down, or who escaped alive. The *Columbia*'s purser, August Mehl, who counted the tickets, and the chairman of the social club that sponsored the trip, Ben Meinen, were able to give Clary only a rough estimate of how many people may have boarded that night—there was no list of passengers by name. Family members crowded the coroner's office searching for loved ones who were either missing or hadn't returned home. "Maybe they were on the boat," they would ask the coroner. Clary simply didn't know.

He submitted a five-line ad that appeared in the paper just days after the wreck:

> Notice. All living persons who were passengers on the steamboat *Columbia*, Friday night, July 5, are requested to leave their names at the Association of Commerce, Pekin, at once. L.R. Clary, Coroner.

The announcement was brief and the print so small that it would have been easy to miss. It appeared with little distinction in the middle of the classified section normally used by citizens for such matters as announcing an engagement, wedding or birth date. Next to Clary's notice was a wedding announcement for a young couple from Kickapoo, a job opening that stated, "girls are wanted [to work] at the Pekin Steam Laundry," and an advertisement for a newfangled cure-all called Sanol. "When you have a backache," proclaimed the ad, "the liver or kidneys are sure to be out of gear. Try Sanol. It does wonders for the liver, kidneys and bladder."

Also in the paper that day, the Transportation Club of Peoria had an urgent message to its members. The Transportation Club was a new organization, established in 1912, to "promote closer relations between the shipping and transportation interests by personal acquaintance and the friendly discussion of traffic issues." In July each year since its conception, the club held an annual picnic, usually outdoors and usually on a boat. In all, nearly 400 members would come from Chicago, Indianapolis, St. Louis and Kansas City to attend the event. Before the very first outing in July of 1912, the *Peoria Transcript* noted: "The picnic is to afford the members, who cannot get away for vacations, a half day off for thorough enjoyment. The boat leaves the dock, foot of Fulton Street at 1:30 PM." However, the notice made clear, the picnic and outing for 1918 would perforce be rearranged:

> The annual outing and election of officers, which was slated for July 9 aboard the ill-fated *Columbia,* has been called off. It will probably be ten days or two weeks before the outing is held. Upon which, it will be held in some form other than a river cruise.

Adding to the air of intrigue surrounding the arrival of state and federal investigators, a man from the secret service office was spotted nosing about the wreck site. His name was Rosen, head of the secret service in Springfield. The reporters recognized him. "Just what a part Secret Service agent Rosen is playing in the unraveling of the tangle of circumstances surrounding the sinking could not be ascertained," a writer from the *Peoria Journal-Transcript* speculated. "Whether or not he was investigating the sinking in relation to the war situation—the principal work of the secret services department in the present crisis—is only a matter of conjecture."

Rosen himself added to the mystery surrounding his appearance. "The less said about my work the better," he told the newspaper.

IF FEDERAL INSPECTORS George Bower and R.V. Downs arrived in Peoria a little on edge, it was understandable considering the circumstances. The *Eastland* disaster and subsequent public hearings had been an embarrassment to the Department of Commerce and their boss, William Redfield. Several men in the same position as themselves—steamboat inspectors—had been indicted and faced criminal charges with lengthy trials.

Bower and Downs had nowhere to hide. They had inspected the *Columbia* just two months earlier and deemed her "the safest boat on western waters." Now they were in Peoria to investigate why that same boat sank and fell to pieces. Was it a structural problem?

Did they miss something in the last inspection?

Their work would be scrutinized as much as the boat's crew. Still, they had a job to do and were fully prepared to do it. They had to take assertive command from the very beginning or the investigation would be compromised. So, unlike state officials who clammed up when they first arrived, the federal inspectors were talking—or spinning, depending on your point of view.

"Our inquiry is aimed especially to see whether there was any carelessness on the part of the licensed officers of the steamer or members of the crew," said Downs. "It was a terrible thing and we want to do everything we can."

Three years before, both Downs and Bower examined the *Columbia* as they had dozens of other boats after the *Eastland* wreck. The Steamboat Commission demanded it. They asked that all excursion boats meet the measures of safety required to carry passengers or remain aground.

The *Eastland* wreck brought few if any changes. In fact it raised more questions than answers. Still, the public demanded safer boats and more stringent inspections. The Steamboat Commission complied. The Peoria boats, including the *Columbia,* were included. The inspectors meticulously examined the hull and boilers and gave them their stamp of approval. The *Columbia* met all federal requirements.

Before the start of the 1918 excursion season Mehl had been told to make improvements, especially to the aging hull. Downs and Bower would not grant Mehl his license that year until the changes were made. However, this was not an unusual request. The *Columbia* was an older boat, and overhauls were common. Mehl spent thousands on the repairs. When the inspectors returned in May they did a thorough examination, including "spending considerable time in the hull," claimed a crew member, before they surprised Mehl with the "safest boat" tag.

Mehl painted the words SAFETY FIRST on the outside wall of the boat's main deck, "where everyone could see it," he said proudly. Now two months later, that same hull was sitting on the bottom of the river and the rest of the boat was a pile of timbers. Downs knew the question was coming and answered it directly.

"She was in good condition," he said. "Captain Bower and myself did our full duty when we inspected her May 7 last."

He added, "We have no fear of anything developing that will get us in any hot water."

If that statement didn't raise reporter's eyebrows, the next one certainly did.

"It was just a case where somebody's foot slipped," Downs said. "The accident which befell the *Columbia* was one such as might befallen any river boat. Even the *Titanic* sank when it struck something too powerful to resist. When an obstruction is encountered in any water only two things can happen—the obstruction is pushed out of the way or the boat is crushed.

"That is fundamental," he added with some authority.

Downs was asked if he considered the *Columbia* seaworthy.

"It had always been regarded as one of the best boats in the district," he answered. "Many boats are rebuilt many times. I know of good boats that have undergone reconstruction several times and will pass any inspection."

Redfield had made it clear that the captain, pilot and crew of the *Columbia* were not on trial, at least not initially. The most severe punishment his department could impose would be loss of license. If they were found guilty of negligence, Herman Mehl and Tom Williams would never be able to own or operate a steamboat again. Upon arrival Saturday morning, the two inspectors immediately sent a letter to Washington:

> *We arrived at port today at 9:30 AM. We found the steamer lying head downstream diagonally across river, pointing towards left-hand shore in from 18 to 25 feet of water, hurricane roof amidships being partly submerged. Part of the crew and quite a number of volunteers were engaged in removing bodies from wreckage by cutting holes through hurricane roof. Seeing that they were weakening the supports of the Texas roof, we suggested and helped tear away said roof and*

remained at scene as long as we thought our presence necessary.

Downs and Bower were waiting for Captain George Greene, the acting district supervisor of the Steamboat Inspection Service, to arrive so they could begin taking testimony. He was running late. Greene had sent word that he had boarded the wrong train by mistake and would now get there Sunday evening, a full day behind schedule. Redfield didn't want the investigation to drag into embarrassment like the *Eastland*. He wanted the inquiry to begin right away. "The captain, pilot and all surviving crew members would be questioned on Sunday, the next day," Downs told reporters.

"It will be a secret meeting," he said, "behind closed doors."

The news of a closed-door meeting meant nothing to the fervent reporters. They had a feeling the captain and pilot would talk to them as soon as the federal questioning was over. Maybe as soon as they walked out the door. The accused always wanted a chance to defend themselves, was their thinking.

They were right.

DIVER EARL BARNEWOLT TAKES A BREAK
MURPHY LIBRARY UNIVERSITY OF WISCONSIN-LA CROSSE

23

ANOTHER BODY

AT NOON ON SATURDAY, Coroner Clary announced that more than 50 bodies, many still unidentified, had been brought to the surface. In just a few short hours, the rescue crew and diver Barnewolt were pulling the lifeless forms out of the murky water at a rapid pace. The first 24 bodies found were mostly women or young girls between the ages of ten and 20 years old. One adult male body had been recovered as well as several small children.

Barnewolt had found five bodies trapped under debris. The rest had simply floated to surface as the heavy boards were pulled away. The men reached in with their pike poles, snagged a piece of clothing and pulled the bodies up. Seven bodies were found beneath the pilothouse. At one point a baby carriage was fished from the water. "Careful there," said Barnewolt, who had surfaced and was taking a break. "See if the baby is still inside."

"The workers exercised care," a reporter witnessed, "but the buggy was empty."

Soon thereafter the bodies of Francis and Albert Grewey were pulled from the water and identified. Albert was three years old;

Francis only two months. They were the son and daughter of John and Jennie Grewey. All four family members had been on the *Columbia*. John survived. Jennie was still missing.

"There's a baby!" shouted one of the workers. A body was spotted floating away. The men caught the "little form" and pulled it out of the water. It was a small girl with a signet ring on her finger bearing the letter 'G.' Grace Harbolt, age four, was no longer missing. Four members of the Harbolt family, including Grace, her mother Iva and sister Mabel, and Katie, her aunt, all perished in the wreck. They were among the first victims identified who had boarded the *Columbia* in Kingston Mines.

Clary used many personal items to identify victims. A gold watch was found on the body of a young man whose "features were unrecognizable." The watch was a gift from his parents, it was later learned. The man, George Schuster, a coal company worker, would have turned 21 in September.

Two women were pulled from the wreckage and placed on the deck for Clary to examine. Both wore watches that had stopped at 12:05 AM. Another unidentified body was taken to the morgue. Clary found a set of keys on the young man, who looked to be no more than just a teenager. The tag on the keys was marked JOHANES ICE CREAM PARLOR. As soon as the keys were revealed someone shouted, "I know him! He works at the ice cream shop." Fifteen-year-old Rudolph Poebel had been found. He was on the *Columbia* with his twin brother Roland, who survived.

In the small rowboats and gas launches that surrounded the wreckage, photographers set up their tripods and snapped away, capturing image after image of the rescue operation in progress. In one photo, Clary and Captain Mehl are standing together on the top deck looking solemnly down as another body is removed from the wreckage. In another photo, a woman's body is seen being pulled out of the debris. A man's arms are wrapped underneath the woman's shoulders in an effort to lift her legs free. In still another dramatic shot, Clary is seen crouching next to the body of a woman and holding her frail limp wrist in his hand. Another man in a derby hat is standing next to the coroner, stooped over at the waist.

He scowls at the camera, silently saying to the man behind the lens to "show some respect." The picture was published Monday, July 10 in the *Pekin Daily Times.*

AT SOME POINT on Saturday, Clary asked reporters to gather around. He had something to say. Clary cleared his throat and told the intently listening crowd how many bodies had been found so far, about 60. He also wanted to clear one thing up. Earlier he had reported one of the missing boys, Jake Becker, had been found dead.

"The body of a boy first identified as that of Jake Becker," Clary said slowly and clearly so all could hear, "was actually a boy named Orville Shyrock." Shyrock had already been reported missing and presumed dead. "The victim looked very much like Becker," the coroner continued, "and his friends thought he was dead. That is until Becker appeared and assured them he was not."

"So Jake Becker is alive?" the coroner was asked, just to clarify.

"That is correct," said Clary, "Jake Becker is alive and well."

The reporters ran to make a call and correct the mistake. They must have felt like they were in for a very long day.

THE CROWD THAT HAD gathered along the shoreline on Saturday was loud and boisterous, much different from the night before. The grieving family members were gone. They had left for home or to the morgue to identify the dead and prepare for burials. The folks who came to the river on Saturday were mostly curiosity-seekers, plain and simple, who wanted to witness the wreck site for themselves, with no other vested interest than just to say they were there. Peoria police chief Randy Rhoades, Tazewell County Sheriff Jack Wilson and Captain Frederick of the Home Guards kept a close watch on the proceedings. So far, the onlookers were orderly.

The word they were getting from Pekin, however, was much different. The saloons had been open since early that morning, and men bound on stirring up trouble had done just that. They were rousing the large crowds into an angry frenzy. The people of Pekin had already been talking and placing blame on the captain and crew of the *Columbia*. They wanted justice. The voices coming from the saloons were fueling the flames.

The commotion emanating from the barroom doors was not uncommon. Neither was the clientele uncommon. The loud and bawdy establishments were owned, operated and attended only by men. For good reason, women mostly stayed away. Here was a place where men could smoke, spit, swear, argue, reminisce, complain, laugh or fight among themselves without the conformities of home or the eyes and ears of a good woman nearby. "Respectable working class women were prepared to drink in private, even in the company of men," wrote Andrew Barr, author of *Drink: A Social History of America*, "but they were not prepared to enter the public drinking place, where men held sway." In some instances, women would turn their noses up and silently protest by walking on the other side of the street. "The salon was the anti-home," writes Barr, "where men went to escape from their homes and their wives, to take 'time out' from their responsibilities."

The dusty floored, smoke-choked rooms with cheap wallpaper and ornate mirrors were open for one purpose—drinking, no questions asked—and while beer was served it was mostly harder drink like whiskey and gin that was being consumed. If a meal was offered, it was usually advertised as 'free lunch' that cost a nickel just to keep out the freeloaders and down-on-their-luck types. And just in case there was any question as to whether the joints were for men only, oftentimes a painting of a naked female would hang over the long mahogany counters. The place was made to make women feel uncomfortable—at least the ones who planned to keep their clothes on.

Saloons in the bigger cities like New York and Chicago had reputations as round-the-clock party houses, filled with late-night drinkers and scantily clad women dancing on dingy, dirty wooden stages. The hooting, hollering and drinking would continue from "the crack of dawn to the crack of dawn," it was said. No one questioned or really cared when and if the place closed, or how much illegal activity occurred as long as the police were paid off and the reformers kept at bay. One saloon keeper in Manhattan, named

Callahan, claimed he threw his keys in the East River. Perhaps he would lock the doors, he supposedly said, if someone found them.

In Pekin, the saloons certainly weren't as big and sinful as in New York, Chicago or perhaps even some of the seedier sites in Peoria, but the purpose was the same. A swig was a swig no matter where it was consumed, and in Pekin the stuff was nearly home-made. The distillery in town was its biggest employer. Some of the men who were slugging it down were the same ones who were making it—or on this Saturday, *had* been making it.

In 1917, three years before prohibition became law, the Lever Food and Fuel Act that regulated food, fuel, and other commodities needed for the war effort was passed. The distilleries that made the whiskey were temporarily shut down. The grains needed to distill alcohol were otherwise needed, according to the Act.

Asbury Lever was the son of a South Carolina farmer, and a Democrat like Wilson who entered the U.S. House of Representatives in 1901, just as the temperance movement was gaining momentum. He had a knack for issues concerning agricultural and rural life. He passed the Farm Loan Act in 1916, making it easier for farmers to borrow money, and a year later sponsored the Food and Fuel Act giving government limited but efficient control over coal, natural gas, oil and alcohol. The anti-alcohol forces leached onto the bill and demanded even stricter regulations be enforced that included a total ban on *all* alcohol makers, including beer and wine, not just whiskey. Wilson knew the bill was doomed with more regulations and asked the prohibitionist leaders to withdraw their demands. Instead of the all-out filibuster threatened by the 'wets,' who were clearly in the minority, the bill passed with only the production of spirits affected. It was not exactly the sweeping prohibition the reformists wanted but a win nonetheless. The bill flat-out prohibited the manufacturing of whiskey nationwide—but only whiskey.

The Peoria-Pekin area was at the forefront, especially Peoria. At the time, Peoria had several massive distilleries and breweries along the banks of the Illinois, and it was one of the largest whiskey makers by volume in the world.

The reformers used the restrictions on production as a springboard to continue their fight for a more extensive and total ban on alcohol's existence. Their tactics weren't always fair. Wayne B. Wheeler, a "small man with wiry glasses, crinkly cornered eyes and a tight smile" was the *de facto* head of an outfit called the Anti-Saloon League, which was an organization run like a racket that targeted churches and politicians to achieve its main objective: eliminating alcohol from the fabric of American life. Nothing but a total ban was acceptable, the Anti-Saloon League preached.

They went state-by-state and picked on vulnerable local leaders in need of support—and votes. Are you 'dry' or are you 'wet?' Come to their side, Wheeler and the ASL demanded, or face the consequences: a fierce backlash of negative press or even worse, an opponent who wholeheartedly accepted their demands. It was political suicide not to abide and Wheeler seized the moment. Many strong-willed lawmakers buckled under the pressure. By 1917, more than half of the 48 states went dry. Wheeler and his cronies were almost there.

Illinois was not a 'dry' state, but due to the war and the Lever Act, whiskey couldn't be produced on its soil. There was no law against selling and drinking it, however. In Pekin that Saturday, the loophole was wide open.

The Local Options Law did provide many counties and townships in Illinois with a choice to go 'dry.' Perhaps pressured by the large number of churchgoers and religious zealots in their communities, many districts—mainly in the southern half of the state—independently declared themselves alcohol-free and pressured local saloon owners to close shop. Hundreds of saloons were shuttered. Peoria and Tazewell Counties, perhaps influenced by the number of urban immigrants and distilleries in town, were not among them, despite strong leadership on both sides of the issue.

In fact the distillers and brewers in Pekin were still doing business during the war years, making yeast products mostly or 'near beer,' which was beer with less alcohol, another government mandate. The papers reported the number of jobs at the distilleries actually went up during this time.

Although the newspaper coverage didn't shy away from mentioning the role of the saloons in Pekin after the *Columbia* wreck, with their "open doors" and constant "chatter," the question of just how much alcohol was being served or consumed is debatable, if not inconsequential. This was still a place to meet, a place to vent, a place to organize and a place to let voices be heard. The men inside, drunk or not, had made up their minds about who was to blame and why.

"The captain, pilot and crew were drinking!" they shouted with irony-challenged conviction.

And there were rumors of women in the pilothouse!

Captain Mehl, they said, is German. "Hun sympathizer!" the men shouted.

The glaring prejudice against German-Americans was not uncommon after the war began, even in a town like Pekin that was built upon the strength of its first immigrants. But with few original inhabitants left, the mostly American-born citizens gave vent to angry bigotry. "An unreasoning anti-German fever raged across the land," noted Irving Werstein in his book *Over Here and Over There.* "Everything Germanic was erased from the American scene."

Nationally, German named foods like frankfurters and sauerkraut were changed to resemble more American sounding labels like 'liberty sausages' and 'liberty cabbage.' Almost overnight, Germans became 'Heines,' 'Fritzies,' 'Krauts,' 'Jerries' and 'Huns.'

"Hun sympathizer!" the more ardent—or perhaps more inebriated—crowd members shouted again. There were reports that Captain Mehl was "hung in effigy," but the story was never substantiated.

Perhaps the angry fervor had been started by a man named C.A. Rau, a Pekin resident who would later repeat a story he was telling around town to the *Pekin Daily Times.* "I went from the dance floor deck to the roof and climbed up the ladder which leads to the pilothouse," he said. "I was seeking an ax to liberate an old man pinned under a seat. I knocked on the pilothouse and a man barred my entrance. He appeared to be in night clothes with a white blanket about the head and shoulders. I was sure he was either drunk or out of his mind." Rau also said he saw a woman in the pilothouse. "She wore a black skirt, a white waist, had black hair and appeared to weigh about 140 pounds."

"She was the last woman to leave the boat," he claimed. Although Rau's tale seems unlikely in the extreme, reporters never pressed him to explain. Who was this woman? Why was she the last to leave?

The chief of police Harry Smith had few options. If the town rioted, the department would be outnumbered. He suggested that all saloons in the city be closed "to prevent men who had lost dear ones from taking the law into their own hands and meting summary vengeance upon the pilot and captain of the *Columbia.*"

Captain Frederick of the Home Guards, who would likely be enforcing the action, listened to the chief's impassioned plea and overruled it. "The threats of violence, if any, were idle," Frederick said. "Besides, none of the crew resided in Pekin."

Perhaps he thought a bunch of angry louts on the loose was worse than keeping them immobilized inside their watering holes. "Rumors of trouble were without foundation," is what he told reporters.

The saloons stayed open.

BACK AT THE WRECK SITE, police closed off the only dirt road that led to Wesley City. It was clogged with automobiles. The order was given to free the path. From now on, authorities directed, only undertakers' cars bearing caskets, boxes and other funeral supplies would be allowed to pass through.

Unfortunately, the task of removing the vehicles was just as chaotic and time-consuming as it was getting them there. The early automobiles, like Ford's Model T, weren't exactly the idling type. The clunky contraptions were left belching smoke, breaking down and getting stuck in the mud. A reported "2,000 cars" jammed the river road, and it took nearly six to seven hours just to clear the "machines out of the tangle," the papers noted.

In the meantime, Coroner Clary got a message. The diver from Chicago was in Peoria. A train was waiting to take him to the wreck site.

HARRY HALVORSEN
CHICAGO HISTORY MUSEUM

24

HERO DIVER

HARRY HALVORSEN—the 'Hero of the *Eastland*'—what an honor.

Coroner Clary's telegram to the Chicago Police Department asking for a professional diver, specifically one with experience in shipwrecks, brought Halvorsen to central Illinois. When the police captain in Chicago received Clary's request he knew there was only one man for the job; he contacted the Great Lakes Bridge and Docks Company. "Is Harry available?" he asked. Halvorsen would take the first train in the morning. The message was relayed back to Clary.

Halvorsen arrived in Peoria on Saturday afternoon, where Clary had made sure a special train car waited, ready to take him to Wesley City. Described as "tall, burly, and chiseled-looking," the good-natured Norwegian stepped off the train and was said to be ready for "a big job."

If someone had described Halvorsen as carrying a 'ton of baggage,' they would have been speaking literally—Halvorsen didn't travel light. Several huge chests were filled with heavy diving equipment. They included an air pump, which was about the size of a large hot-dog cart, his one-piece waterproof suit, weighted shoes, helmet and a large diving bell. Handy though the diving bell was, it couldn't replace the flexibility of wearing a suit. Halvorsen had used both the bell and the suit effectively in his work on the *Eastland* and spared no expense on his trip to Peoria. He brought the whole shop.

Halvorsen's valiant work on the *Eastland* had made him a household name. He was personally responsible for bringing up more than 250 of the 844 (or more) persons lost in the disaster. The brave diver didn't save any lives, but he gave families back their loved ones for burial. Without Halvorsen's help, the trapped bodies might have remained in the underwater tomb for days, possibly weeks.

Now with celebrity status and a solid reputation, he was in Peoria. The papers were all over it. The name Halvorsen was good print. A reporter was waiting for him when he boarded the special train from Peoria. Halvorsen told the writer he was working on raising a coal boat when the call about the *Columbia* came. He also told the story of recently bringing up four bodies that were pinned in a submerged auto that plunged off the 12th Street Bridge in Chicago.

Halvorsen had some concerns about the new job. He said the *Columbia* wreck posed risks he didn't encounter on the *Eastland.* Those who perished on the *Eastland,* for example, were overcome by rising water and drowned before they could find an escape route. The metal steamer itself remained fairly intact. By contrast, the *Columbia* was broken into pieces, and bodies were trapped by heavy beams and woodwork. Searching through the unstable debris would be a risky undertaking. Halvorsen had no idea that a local diver had already been under the water and briefly trapped by the twisted wreckage.

At the wreck site, Halvorsen was all business. A writer for the *Peoria Journal-Transcript* recorded his every move:

> In his diving bell he went under and through the wreck, and when he came back up said: "They are packed in thick

in the barroom. There must be dozens of bodies down there. [The authorities] need the assistance of two or three good professional divers because in my opinion the job is really more dangerous than cleaning out the *Eastland*. The *Columbia* is so badly shattered and piled up that only experienced men should be allowed to work on her below deck. The whole thing could go to pieces and the diver loses his own life."

Halvorsen immediately found Clary and told the coroner about his shocking discoveries. What happened next was just as shocking. Clary thanked Halvorsen for his time then told the diver that his services were not needed.

Not needed? Halvorsen must have thought, confused.

Clary had made up his mind.

The day before when he called for a diver, Clary wasn't sure how many bodies lay in the wreckage. If there were only a hundred or so, as he was being told, then more than half had already been brought to the surface. The local diver, Barnewolt, was doing good work, better than Clary had expected. Halvorsen came at a high cost, which Clary wasn't willing to spend. Halvorsen was gracious. He thanked the coroner, the people of Peoria who greeted him at the railway station, and apologized for not having the time to "shave off a stubby beard." He loaded up his heavy trunks and boarded the next train back to Chicago.

Meanwhile Barnewolt continued the search for bodies and found someone he recognized, Maurice Feinberg, a Peoria man. The 18-year-old had moved to St. Louis and recently returned to visit family and friends. Until he found Feinberg, Barenwolt had no personal connection to the bodies he was pulling out of the wreckage. Most were from Pekin or farther south, while Barenwolt lived in Peoria. He also ran a business in Peoria. Feinberg was the first victim he knew. Later Barnewolt would find out that his friend was last seen alive on the top deck of the boat right after it sank. He had been with a companion who jumped in the water and shouted back at Feinberg, "Take off your shoes and swim to shore."

"No, I can't swim," was Feinberg's reply. "I might just as well die here."

He did.

THE FEDERAL INSPECTORS had made another important decision. "The diver who inspects the hull should be a disinterested party," they said. Another diver was on the way, Clary was told, this one appointed by Governor Lowden. His job wasn't to recover bodies like Barnewolt, but to inspect the hull and determine what may have caused it to leak. His expertise would prove to be invaluable.

While the town of Pekin was stewing over wild allegations against the crew and captain of the *Columbia,* men with cooler heads—and state and federal job titles in front of their names—were sitting down and discussing theories as to why the boat sank and collapsed. They needed to know how the water got in the hull. It wouldn't be long before the state's diver would arrive and find "the hole."

ALTHOUGH DISHEARTENED by the circumstances, Clary must have been pleased with the efforts so far. He had arrived the night before, shortly after the wreck was first reported, and took charge of operations. He ordered the rescue work to stop and resume in the morning. He called for several divers to begin the search for bodies and opened a temporary morgue site in Pekin. Everything he had asked for so far was being done with efficiency and order. But Clary soon faced another problem, one that was completely out of his control.

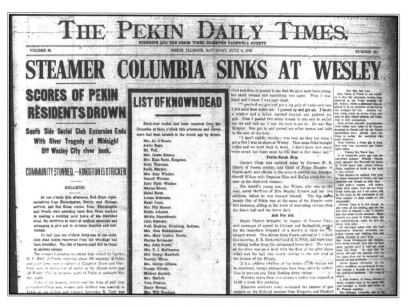

PEKIN DAILY TIMES FRONT PAGE HEADLINE
JULY 6, 1918

25

THE STORM

THERE HAD BEEN A steady rain all day. The river was up and running quickly. But something more was in the air. The rescue crews aboard the *Columbia* could sense it. The clouds were thickening, the wind picking up. They continued working and kept looking up at the darkening sky. Then shortly after 9 PM, it hit.

"The storm swept up with almost hurricane velocity," was the way the *Peoria Evening Star* described it.

Coroner Clary and the rescue crew on board the wreckage had difficulty getting away from the rapidly increasing winds and drenching rain. "Get her out of here!" cried Clary as the government steamer *Comanche* with its extended crane was lowered and safely pulled away from the sunken steamer.

The launches and skiffs that were tied together and surrounded the wreckage swayed back and forth like rocking cradles. Clary feared the *Columbia* would break apart, perhaps releasing the trapped bodies below. "Get someone on the wagon bridge," he ordered.

In a farmhouse near the wreck site, Clary placed a lookout. The

man's job was to report back to Clary any shift in the boat's position. The rest of the rescue crew and stragglers still on the shore
ran for cover. They were the only ones left. Most of the sightseers
from earlier in the day were gone. They had either hopped on the
last train or went home after the police shut down the road.

Clary said he would be in contact with both lookouts overnight.
The brave men who volunteered for the job hunkered down. They
pledged to let Clary know if there was any movement overnight.

The storm was as brutal as its ominous appearance suggested.
"The big wind with heavy rain and lightning that broke upon Peoria Saturday night did a lot of damage," the *Evening Star* reported
the next day. "Telephone and telegraph wires which by lightning
and wind were put out of commission. Probably 1,000 telephones
were on the hummer. Two tents of the carnival company at the
river bank were blown over, but no one was hurt."

Clary could only make a run for it, wait and hope. He would find
out in the morning if the *Columbia* held.

BY NIGHTFALL, the line at the morgue was thinning out. Most of the
nearly 70 bodies that had so far arrived at the building on Court
Street had been identified. To help speed up the process and prepare the bodies for burial, several dozen undertakers were called
from a wide region, even from as far as Decatur, 100 miles away.
Caskets were in such short supply that a special boxcar-load was
rushed over on the Chicago, Peoria and St. Louis Railway.

But not all bodies made it to the morgue.

Back at the wreck site, the body of a small boy was found floating in the debris. A rescue worker gingerly picked up the corpse
and was carrying it away when a man approached. The man had
been helping rescue crews on the boat since sun broke that day.

He stared at the small lifeless figure in the worker's hands and
reached out. The baby was placed in his cradled arms. Then he
turned and walked away. The man had done a similar thing earlier that night when he dropped off his eldest son at a neighbor's
house. "Watch Henry for me," he asked the kind folks, then turned
and walked away. He had returned to the wreck site and was told

that his wife Martha and son Melvin were both dead. Now John Diepenbrock was holding the body of his youngest son, the baby, Norman. "There wasn't a dry eye among the rescue workers as the man took the boy home," a reporter wrote.

RUTH BROWN WAS TOLD her son's bride-to-be was among the victims. Louise Neaver would have turned 18 in October and was a "most likeable miss," according to her family. She and Floyd Brown were scheduled to be married as soon as Floyd returned from the war. He was one of four Brown brothers in the service. "Now the Spartan mother of soldiers," the papers reported, "would have the unpleasant duty of breaking the sad news to her son."

IN THE STREETS OF PEKIN, as the sunlight faded, so did the grumblings coming from inside the saloons. The armed Home Guards lined the streets and kept the lawless from getting out of hand. Pekin Police Chief Harry 'Harm' Smith helped suppress the angry mob with words of encouragement. "Reports have come to me that drinking on board the *Columbia* was carried to extremes," he said. "This phase of the case will receive rigid attention after we have buried our dead."

"The results may be amazing," he added.

But not all the news out of Pekin had such a revengeful tone.

"Survivors of the catastrophe were on the streets for the first time since being brought home," was the report in that day's *Evening Star*. "In conversation with friends and reporters they told and retold their recollections of the tragedy and instances of heroism on the part of those who were saved and those who lost their lives in trying to save others." One name that came up frequently was a young man by the name of Joe Kumpf.

His story was told by others.

"He smashed out a window, and might have easily escaped, but aided a half-dozen women," said one witness. Another person added, "He was an expert swimmer and could have went straight for shore, but helped save many people instead."

"He could have made his way to safety," still another recalled, "but instead helped three others up the companionway."

Joe Kumpf was on board the *Columbia* with his brother Bill. When the boat went down, both Kumpf brothers made it safely to shore. But Joe kept returning, recalls Bill, who would wait for his kid brother to return after making several trips back and forth, each time bringing another struggling victim with him. But after one such trip, Joe failed to come back. "Unfortunately, one of the men he tried to save panicked and ended up drowning them both," Bill said.

Later, Joe's family would put three simple words on his tombstone. A *COLUMBIA* HERO, it read.

There were other amazing stories of survival and heroism being shared around town. "A young woman coolly refused all proffers of rescue and cried over and over again for the rescuers to save the ones who were 'more scared,'" reporters were told. "The young woman remained on the boat until she was dragged off and when the water was up to her chin." A man who witnessed the woman's brave actions said, "Certainly she was a true heroine."

Another girl, 15-year-old Frances Poebel, was said to have saved the lives of four women. And Mabel Rue, only twelve years old, rescued her friend and playmate Gladys who was 13.

Two brothers, Oscar and Robert Gehrig, rescued several women at their own peril. Oscar was thrown into the river when he heard a woman crying out, "Oscar come get me!" He swam back to the boat, climbed up and found her safe but shaken. He pulled her and several other women to safety. Robert was dancing when the listing boat "threw us all into a heap," he recalls. He reached the skylight and pulled three women out.

The Peoria papers sometimes carried the praise to extremes. "A man with only one arm," one story went, "bravely rescued a half-dozen women!" Even if some of the rescue stories were exaggerated or worse yet, fictitious, there were still plenty of heroes of the *Columbia* disaster and plenty of Pekin residents to thank them.

AS THE CLOUDS CLEARED the next morning, there was good news from the shoreline. The *Columbia* had weathered the storm. The lookout in the farmhouse across from the wreck site reported no movement overnight. There were no sign of bodies floating downriver.

While it put a crimp in the recovery efforts, the storm was s relief for the workers who had been laboring nonstop since daybreak. They needed a rest, both physically and emotionally. The storm allowed many to return home for the first time since the wreck occurred the night before.

Rube Collender was one of the first men to arrive at the wrecked boat and one of the last to leave. He lived in Wesley City and came running when he heard the cries for help. He later spoke about his experience. "They called for help in many different ways," he said of the victims. "Some were loud, others only asked by the outreach of their hands. We crawled all over that wreck and into places we shouldn't have.

"We rejoiced when the hand responded with life. But the hands that did not respond were a pain in my heart."

Collender arrived home that night and was unable to take off his shoes. "The buckles were so full of human hair that I had to cut the laces," he said.

JOE KUMPF'S TOMBSTONE
COURTESY LINDA TILLMAN

26

SPECIAL PRAYERS

CLARY BREATHED A SIGH of relief. The *Columbia* hadn't moved an inch. *A small favor,* he must have thought. Just a day and several hours before, the boat had sunk and collapsed into a pile of broken boards. Now the crumpled mass, despite how unsteady it may have looked, had some stability. It had survived gale-force winds without budging. The rain was still coming down when morning broke, but the worst was definitely over. Now it was time to get back to work. There were still more bodies trapped below, Clary was sure of it. The diver and crew could safely return to the wreck and resume the search.

It was Sunday.

Oh, Earth, Earth, hear the word of the Lord. The Reverend George W. Goebel stood at the altar of St. Paul's Church at Seventh Street and Ann Eliza. He read from Jeremiah 22:29: "Oh, Earth, Earth, hear the word of the Lord," he repeated. He applied the Bible verse to the *Columbia* disaster, telling parishioners "of the peculiar ways in which special visitations are made by the Lord."

It was a scene repeated all over town. There were almost 500 passengers on the *Columbia,* nearly all from Pekin. Every church in the close-knit community had at least one of their members on the boat, many had several. They were either saved, injured, missing, or worse.

"Gloom that only death tragedy can shed, was to be seen on all sides," the *Peoria Journal-Transcript* reported later that day. "The saddest Sabbath this pretty little city ever experienced."

Despite vast disparities in wealth and social standing and regardless of the true stew that made up the American 'Melting Pot' at the time, one thing almost all Americans shared in the early part of the 20th century was the role of organized religion in their lives. In addition to their function as houses of worship, Christian churches and Jewish synagogues were a social meeting place that offered members a place to gather and participate in clubs, picnics, potluck dinners, and even sporting events. Most embraced the sanctuary as a second home and the congregation as an extended family. A general wave of Christian rebirth was spreading across the country as churches of all denominations—Methodist, Protestant, Presbyterian, Episcopalian, Baptist, Roman Catholic and others— were being built. Large numbers of Jewish immigrants who came to America in the late 19th century settled in upper Midwestern cities as well.

The importance of God and religion didn't stop at the bottom of the church doorsteps, either. Americans of all classes, noted author Harvey Green in *The Uncertainty of Everyday Life 1914-1945,* "included some physical reminders of religious affiliation in their homes...walls were often decorated with items such as framed prints, calendars depicting biblical events, needlework or printed mottoes such as GOD BLESS OUR HOME, and crucifixes.

"When death visited a family," Green noted, "it brought them together in a community of grief. Nearly all religions, ethnic groups, and classes in some way gathered to honor their dead at graveside services."

Pekin would need to bury its dead, but on this Sunday before interments began, it was the living that urgently demanded attention. "The congregations couldn't contain the parishioners' emotions as special prayers for the dead and rescued were offered," the evening's *Transcript* reported. The passionate sermons echoing from the altars "brought some comfort to the sorrow." The children at the Christian Church at Broadway and Elizabeth Streets were so saddened by the disaster that Sunday school lessons that morning were "impossible to conduct."

Reverend Earnest C. Poole of the First Baptist Church preached a special sermon that day, taking his reading from the first verse of Psalm 21: *The King shall joy in thy strength, o'LORD; and in thy salvation how shall we rejoice.* The Rev. Poole had just returned to the Pekin parish after serving a church in Rantoul.

The First Baptist Church was one of the town's oldest, built in 1855.

WHILE SOME FOUND SOLACE in the solemn and respectful services, others were just too overcome to attend. The night before, victims' families had spent several hours at the morgue and returned home late. They walked through the rows of white sheets, identified their loved ones, then waited for an undertaker to prepare the body for burial. The work was carried out "rapidly and systematically," it was reported, and "shortly after midnight, every body recovered was ready for transportation to the sorrowing homes."

"Every available hearse and ambulance in Pekin was occupied in moving the corpses," the *Pekin Daily Times* noted. Instead of early church services, families chose to stay home with their fallen loved ones who in repose lay peacefully in the front parlor or living room.

The church pews were only half-filled. The *Journal-Transcript* reported that several pastors "of many churches" stated that there were "a smaller number at their morning services than has been noted on even the most stormy of days."

The first funeral would take place that morning at the Presbyterian Church. Most of the rest were scheduled for Monday, Tuesday and Wednesday of that week. The Red Cross was busy working with families on the arrangements. Five members of the St. Joseph Catholic Church perished on the *Columbia*. "It is probable all five funerals will be held at the same time," Rev. Father J.D. Sullivan announced in his sermon.

The bodies of two men from Peoria, Maurice Feinberg and Kenneth Sanders, were brought back home from Pekin the night before, the *Journal-Transcript* reported. "The remains were accompanied by relatives." On Monday, the *Transcript* carried an ad from the local musicians union. Sanders was the orchestra drummer on the *Columbia*.

The ad read:

> All members of local No. 26 of the musicians union will meet at 306 Garfield Avenue to attend the funeral of Brother Kenneth Sanders.

The union asked members not to wear uniforms, but had one special request. In a fitting tribute to a fallen musician, it read, "bring instruments."

THAT SUNDAY AT THE federal building in Peoria, steamboat inspectors Downs and Bower waited along with assistant U.S. District Attorney John Dougherty for the captain of the *Columbia,* pilot and several members of the crew. All had been summoned for depositions. The captain and pilot faced the loss of their operating licenses in the federal investigation. Dougherty was there to determine if any criminal charges were warranted.

It was rare for such proceedings to occur on a Sunday afternoon, but federal investigators did not want to waste any time. Captain Mehl arrived shortly before 11 AM. The rest followed. They included pilot Tom Williams and assistant pilot Dell Sivley, who was 'off watch' at the time of the wreck but still on the boat. The boat's engineers, Allen Davidson and L.W. Logan, were called. Davidson was considered the man 'at the throttle' when the steamer struck the bank. Along with Henry Trippler and first mate W.C. Edwards, Davidson was also the first to discover water in the hull. Trippler and Edwards arrived at the courthouse along with several of the other deckhands who had been on duty that night.

Also appearing was a man the inspectors added to the list after allegations surfaced concerning drinking by the crew. His name was Charles Stedman, the *Columbia*'s bartender.

The only crew member not called was George Stewart. He was still missing.

"Pale and shaking," a *Peoria Journal-Transcript* reporter noted, "the crew talked in subdued tones while awaiting their interviews with officials."

One at a time they entered the interrogation room. Mehl was the first to be questioned. The rest were sitting ducks for reporters as they waited outside the closed doors. They didn't need to be prodded.

"The hull was pierced by a stationary log," the soft-spoken Williams told reporters when asked what he thought may have caused the wreck. "The turn in the river opposite Wesley City is a particularly dangerous one. It is a place of swift currents and whirlpools. I always feel a sense of relief when I get past that death trap." Pencils were scribbling furiously as Williams was asked why he didn't try to ground the boat. "There was no time," he said. "It was a battle against the current. The current had swung us over too close to shore. I was trying to turn the boat back again to the channel, that's when the snag caught us."

"Did you hit the sand bar?" a reporter asked.

"No," Williams answered. "A log went through it–the hull that is–like it had been made of paper. When a ship strikes a hidden obstruction like that something has got to give–either the snag or the ship. In this case it was the ship," he concluded.

The door opened and Mehl stepped out. He had been answering questions for about a half-hour. Williams was next. The reporters swarmed on the captain like moths to a light. Mehl had something to say. "We are doing everything in our power to assist the federal investigators of the terrible disaster that overtook our steamer," Mehl said. "These investigations will show that the *Columbia* was properly inspected. They will bring out the fact that we were running on a slow bell and taking every possible precaution. It was a terrible thing–I am heartbroken about it–but it seems to be one of those things which sometimes overtake the most careful navigators.

"You will find every man from the *Columbia* ready to testify before any investigating committee at any time," he added.

"What about the condition of the hull?" he was asked directly

"She was the best on the Illinois River," the captain retorted. "The hull was purchased from Captain Walter Blair of Davenport. She was never condemned."

"Was the crew drinking?"

"As for the crew being drunk," Mehl shot back, "or whether there was any woman in the pilothouse with Tom Williams? Those are lies too. Our engineer hasn't taken a drink for months, neither has our pilot."

Some of the crew may have had "a few bottles of beer," Mehl stated. "But nobody was drunk," he said. "The crew behaved like gentlemen."

Mehl was asked about his loyalty to the U.S. and accusations that he was a supporter of the German cause.

"I am not an enemy alien!" he said, raising his voice. "I gave seven trips to the Red Cross last year as promised and this year we have already given five, and there were five more to come."

"On these trips," he said mocking the reporter's previous question, "the bar was always closed."

While the question of nationality and loyalty may or may not have been justified in this case, it was not an unusual one. The angry mobs in Pekin continued to accuse the captain of being a 'Hun sympathizer,' but the reporter's question had a much deeper connotation.

At the time, anarchists and militants were becoming active in the country, pitting workers and labor unions against evil capitalist bosses. Crude homemade bombs had exploded in protest. In fact, a bomb that was set off in the railyards of downtown Peoria was used by detectives to nab the two men accused of setting off a similar type of dynamite explosive that killed several dozen workers at the *Los Angeles Times* building in 1910. The capitalist owners fought back. Their chief target was the militant group Industrial Workers of the World, popularly known as the 'Wobblies.' Unlike the more streamlined and neutral American Federation of Labor, the 'Wobblies' were especially hated because they were also against the war. There was bloodshed on both sides.

While Mehl was certainly no anarchist, he was an immigrant, and in time the lines between anarchist, socialist and eventually communist—especially after the war ended—became blurred in the popular imagination. The immigrants felt the wrath. Most foreign-born Americans were pigeonholed by the capitalists and accused of supporting the workingman's cause, since they were the ones that labored in the meager, menial factory jobs and came from socialist and supposedly communist regimes. Mehl was a businessman who hired and fired workers rather than ran with them, and the 'Red Scare'—a communist blacklisting supported by the government—was still a year or so away. But as the labor movement and the war dominated the news, it wasn't uncommon for the media to question the loyalty of a man of German descent since Germany and its allies—'the Huns' —were killing American boys overseas. Mehl answered the reporter's question directly but was clearly agitated by it. He motioned for the reporters to move back and walked away.

After each participant had been questioned and the inquiry came to a close, Downs, Bower and Dougherty emerged. Dougherty made a short statement first. "If there has been a violation of the law," Dougherty told reporters, "there will be prosecutions enough to satisfy everybody."

"We cannot disclose the nature of the depositions until after we make our report to the head office," Bower added. "The witnesses testified under oath and their evidence was made into the first record. Until we make our report and the trial is on, the blame—if any is fixed—and what they told us is an inviolable secret."

Before the reporters left they caught first mate W.C. Edwards heading out the door. They asked him what he thought of allegations that the crew had been drinking. The captain said some of the crew may have had a few beers, he was told.

"Neither of the pilots or myself touch a drop," he answered back, "and the other men do not drink while they are on duty. I was in charge of them and know it to be a fact.

"They never had a drink on that trip," he said sternly.

VIEW OF THE COLUMBIA WRECK FROM THE TAZEWELL COUNTY SHORE
MURPHY LIBRARY UNIVERSITY OF WISCONSIN-LA CROSSE

27

PICNIC DAY

THE HOME GUARD and local authorities had done their jobs well. On Saturday, when hundreds of automobiles choked the only river road heading into Wesley City, the road was shut down and the vehicles cleared. The sightseers who lined the shoreline that day for a glimpse of the wreck were said to be respectful: talkative, but orderly. Many leaned over the shoreline and shouted across the river at the workers. "How many do you think are down there?" they asked. The papers reported that some of the rescuers even obliged the curious with an answer.

By nightfall, the crowds had thinned out. Many had already left before the storm hit. No one, especially the authorities, had any idea what to expect the following day.

Sunday proved to be even busier.

"From early on in the morning until late at night," the *Peoria Journal-Transcript* reported, "the river bank was a scene of sobbing groups. Some were awaiting anxiously, hopeful. Others came to offer consolation to their friends or for their [own] curiosity sake."

This was not particularly surprising given the nature of the time.

In 1918 the social order isolated Sunday as a day of worship and a time of unity with the family, especially in smaller cities like Pekin. The Sabbath laws and customs and even 'Blue Laws' in many states reinforced the tradition. By law, theatrical performances were not permitted on Sunday unless they were religious, for example. There were no professional sporting events like baseball, boxing or horseracing on Sundays. And the saloons were closed. There were exceptions, especially when it came to drinking (the watering holes sometimes had 'secret' side entrances), but for the most part Midwestern families stuck to the religious rules on Sunday and spent the day together at picnics or other 'wholesome' social events. Even women who slaved over household chores during the week would leave Sunday open to rest. So it was perhaps unsurprising that after church Sunday morning, families in Peoria gathered up baskets filled with cold veal sandwiches, devilled eggs and spiced pickles and boarded a train to see the great boat wreck on the river.

"Wading in the sticky mud of the Pekin road," the *Journal-Transcript* reported, "thousands of men, women and children crowded toward rifts in the willows which lined the bank to get a view of the ill-fated steamer."

Since the roads were closed, the privately owned P&PU Railway—either bowing to demand or recognizing a good business opportunity—offered eight special coach trains on Sunday that ran continually from Peoria to Wesley City. The trains were said to carry 1,500 passengers each. The coach cars were so crowded that the train was forced to stop between the two cities and wait for conductors to catch up in collecting all the fares.

"The far-off shriek of an approaching train sent the folks scurrying back to the station, a mile away, and a new thousand took the place of those whose curiosity had been satisfied," the paper reported. The train company estimated 5,000 persons boarded the special trains that day.

The atmosphere had changed too. Despite the papers assertion that there were "sobbing" groups, the crowds on Sunday were different; without any connection to the victims of the tragedy, these onlookers were brash and noisy. The children played and parents mingled, like it was a day at the fair.

A writer for the *Journal-Transcript* put it this way:

> It was different than it had been 36 hours before. Then all
> was a fearful hurry. Rescue workers with blanched faces
> frantically pulled on yielding oars in their hurry to get back
> for more survivors marooned on the upper decks of the ves-
> sel. Half-crazed mothers sought their children in the weird,
> shifting light of a policeman's lantern. But today there were
> people who laughed. The curious wanted to know how many
> bodies were in the lower half of the boat, photographers
> saw an opportunity for the picture of a lifetime, old river-
> men reminisced of shipwrecks past and children dressed
> gaily in spring and summer clothes played tag with cast
> away life preservers as safe bases.

Still, the reality of the wreck and its dead was not lost on some
gawkers who braved the chilly, rainy weather to pay their respects.
"Occasionally, there were persons who gazed in silent awe at the ill-
fated steamer. 'It's too terrible...let's go back' was not an uncommon expression."

But that was the minority view. "Many brought their lunches
and picnicked at the spot," wrote a correspondent for the *Peoria
Evening Star,* "making a Roman holiday out of a tragedy which
had brought a black pall of a terrible grief to hundreds of homes."

The crowd packed the shore and watched as rescue workers and
divers went about their business of removing bodies and debris
from the wreckage.

"On board, all was orderly industry," the *Star* reported. "The big
government steamer *Comanche* poked her nose into the twisted
boat and the huge derrick lifted unwieldy pieces of the boat corpse
and deposited them on barges, anchored nearby." The pilothouse
had been removed and the dance floor "rose almost sheer now, out
of the water."

"Life preservers, folding chairs, benches—which held couples
who whispered of love—ice cream tables, beams, stairways and
loose pieces of filigreed railings were stacked in orderly piles."

CLARY'S DIVER BARNEWOLT arrived back at the wreck site. He donned the heavy suit and prepared to go under for a second day.

"I'm hoping the water is clearer this morning," he said.

"I had no opportunity of exploring the rear part of the dancing pavilion or the ladies rest room yesterday," Barnewolt told reporters. "I am inclined to believe that there are 25 bodies back there in the rear. There may be very few bodies in the main deck, as reported, but my judgment is that there are a few, if any."

Captain Mehl arrived back at the wreck site after testifying to federal authorities earlier in the day. He told reporters he had very little sleep over the past couple of days. "I ate my first meal since the sinking," he said. "And only because I realized I had to keep up and going. I'm keeping on my feet by exercise of all my will power."

Personally, Mehl had a lot to be thankful for. His wife Ethel, who was injured in the wreck, was home recovering from a minor cut. His two young daughters, Naomi and Ruth, were not on the boat, and his brother August and wife escaped unharmed.

"The only grain of relief I've got, is to know I did the best that I could do when she started to go down," he said. "If I hadn't there would have been a 150 more drowned. I never saw a boat go down so quick. I know her hull was alright. I spent a barrel of money on her. She was in first-class ship shape."

Just then the *Columbia*'s bell tolled across the water, the same sound the coal miners and fisherman of Wesley City had heard two nights before when the pilot reached for the bell tap and pulled on it shortly after the boat collapsed. The bell's ringing that night woke the men up. They were the first to arrive at the wreck. This time, the tolling of the bell was unintentional. The heavy iron cast was being carried from the wreckage when it shifted and rang out. The unexpected ringing startled Mehl. He turned and pointed to the men carrying the large bell.

"Muffle that tongue!" he cried out. "I don't want to hear that again."

The ball-shaped tongue was wrapped in a blanket and the bell was carefully "rolled over" to the deck of the salvage barge.

"The captain gave his last direct order as master of the *Columbia*," the *Journal-Transcript* reported.

ONE MAN IN THE SHADOWS was William B. Elliott. The 48-year-old coroner of Peoria County had been at the wreck site on Saturday as promised, but he remained mostly unnoticeable by the press. Coroner Clary had called his colleague Elliott the night of the accident. It was mostly a courtesy call. Clary told Elliott he was sure the boat went down in Tazewell County, just east of the dividing line, which was right down the middle of the river. The responsibility of recovering, identifying bodies and determining cause of death would likely fall under Tazewell County jurisdiction. That was Clary's assessment, at least, and Elliott agreed. He also agreed to help, if he could.

Elliott must have felt like there was some professional duty he could perform. Most of the victims were from Pekin in Tazewell County, but the men who were responsible for the operation of the *Columbia*, its captain and many of the crew members, lived in Peoria County. The boat was moored each night along Peoria's downtown riverfront. In the winter, the boat was dry docked in the town of Chillicothe, north of Peoria, but still on Peoria County's side of the river. The boat made frequent stops at the Al Fresco Amusement Park, in Peoria Heights. Captain Mehl, the owner and captain of the *Columbia*, had several businesses and paid taxes in the county Elliott was elected to serve.

Elliott lived in Peoria too. A cooper by trade, he was born in Lafayette, Indiana and moved to Peoria in 1888 at the age of 18 to work at the Great Western Distillery. Soon, Elliott found public service more his calling. In 1904 he was named deputy coroner and four years later became the county's coroner serving a four-year term. He would return to the coroner post in 1916. In the eight years in between, he served as Peoria's school inspector. In December of 1890, just two short years after arriving in Peoria, Elliott married Catherine DeWald. Eventually they had three daughters and two sons.

Although he desired to get involved in the *Columbia* investigation, Elliott kept his distance. It was the right thing to do. Clary's signature would be on each and every death certificate, he thought, and it would be up to Tazewell County to determine any criminal charges. Elliott would have no say or influence in the matter. Unless something unusual happened.

Elliott knew there was only one conceivable way the Peoria County coroner could legally get his hands on the case. So he waited, out of the way, just in case something came up.

It did, in the form of a man named Harry Brown.

Harry Brown lived in Pekin and worked as a coal crane operator at the sugar factory. He was also on the *Columbia*. When he didn't show up for work on Saturday, it was noticeable. In fact, without poor Harry, the plant nearly closed up shop. "His absence caused the crane to suspend operations," the papers later reported. Apparently, no one else but Harry Brown could operate the heavy machinery. "More than 20 extra men were needed to shovel the coal [by hand] to prevent the big plant from being shut down."

Harry's wife Catherine was the first to receive the bad news. "Does your husband wear a gold watch with the name E.J. Hoffstetter?" she was asked.

"Why, yes," she replied.

A man at the morgue had identified the body by the watch with that name, she was told. The man informed undertakers that he knew Harry Brown and remembered the plant worker carried with him a watch with an inscription which did not match his name. A guardsman then called Brown's wife to confirm it. The next call was to the county coroner.

William Elliott picked up the phone.

Harry Brown's body had floated away from the wreckage, the coroner was told, and found on the west side of the river—*the Peoria County side!*

"Get a room ready," Elliott must have told anyone who was listening, "we have an inquiry to conduct."

While Elliott was busy preparing to call witnesses, Captain Mehl had dropped a bombshell of his own. He told reporters that he had planned to sell the *Columbia* later that year and get a bigger boat.

"I had completed the sale for $32,000," Mehl declared. "She was to have left for the Mississippi River September 5 at the conclusion of the excursion season. I had just about completed arrangements for the purchase of the *Homer Smith* from the Ohio River for $65,000."

By way of explanation, he added, "The *Columbia* was not large enough for business here," he stated, and the *Homer Smith,* a much larger boat, "was too big for the Ohio River business."

For obvious reasons, the deal was off. The *Homer Smith* stayed in Ohio and continued to run excursions the following year including popular day trips from Pittsburgh to a resort called Walnut Beach in Sewickley, Pennsylvania, twelve miles downriver from the steel city. In 1928, the boat was sold to a Pittsburgh amusement company and renamed the *Greater Pittsburgh.* Four years later, in April of 1932, the *Greater Pittsburgh* caught fire rather mysteriously, while moored at Manchester on Pittsburgh's north side. The watchman was jailed for arson, but released for lack of evidence.

As for the *Columbia,* a reporter asked Mehl what he planned to do with his boat now. Mehl looked at the wreck. "I have not thought about what I am going to do or about any salvage. My whole attempt has been to get out the bodies. I think most of them are out now.

"Financially, I'm flattened out," he added. "But I would have willingly given every dollar if no lives had been lost."

Mehl wasn't through. The questioning at the courthouse in Peoria had obviously rattled and angered him. He chastised the newspapermen for harshly judging his actions and that of his crew. "See where I was heading," he said, raising his voice and pointing to the Tazewell County side of the river. "I was doing the only logical thing. I think experienced river men will bear me out in trying to reach the Tazewell shore. The water on the Peoria side is deep and the current swift."

He paused and took a deep breath.

"Oh, if I'd only had two minutes more—yes, a minute, I could have made it and there would have not been a single life lost."

The reporters wrote down every last word. Despite being reprimanded, they had a good thing going and knew it. Captain Mehl, the star witness, was good copy. And he wasn't even in court, under oath, or talking to a judge yet.

HOME GUARDS MARCHING IN DOWNTOWN PEKIN
TAZEWELL COUNTY GENEALOGICAL AND HISTORICAL SOCIETY (TCGHS)

28

OVER
THERE

AMONG THE THOUSANDS who lined the shores of the Illinois River to get a glimpse of the wreck that Sunday was Roscoe Maxey, who ran an engraving business in Pekin. Maxey was different from most of the sightseers who came to the sunken boat that weekend. They were witnessing the carnage for the first time. Maxey had come back for another look. He had been aboard the *Columbia* that fateful night with his two sisters Elva and Irene. They also survived.

Now the man upon who Pekin residents depended for engraving their names on heirlooms like "pianos, talking machines and jewelry," wanted something for himself, a keepsake to remember the tragedy by. Maxey noticed a flag pole sticking out of the wreckage. The American flags on tall masts, more than a dozen, flew from stern to bow. Captain Mehl had made sure his boat looked the part on the Fourth of July. There were several still visible on the top deck.

According to the story Maxey told his family throughout the years, he jumped in the water, swam out to the boat, climbed up one flag pole and removed the flag.

"He thought it would be a good souvenir," his son would later say in a newspaper article about Roscoe in 1986, nearly 70 years after the wreck and 30 years after his father's death. "He would proudly fly the *Columbia* flag from the family home every July Fourth." Maxey had good reason to choose the Stars and Stripes as a souvenir from the boat that night. In the summer of 1918, the news from overseas was promising. The doughboys were making good progress. The war in Europe was finally swinging in favor of the U.S.

It was no ordinary July 4th in 1918.

Across the country, in bustling big cities, rural farm communities and industrial working-class towns like Peoria and Pekin, Fourth of July celebrations took on an air of patriotism and brotherhood like never before. The bombastic affairs featured rousing marching bands, spectacular fireworks and mile-long flag-waving parades highlighting the spirit of unity among fellow nations, nations that were fighting together as one.

In Mount Vernon, Virginia, standing in front of the home and tomb of George Washington and before a packed, attentive audience—including representatives of all the countries allied with the United States—President Woodrow Wilson inspired everyone: "The United States entered the protracted affair to uphold the civilized world's Declaration of Independence," he bellowed. "The settlement must be final. There can be no compromise."

The President echoed much of his Fourteen Points speech from earlier in the year and stressed that the allied forces "in the cause of liberty" must fight to the end against governments "clothed with strange trappings and the primitive authority of an age that is altogether alien and primitive to our own."

The *New York Times* reported "the crowd of 10,000 was quick to grasp the significance of the President's statements and supported him with applause."

In a "spectacular touch," as one correspondent called it, just before the President spoke, popular opera singer John McCormack was given the honor of singing *The Star Spangled Banner.* What a thrill for the Irish-born tenor who had just become a naturalized U.S. citizen a year before. He didn't disappoint.

Now with his smooth falsetto soaring like an eagle over the lush green hillside, McCormack continued a second verse of Francis Scott Key's battle anthem and sang the line "for conquer we must." The slight elevation in his voice was noticeably moving as he held the last ringing note; stretching its significance and putting the astonished crowd in a stone silence until President Wilson stood up and wholeheartedly extended his hand in approval. The *Times* noted that the 1,000 or so soldiers in attendance seized the moment and "stood rigidly at attention."

"Never did patriotism surge within in me as it did that day," McCormack would later write in his memoirs. "I saw nothing, heard nothing, felt nothing but the grandeur of what the poem meant. My eyes were closed all the while I sang."

After the rousing performance, Wilson leaned into McCormack and said something in his ear. The words were out of earshot of the reporters who hardly noticed as they cheered along with the crowd. McCormack was visibly moved by the message and kept it a secret until years later when he finally revealed the heartfelt praise he received from the president that day. "I've never heard *The Star Spangled Banner* sung as you sang it," McCormack says Wilson told him. "Thank you from the bottom of my heart."

Thanks also in part to Wilson's insistence that *The Star Spangled Banner* be played at all military gatherings during the war, the song later became the nation's official anthem by order of a congressional resolution on March 3, 1931.

The stirring festivities at Mount Vernon were everything the 28th President of the United States had hoped for and more. The road to war had been a long and arduous one for Wilson and most Americans who patriotically stood by the president's attempt to stay out of the fray in Europe and broker peace from afar.

In August 1914, when Germany declared war on Russia, then France, and Great Britain declared war on Germany, Wilson told the European communities that the U.S. could offer its services as mediator only. Soon after that he issued a proclamation of United States neutrality. An order he signed with a heavy heart. Just the day before, on August 5, Ellen Wilson, the president's beloved wife of 29 years, passed away after a battle with Bright's disease. "Please take good care of Woodrow, doctor," was Ellen's final request as the president held his wife's hand and watched as she took her last breath.

Around this same time, war drums were beginning to beat. But public opinion among the American people was still on the president's side. That changed in May of 1915 when the British ocean liner *Lusitania* was torpedoed and sunk by German u-boats. Some 1,200 people traveling between the U.S. and Great Britain were killed in the attack, including 128 Americans. Wilson proclaimed defiantly that "there is such a thing as a man being too proud to fight," and continued to wait, but sentiments were shifting. The president's neutrality was severely tested. After the *Lusitania,* several more ships were attacked by the Germans even after they briefly acquiesced. This time even Wilson knew America needed to be prepared for war. His abrupt stance from world peacemaker to war advocate, although seen as unavoidable by many, was met with jeers from neutrality groups and many congressmen who vehemently opposed U.S. involvement overseas.

At the outset of the New Year, Wilson tried to drum up support for preparedness by traveling West and making stops in mostly larger Midwestern cities like St. Louis and Kansas City. He was shocked by the "almost apathetic [attitudes] regarding the possibility of war."

He told a crowd in Des Moines: "America cannot be an ostrich with its head in the sand. America cannot shut itself out from the rest of the world.

"I have spent every thought and energy that has been vouchsafed me in order to keep this country out of war," he added. "Yet there is a price which is too great to pay for peace, and that price can be put in a word, self-respect."

At the next stop, in front of a record crowd in Kansas City, the *New York Times* reported, the president was so deeply moved that he asked the crowd to join him in singing *America The Beautiful.* Later in his address to Congress asking for a declaration of war, Wilson summed up his feelings in one sentence: "Right is more precious than peace." He asked the American people to join him.

IN 1916, THE SELECTIVE SERVICE ACT became law, forcing young men to sign up for the possibility of a draft. Hoping to avoid conscription, Wilson had asked for 500,000 young men to volunteer, but he soon found that business at the recruiting booths was slower than expected. Times were good at home, and men were working. Why risk it all in a trench overseas? Wilson had to swallow his pride. A few months earlier he was questioned about the possibility of falling short of volunteers. "I would be ashamed of America," the president said. Now, the draft was imminent. America was preparing for war. It wouldn't be long. That same year, Germany resumed unrestricted u-boat attacks against passenger ships in open waters. Wilson could wait no more. On April 16, 1917, America entered the 'war to end all wars,' and induction letters went out immediately.

In Pekin, the boys who received their draft papers hardly had time to finish breakfast before they were summoned to the county courthouse in the downtown square. One by one they arrived until there was a group of 30 or more, all dressed in their finest suits as if they were going to church that day. They posed for a group picture on the courthouse steps, walked past a crowd of family members and well-wishers, reached the train depot, boarded and left. It was that quick.

The crowds that gathered to send the boys off were confused, not knowing whether to cheer, cry or scream. "The average American had no realistic conception of war," wrote author Irving Werstein. "For him it seemed like a football game or World Series."

The fantasy was disabused on October 23, 1917 when Battery C of the First Artillery became the first American unit to taste combat. OUR BOYS ARE FIGHTING, the headlines proudly read, but Americans, writes Werstein, were about to realize that war "was not a sand-lot baseball game." Mortar shells blasted from afar, and the unit was bombarded. By the time the shelling stopped, three U.S. soldiers lay dead in the trenches, the first American casualties of the Great War.

Roy King was a Pekin native who was called to duty. The handsome former high school football star received his induction notice shortly after America's war began, and he proudly served. King was a member of the 1909 Pekin High School football team that charmed the city by going undefeated for a full season. They were beasts on the field—no opponent even scored a point against them— and crafty competitors too. When the team needed a large trunk to store and move equipment, they sought help from a local funeral director who promptly lent them a coffin box. The rather macabre makeshift locker, perfect for holding balls, pads and helmets, likely gave the rival team pause when before each game it was carried across the field in front of the opposing player's bench.

Nine years later, the team's star player went to France and never came home, one of Pekin's first casualties of the war. His memory is still honored today by the local chapter Roy L. King v.f.w. Post.

Now on the second Fourth of July holiday since entering the war, President Wilson tried to convince a nation—and its allied partners—that there was still discernible cause and a steely resolve. He proclaimed that "no half-way decision would be tolerable," and just a day before urged all Americans to "observe this Fourth of July as it has never been observed before."

The *Times* reporter summed it up: "Not a moment of time was lost by the President in making the day one in which would play a big part in cementing the allied nations together and move nearer the day when Germany will be crushed."

America's late entry in the war and short foray into combat kept the number of causalities down, but the war still cost the nation more than 100,000 dead and nearly 300,000 wounded. The war would eventually end in November 1918.

THAT SAME MORNING, as Woodrow Wilson addressed the throng at Mount Vernon, in a slip at the foot of Peoria's Main Street, Captain Mehl was readying the *Columbia* for another holiday excursion on the Illinois River. He had no idea it would be the ship's last. On the top deck just ahead of the pilothouse, Mehl placed two large American flag decorations he had saved just for this occasion. The electric flag lights looked frozen in time, stuck in a pose—a folded flap in the wind. The stars and stripes were brightly lighted by hundreds of small red, blue and clear 'globe-shaped' bulbs. There were other flags on poles that adorned all sides of the ship, but the lighted flags really stood out, especially on an evening cruise, and especially on this Fourth of July holiday.

At dawn the day after the tragedy a reporter for the *Peoria Journal-Transcript* noticed the lighted flags again, "flaunting their imitation waves in the faint breeze." The reporter was struck by their significance among the rest of the battlefield-like debris that lay in the water. An incongruous image silhouetted against the morning sky, the stars and stripes had stood tall and survived. "Not a globe of them was broken," the paper reported the next day.

It was no ordinary Fourth of July.

COLUMBIA'S LIGHTED FLAGS STOOD TALL
"NOT A GLOBE OF THEM WAS BROKEN"
MURPHY LIBRARY UNIVERSITY OF WISCONSIN-LA CROSSE

29

THE
TRUTH

THE FEDERAL INSPECTORS, state investigators including Assistant Attorney General Mansfield, Tazewell County State's Attorney Black and Coroner Clary all agreed to work together in an effort to move the judicial process along. There would be three investigations in all and three separate rulings, since each government agency was investigating a different aspect of the wreck. In theory, the combined efforts would help simplify the proceedings by avoiding overlapping testimony and witnesses appearing before multiple committees to repeatedly answer similar questions.

The *Columbia*'s captain, pilot, and crew were excluded from this relief. Mehl, Williams and the rest of the boat's crew had already testified in front of federal investigators and were expected to do the same before the coroner's jury. The swift start to the federal investigation was unavoidable. It was ordered by Secretary of Commerce William Redfield. Neither Clary nor the governor's men were about to defy Redfield, but they didn't want to rely only on testimony they had not personally conducted or attended. The federal hearing was behind closed doors, Clary argued. The demanding public never got a chance to hear from the two main witnesses. Clary didn't have to push too hard. The captain and pilot would be subpoenaed to appear before the coroner's jury and answer questions under oath. Whether they chose to talk or not was another matter.

As for other witnesses in the hearings, the state lawmen, including Mansfield and Commissioner of State Waterways Superintendent Sackett, agreed to sit in during Clary's inquest hearings and assist in questioning. They also would attend hearings conducted by Peoria County Coroner Elliott, who was organizing hearings of his own and setting up a potential list of witnesses that included—much to everyone's surprise—the two federal steamboat inspectors, Captain Downs and Bower.

Clary was eager to get the coroner's inquest started, but he wanted to wait until all of the bodies had been accounted for. By Sunday, most of the bodies in the wreckage had been removed, but a dozen or so people were still considered missing, including *Columbia* deckhand George Stewart.

"The inquest will not be held until the latter part of the week," the level-headed Clary told reporters. "The work of securing the bodies is not finished. When it is done I will begin to collect a list of witnesses covering every possible angle.

"What I want is the truth. My office is that of an inquisitor purely and that is what I will do. If I find any facts that would warrant holding members of the crew they will be held for further investigation."

"What about criminal charges?" he was asked.

"The jury is the judge of the facts and makes the recommendations," Clary answered. "If I have found any evidence that would show criminal carelessness, I could not so state at this time. The crew is all within access and Captain Mehl has volunteered the presence of all his men when I call them."

In the meantime, Clary continued to console victims' families and in the process do a little detective work too. He was asked by relatives of two victims to investigate the loss of several pieces of jewelry. A brooch set with two diamonds was missing from one woman's body, and a large cameo ring was no longer on the finger of 25-year-old Louise Berends, a glove-factory worker. The ring had turned up missing when Berends' body was identified at the morgue. Clary tried to explain to the woman's family that the water entered the steamer with such force that many pieces of jewelry and clothing were swept from the bodies.

They weren't convinced. "Why then," they inquired, "was only one ring missing when the other rings she wore were not disturbed?"

Clary may not have had an answer for that.

In fact there were several circumstances that went beyond Clary's jurisdiction as a coroner. He deferred them to the Tazewell County Sheriff.

Sheriff Wilson also had some unclaimed property on his hands. In the wreckage, two suitcases and an iron safe had been recovered. The safe contained nearly $3,000 in cash and was believed to be Mehl's personal bank. The heavy submerged safe was raised with ropes. The currency was "badly water-logged." The suitcases found near the engine room contained no money, but they had several hotel keys and two life insurance policies inside. The policies belonged to a man named Ernest Hines of Springfield. The receipt book showed it had been paid up until July of 1918 with the last payment dated June 25. Earnest Hines was a *Columbia* crew member, a deck watchman. The life insurance policy had not expired, and neither had Hines. He was alive and well.

"In spite of every precaution," the *Peoria Journal-Transcript* reported, "vandals have been working about the wreck." Even Mehl and his wife Ethel were victims of random thievery. "I had a suitcase filled with Mrs. Mehl's clothes," the captain said. "I sat it down beside me to talk and when I reached for it five minutes later, it was gone."

Perhaps the most bizarre story was that of a priest who came to the wreck site to offer last rites and pray for victims' families. While the pastor was doing his priestly duties, someone burglarized his home. The resourceful thief tried to elude police by wearing the preacher's clothing that he stole, but the several layers of clothing slowed him down as he ran. He didn't get very far before he was caught.

THE FEDERAL INSPECTORS may have grabbed the headlines so far with their hasty closed-door questioning of the crew, but state investigators, who were being patient and mostly tight-lipped, would soon have their turn. The diver appointed by the governor had just arrived.

W.F. Dunscombe of St. Louis came with a solid recommendation from General Bixby, chief of the Mississippi River commission. Bixby was a retired U.S. Army brigadier general who was recalled to service "by the press of war business." When he called, Governor Lowden listened. Dunscombe was a good diver, Lowden was told, and had a keen eye for detail. His job was to examine the bottom half of the boat and determine its condition both before and after the wreck. The governor also ordered several engineers to survey the river and take soundings.

The state's responsibility was the river itself and the passenger safety precautions required by law. There were certain 'rules of the river,' and the state investigation team was there to determine if the pilot, captain and crew had followed them. This included the number of life jackets and lifeboats on board.

Their findings could mean changes in how steamboats operated on the river in the future. "The idea is to investigate and ascertain if the law has been complied with," said C.N. Posegate, a veteran railroad engineer and head of the state's public utilities commission. "Only by investigating such accidents can we make recommendations for future laws. It is our duty to investigate all such accidents since river transportation is under our supervision as well as railroad transportation."

"Might this disaster suggest some new legislation?" he was asked.

"Possibly," he replied. "When the *Eastland* disaster occurred we prepared some bills we thought ought to be passed but never were."

Posegate told them that the state would investigate reports that the *Columbia* "broke in two" as a result of going aground and hitting a sand bar or an obstruction in the river. It was important, he added, that state investigators find out what struck the boat and how much damage it did. He was told a man who was on the *Columbia* had seen a large log before the boat scraped the shore.

Walter Fluegel was the man's name.

The reporters had already spoken to him.

"Find him," Posegate ordered. "Mr. Fluegel is about to take another boat ride."

Meanwhile, the state's appointed diver was getting ready to make his first underwater inspection.

IN PEKIN, AS SUNDAY was coming to a close, the grim reality of the upcoming week was beginning to settle in. In homes and churches throughout town, funeral services were being planned. Nearly all of the victims so far, a little over 80, would be interred over the next three days. The few bodies that were left unidentified at the morgue were taken to nearby funeral homes. A list of the dead was placed on the morgue's window.

In the early edition of the *Peoria Journal-Transcript,* there was an urgent plea from the Red Cross. They were facing a shortage of workers to perform an unenviable task. The Pekin Street Department, under orders from the mayor, volunteered their services. Several janitors from local schools also offered to help. They would all bring shovels. But it wouldn't be enough.

The headline read: TWENTY MEN NEEDED TO DIG GRAVES.

Sad days were ahead.

CLARY IDENTIFYING A WOMAN'S BODY
THE PEKIN DAILY TIMES

30

SAD SCENARIO

IN THE SULTRY, CONFINED barracks of the 308th Calvary at Camp Douglas in Arizona, private Walter Soady received a letter. It was addressed from his parents, Fred and Laura May Soady in Pekin, Walter's hometown. Normally a cheery letter from home was a welcome break from the grind of training camp, but this letter was different:

> Dear Walter,
> We read all about these horrible disasters in the papers and pass them out of our mind, but when it is right at home, it is different. The South Side Club ran an excursion boat on the Columbia last night and we were down to see it. At Wesley City, coming home last night about 11 o'clock, something happened and the boat crushed to pieces. I don't know if you care to hear about so much about it, but it is the news and only news in Pekin since last Friday night. I thought you would like to know what is going on here, the good and the bad.

Walter would receive several letters from his parents over the next couple of weeks, each one describing a different aspect of the wreck, the people affected and the lives that were lost. The letters remain a snapshot of the town's terrible grief at the time. They give us a picture of a community that came together to remember, mourn and ultimately bury its dead.

> ...*Most of them drowned on the Dance Hall [of the boat]. They did save a lot of people, but the boat sank in five minutes and some of them were killed when the boat broke in two...Many of them we knew real well.*

Throughout Pekin, in homes along streets that were named after the town's early settlers—Margaret, Caroline, Ann Eliza—crêpe paper bunting was placed in front windows signifying a loved one or relative had been lost in the accident. "Sorrow enveloped Pekin like a pall today as it laid to rest the first of its many victims of the ill-fated river steamer *Columbia*," the *Peoria Evening Star* reported.

The South Side Social Club that sponsored the fateful cruise was located in the southwest part of the city. Most of its members lived there. "Beside the clubhouse," the *Pekin Daily Times* reported, "a husband and wife lay dead; across the way on Second Street a mother and daughter. A block north a mother and two children. On South Second Street and several cross streets there were blocks in succession with one or more houses where emblems of mourning were in evidence."

> ...*Chris 'Kid' Sickles was drowned. And Casey Jacob's wife is drowned. 'Chuck,' I don't know his other name, the fellow that was hurt at the railroad a while ago, was on the boat. He was rescued. He told us there were six of his c.p. [Corn Products Co.] workers still missing. When you read the names you will find that you know many who worked at c.p. or their folks were lost. Anna and Louise Lucas were on the boat but were saved o.k.*

The funerals started early in the morning and continued into the evening. The services were mostly private. "Morbid curiosity seekers were absent," the *Evening Star* reported. The churches remained closed. There was no mournful, measured tolling of church bells so as not to "freshen minds of the awful tragedy that befell citizens."

As always, the Red Cross was there to assist. "At the present we will leave each family to decide its own arrangements, though we will aid in every way and send workers to every home," said Walter Lautz, chairman of the Red Cross relief committee.

The same sad scenario played out throughout the town, on every other block on every other street. Families stayed quietly in their homes, beside the caskets of their loved ones and waited for the minister or priest to arrive. The burials were scheduled in relays—four at 2 o'clock and five at 3 o'clock—so the clergymen could administer last rites over the bodies of the first relay then be "hastened to other homes to perform again their grim task."

> *...That Jacob that worked with Jimmie Schwartz lost his wife and her mother and brother. You know, they are the Hill's that lived in our house. Papa says he thinks he and Jake are cousins...Verah Flowers is the girl we brought down from Peoria in the car one time. She drowned. Esther Bellville was on the boat. She escaped but was bruised up...The one, or rather two, funerals at 12 o'clock is for Sam Neaver and his daughter on Suzanna Street. Did you know him?*

There were double, triple and quadruple funerals since, in many cases, more than one member of a particular family were lost. The services for 36-year-old Phoebe May Thurman, her 14-year-old daughter Ruby Ann and two-month-old baby Clyde were held at the Union Mission in Pekin. "It was one of the sorrowful events of the day," a reporter wrote in the *Evening Star*. "The minister spoke words of comfort to the bereaved ones and held out to the hope of the reunion in the bright beyond." Three friends of the family sang *Beautiful Isle of Somewhere* and *Till We Meet Again* as two gray caskets—the mother and baby in one and teenaged daughter in the other—were carried to waiting hearses. Six "young ladies" around the same age as Ruby acted as pallbearers for their fallen friend. Fifteen automobiles filled with friends and relatives followed the two hearses to the cemetery.

At another funeral in town, nearly all the mourners who attended had a musical instrument in hand. "Every member of the local musicians union turned out to pay their last respects to Kenneth Sanders," the *Journal-Transcript* reported. Sanders was the only local member of the boat's orchestra who died in the wreck. "They attended in a body without uniform and played a funeral dirge from the home to the cemetery gate."

THE PAPERS LISTED them all. Not only a daily count of the identified dead and missing, but announcements from families, funeral directors and organizations on each burial—who, where and when. In most instances, it was informal to use the woman's first name in print, only her married title by her husband's name:

> Mrs. Clyde Witcher and her sons, Donald and Richard will be buried tomorrow afternoon from their late residence on Fayette Street.

> Mrs. Leona Moldenhauer and her babe and Mrs. Phil Mauser will be buried from the Mauser Residence on the East Bluff in Pekin.

> The remains of Mrs. John Diepenbrock and her two sons will be laid to rest on Tuesday afternoon from their residence on Caroline Street. Rev. Mr. Hahn will officiate.

> At 9 o'clock a common funeral was held from St. Joseph Church. The Rev. Father D.J. Sullivan sang the solemn requiem high mass for the repose of souls of Mrs. Ivy Brown O'Hern, Mrs. Frank Callahan, Miss Mary Holden and Joseph Kumpf.

> At the same hour, services for Louise Behrens were held from Sacred Heart church. The Rev. Fr. Grusel was in charge.

At 5 o'clock, services for Dorothy White were held from the residence on 1225 Court Street. A Christian Science reader from Peoria was in charge.

All Eagles are requested to meet Tuesday afternoon at 1:30 o'clock at the hall to attend services for the late James Blackburn; services at 3 o'clock.

Mrs. Amelia H. Loomis and Mrs. Mary Luther will be buried from the home of the former's son, Walter Loomis 227 S. Mary Street, at 2 o'clock Wednesday afternoon, the Rev. Munns officiating.

Mr. and Mrs. William Capoot; 212 Washington Street; member E.M.E. church service July 9; burial Lakeside, minister E.M.E. pastor of East Peoria.

Since there were only two funeral homes in town, there weren't enough hearses or funeral cars. The Red Cross put out a call for vehicles. "Each family will be allowed five automobiles to accompany the casket," Lautz of the Red Cross told them. The volunteer vehicles were not hard to find.

> *...Papa said to tell you that he has a Red Cross Card on his car today. They all have them that donated cars. Papa had calls yesterday for funerals at 11 AM, noon, 4, 5 & 6 PM. His first call this morning was at 9 AM. And he will be going until 3 [without a break].*

Most of the victims were laid to rest in Pekin's Lakeside Cemetery, the city's largest. There was one burial at the cemetery every hour, the papers reported. The graveside services were said to be "quiet and peaceful."

> *...After dinner MaMa Bob and I went out to the cemetery. You can't imagine what a sight it was. The new part looked like it was dug up all over. They couldn't possibly remove the dirt from so many graves and it lay in great piles all around. There were the new graves*

> *and the graves ready for today and boxes, sticks and*
> *cement caskets standing where more graves were to*
> *be dug.*

In the *Evening Star,* a writer summoned up the sad feeling of the city in one unattributed quote: "Let us bury our dead quietly, comfort our survivors, feed our hungry and find home for orphans." "And that is exactly what is being done," he wrote.

THE PEKIN CITY COUNCIL held its regular meeting as usual on Monday, the first day of burials, and in a gesture of sympathy from the city and its citizens they adopted resolutions of condolences. Mayor Charles Schaefer read the letter aloud in council chambers, and it was printed verbatim in the paper the next day:

> Whereas, our city is overwhelmed with sorrow occasioned by the death of approximately 100 persons who lost their lives on the steamer *Columbia,* most of whom were from Pekin and while the sorrow is most keenly felt by relatives who mourn the death of their loved ones, this catastrophe has plunged the entire community into deep sorrow because of the terrible loss and the sudden taking away of so many of its estimable citizens. Therefore be it received that this resolution be spread at length on the record of this council and that the same be made to appear in public press, and that flags on all public buildings be at half-mast until those who lost their lives have been buried.

The paper was signed by the mayor and four council members. The council then went a step further by approving a memorial relief fund of $500 to the Red Cross for help in aiding the victims' families. Council member H.J. Rust explained that the appropriation measure was agreed upon by each member "as a committee of the whole," provided that "each commissioner takes out one hundred dollars from the appropriation [fund] for his department to make this sum."

The measure was passed unanimously.

PRIVATE WALTER SOADY must have read every letter from his parents with a heavy heart. He was far from home and might be shipping out soon to join the war effort overseas. He likely would not see his grieving hometown friends and families for some time.

> ...*Cora Johns Haschert, Minnie Voll's brother Edwin, Letha Black, Mrs. Sapp and daughter Addie, they are Len Peterson's sister and niece, are all to be buried this afternoon...I guess the greenhouses have sold every flower they had. Mr. Schantz [the florist] wouldn't answer the 'phone' anymore yesterday.*

In one of the last letters Walter's mother would send about the *Columbia,* she mentioned an oddity:

> *It seems strange that the only two things not broken [on the boat] were the two lighted flags. Maybe we can take that as a good omen, that the Stars and Stripes cannot be drowned! Let's hope so anyway.*

Private Walter Soady would eventually return to Pekin and later serve his country again as a member of the U.S. Army in World War II. In May of 1931, between stints in the service, Soady married a local girl, Agnes Smith, who had her own story to tell about the wreck of the *Columbia.* She was the girl who was supposed to be on the boat with her neighbors, the Diepenbrocks, but was late leaving the drug store where she worked and never made it. Later that night, John Diepenbrock left his oldest son Henry with Agnes and her family so he could go back to search for his wife and two other boys, who were still missing. Agnes would later learn that they had all perished. The next day Agnes went back to work at the drug store where her job was "one of trying to calm the public," she recalled. "Business elsewhere was at a standstill," Agnes said. "But [at the drug store] there was a steady demand for nerve pills, pain relievers and prescription drugs."

Walter and Agnes would eventually have a son of their own, Fred Soady, who over the years would write many definitive articles about local history, including several on the wreck of the *Columbia.*

JUST DOWNRIVER from Pekin, in the small mining town of Kingston Mines, more funerals were taking place. Kingston Mines was the first stop by the *Columbia* on that ill-fated night. Of the 40 or so people that boarded at Kingston Mines, 14 had perished. There were ten survivors from the nearby town of Glasford. They told their stories to the local *Glasford Gazette.*

"Those who were in the dance hall managed to fight their way to the top and crawl out through the windows," the *Gazette* reported. "Faye Tindall happened to be in one corner of the dance hall where the ceiling was about a foot above water. As she came up her hand came in contact with an electric light bulb, to which she clung for a long time, until discovered by rescuers. She was one of the last taken off. Mrs. Grace Wood was thrown from the top of the boat and was caught by Wm. Lanan as she was going down the third time."

As small town papers often do, the local scribe's coverage of the wreck was peppered with folksy comments and criticisms:

> One or two boys were not in shape to take care of themselves, and owe their lives solely to the fact that they happened to be on top when the boat sank. We hope the boys will take a lesson from this and keep themselves ready in a case like this, especially when accompanied by girls who have the right to expect their protection.

In Kingston Mines, the bodies of the dead were escorted home by barge. They included the four members of the Harbolt family, Mother Iva May and three children: 16-year-old Mildred, three-year-old Gracie and the youngest victim of the *Columbia* tragedy, 18-month-old Mabel. Charles, the grieving husband and father, and his son survived. They were on the top deck when the boat went down. The girls, Charles later recalled, were on the dance floor. "The water came in and it got dark. Someone yelled, 'all hold yer heads, she's alright, nothing wrong.'" Charles managed to save himself and his boy, but his wife and the three girls he never saw alive again.

The town packed the shore just like they had done many times before when the steamboats arrived, only this time it was under very different circumstances. "Less than three weeks ago," the *Evening Star* reported, "the steamer *Columbia* landed a crowd of merry makers on an excursion for the benefit of the Red Cross at the dock in Kingston Mines. This morning a barge with 13 caskets containing the bodies of victims of the sinking steamer will land at the same dock. This time the barge will be in charge of members of the Red Cross. The cortege will be escorted over the same dyke the merry makers from Peoria took to the village almost a mile from the river to the Kingston Mines cemetery nearby."

The Kingston Mines cemetery was located on a sleepy hillside along the river. The mourners trudged up the muddy slope and stood silently as the minister delivered the commitment rites. "Probably a thousand people were gathered in the cemetery to pay their last respects to the dead," the papers reported.

The service for eight victims was held under the trees. The eight bodies in pearl gray caskets were carried up the winding hill to the cemetery entrance, with twelve pall bearers to each casket. The skies darkened as organ music filled the air. The organ, like the caskets, had to be lifted up the steep hillside.

"Just as relatives gathered around the graves, a fierce rainstorm broke, drenching everyone," read the *Glasford Gazette*. "The approach of the storm as the services were in progress had further depressing effect on everyone."

THE IMMENSE GRIEF and solemnity felt by the communities during the three days of burials helped quell some of the anger and resentment that was being expressed shortly after the wreck. In Pekin, the incessant chatter from the saloons finally fell silent and the angry mobs dispersed. The town seemed to accept its fate.

Now that the dead were buried, the business of blame and restitution would begin in earnest. Coroner Clary, who would lead the proceedings, had a special request. He wanted to use the biggest room in the Tazewell County courthouse for the inquest hearings.

His reasons were sound.

In 1904 a similar inquest was held for the victims of the *Gen-*

eral Slocum, a pleasure steamer that caught fire and sank in New York's Long Island Sound, killing more than 1,000 passengers. The captain, William Van Schaick, was accused of criminal negligence. On the first day of the hearings, the victims, even the most severely injured, showed up in droves.

"Everyone stared as the forlorn mass shuffled into the spectators' gallery," wrote author Ed O'Donnell about the *General Slocum* hearings. "Many were wrapped in bandages and used crutches and canes to walk. Others showed no indication of physical injury, but their haggard faces and red, sleepless eyes told of their suffering and loss. They were there seeking answers."

In terms of lives lost, the *Columbia* was not on the same scale as the *General Slocum,* but there were still victims, family members and townspeople in general who were hell-bent on justice and seeking answers.

"Get me some extra chairs," Clary ordered. He anticipated an overflow crowd.

WORKERS ON COLUMBIA WRECKAGE
MURPHY LIBRARY UNIVERSITY OF WISCONSIN-LA CROSSE

31

SHIFTY POSITIONS

THE BUSINESS OF REMOVING wreckage and bodies resumed on Monday, the first burial day, and continued for several more days, even though the newspapers virtually ignored it. The stories of victims and grieving families putting their loved ones to rest understandably dominated the headlines during those three sad days.

Even the gawkers were gone. After the large crowds and ghoulishly 'picnic-like' atmosphere on Sunday, the shoreline was quiet and mostly empty during the middle of the week.

All week long, Clary repeatedly reminded the press why he was delaying the start of the inquest hearings. He was adamant that the jury would not hear from witnesses until all the bodies had been removed from the wreckage. Although he was hounded by reporters, who were eager for the testimonies to begin, Clary stood his ground.

The federal inspectors had trumped them all in any case. Their closed-door interrogations of the captain and crew took place on Sunday, barely 36 hours after the wreck. By Thursday, rumors circulated that Bower and Downs had already reached a decision and would be sending a telegram soon to Secretary Redfield. The Commerce Department chief would have the final say on the matter, but it was clear from earlier telegrams to his subordinates that the decision of the two inspectors in Peoria would stand. The livelihoods of the captain and pilot depended on it.

The next logical step in the investigation was the coroner's inquest. More than anything else the hearings would determine whether or not criminal charges could be brought against the captain, pilot or crew. The coroner's job was to determine cause of death, and the jury was called in to help Clary decide whether any negligence had occurred or if laws had been broken in the process. The captain already had a lot to say—to reporters, anyway—but under oath, in front of the jury, the pressures would be *different*, more public and potentially more damaging. Plus, the room would be full of despondent and angry Pekin residents. A friend of Mehl's remarked that the captain was worried about going across the river for the hearings.

But as long as three people were still missing, Clary would not allow the inquest to begin. The three unfortunate individuals whose bodies might still be in the wreckage were George Stewart, a deck hand, Charles Race, a railroad worker and Eugene Bailey—known by his friends as just 'Gene'—the 29-year-old 'piano player' on the *Columbia* who was last seen telling his brother Ben to "beat it" after the boat collapsed. Ben survived and believes his brother got caught in debris when he tried to jump. Eugene Bailey was not an employee on the boat or officially part of the orchestra that night. A friend, Leo MacDonald, says 'Gene' just liked to play, "that's all," and since there was a piano on board the *Columbia*, Bailey would often engage patrons with a tune. He couldn't help himself, is the way MacDonald described it.

In the middle of the river the pile of sheared timbers that was once a steamboat was a dangerous nuisance. The debris field was as wide as the boat itself, and some of it was still sticking out of the water. Initially, river traffic was halted when it was feared bodies may have drifted downstream. Once it was clear that drifting corpses was not an issue, barges and freight boats were allowed to pass the wreck site, but slowly, and only under the U.S. Marshall's supervision. But commerce had to be allowed to resume, the tragic circumstances notwithstanding. While generally sympathetic and patient, the river industry along the Illinois was taking a serious financial hit.

The steamboat excursions that had been planned for the rest of the Fourth of July weekend were grounded too. Ordinarily, three or four excursion boats would have been merrily drifting past each other as happy patrons waved with delight. But the river, especially the wider stretch of Peoria Lake, was eerily quiet over the holiday weekend in 1918. The large Swain boats, including the *Julia Belle Swain* and the *David Swain,* rocked back and forth in the water, side-by-side, as they sat docked and empty along Peoria's riverfront. The only steamboat in motion that weekend, and the most unexpected, was the "broken beauty" in the middle of the Illinois River.

"Removal of the heavy superstructure and the action of the current of the river has caused the *Columbia* to shift her position," the papers reported.

Coroner Clary, Sheriff Jack Wilson, Earl Barnewolt, his brother Ora, who supervised the removal operations, and two workers, William Parker and Pete Sansone, who owned the small barge used to tow away the debris, were all on top of the wreck when the *Columbia* "started its journey." It was reported that none of the men were thrown in the water, "although there was some lively scrambling."

A small barge, a launch and the crane steamer *Comanche* were all attached to the wreck by ropes and pulled along by the *Columbia* when it started to drift. The boat rose out of the water, rolled, then floated downstream about 100 yards before coming to a sudden stop. The boat turned as it moved and the bow, not the stern, was now headed "slightly upstream with the stern below."

In another ironic twist, it was the *Columbia*'s own unused cargo that stopped its progress. "The 25 tons of coal spilled into the stream below the bow and prevented it from going any further," William Parker explained.

Later that night, Sherriff Wilson was awakened by an urgent

phone message that the boat was floating unobstructed down-stream and heading straight for the landing in Pekin. Wilson immediately called Peoria and Pekin police and advised bridge tenders to be on the lookout. But the report was false, possibly a prank. After its earlier unexpected shift in position, the *Colum-bia* was going nowhere—stuck in its own mud, so to speak. "The *Columbia* had made its last voyage the night before," was the way the papers reported it the next day.

"The hull has sunk again," is how one writer put it.

The day before, the state's appointed diver—Dunscombe—arrived with little 'Harry Halvorsen-like' fanfare and went under for the first time. The reporters keenly observed his movement: "Bubbles indicated that he was about the vicinity of the paddlewheel," they wrote.

After a half-hour underwater, Dunscombe came up with a con-cerned look on his face. He removed the diving suit and politely waved off the swarming press. He was under strict orders not to discuss his findings with anyone other than Coroner Clary or Sack-ett and Mansfield, the two state investigators. But the diver made an honest mistake. He muttered something to himself, something he thought no one else could hear. Someone did. An unidentified man who was on the *Comanche* at the time was in earshot and raced to the reporters with the news. Excitedly he told them what the diver had said in passing. "'I will not go down again until the wreckage is towed to a safer position,'" the man exclaimed. "That's what I heard."

It wasn't the earth-shattering, stop-the-presses kind of informa-tion the reporters were hoping for, but the diver's own prophetic words were a good indication that the boat was unstable and per-haps unsafe as well. Clary may have known it too and was prepar-ing to do as the diver suggested, but he also may have dismissed the warning altogether. After all, the resilient boat had held its own during a fierce windstorm just a few days before. Thanks to the boat and the river, the issue was moot. The unexpected move-ment meant something else for Clary as well—the inquest could start soon.

"When the hulk rose last evening," the *Peoria Journal-Transcript* reported, "two bodies were dislodged." Charles Race, the railroad worker, and Gene Bailey, the 'piano player,' were no longer missing. The report continued, "One floated downstream, the other remained near the boat and was brought ashore with the other after it had been found."

As it turned out, the last missing person, deckhand George Stewart, had already been found. After discovering a suitcase that belonged to another deckhand in the twisted maze of broken pipes, gauges and dials that were the remains of the engine room, a rescue worker claimed he felt something, a limb perhaps, but it was wedged beneath a wall of debris. The boat's shift in position revealed the shocking truth. George Stewart had gone down with the boat. Clary was given the sad news.

"So the last body is out of the wreck, you're sure of that?" Clary asked his men.

Sort of, Clary was told.

Bewildered by the response, Clary asked again.

He was told only the lower half of George Stewart's body, the legs and a part of the torso, had been recovered. The upper half, including the head, was still missing. *That will make an official identification difficult,* thought Clary. Still, it *was* Stewart, he was told, they were sure of it. No one else would have been in the engine room at the time, and everyone else was accounted for.

That unsettling piece of information about George Stewart's missing head and upper torso was not what Clary wanted to hear. The coroner had hoped to announce to the people of Pekin that *all* missing persons had been recovered and reassure them that no bodies would unexpectedly wash up on shore in the days, weeks, maybe even months down the road. There were no more missing persons, but that matter of missing body parts was disturbing. All he could hope for now was that it wouldn't be a distraction. There was to be no more waiting. "The inquest will start on Friday," Clary told reporters. The coroner was ready to call his first witness.

Later that day in Pekin, at the same spot the *Columbia* had launched with cheers before making its final voyage, several pieces of the wreckage had washed ashore. Thankfully that was all that came ashore. The broken boards came loose when the boat shifted position and floated downstream. "Under a heavy coat of paint," the papers reported, "the woodwork was found to be in poor condition."

TOP: PEORIA COUNTY CORONER WILLIAM B. ELLIOTT
PEORIA PUBLIC LIBRARY
BOTTOM: TAZEWELL COUNTY STATE'S ATTORNEY E.E. BLACK
TAZEWELL COUNTY STATE'S ATTORNEY'S OFFICE

32

VERY PECULIAR

WITH THE DISCOVERY of what was left of deckhand George Stewart's mangled body, Clary declared that all the victims of the *Columbia* had been recovered. There were no more substantiated reports of missing persons. In all, he announced, there were 86 victims. But he was wrong—87 people perished on the *Columbia*. There was one more victim, the one and only soul for whom Clary was not officially responsible: Harry Brown.

Brown's body had been found on the west side of the river and thus was under the jurisdiction of Peoria County coroner William Elliott.

It was Friday, July 11, a full week after the *Columbia*'s ill-fated voyage. The dead had been recovered from the wreckage, and most of the victims had been laid to rest. In Pekin, the rage that had boiled over earlier in the week was finally tempered by the solemnity of prayer and the quiet respect of burying the dead.

It was finally time for justice to be served. The coroner's inquest would finally begin. Or rather, the *inquests* would begin.

In fact there would be two simultaneous coroners' hearings, one on each side of the river, in two different counties. Peoria County coroner William Elliott had every right to conduct his own investigation on behalf of Harry Brown, whose body happened to wash up on the Peoria County side of the river. Elliott wasted no time gathering a list of passengers and expert witness to testify. Clary did the same. He was responsible for many more victims, and his ruling would likely carry more weight, but the hearings—as they played out in the papers each day—were very similar in tone and style. State investigators Mansfield and Sackett had planned to attend and direct questions at only Clary's hearings, but now they were forced to do the same for Elliott.

Over the next several weeks, in hearing rooms on both sides of the river, back and forth testimony and contradictory statements would play out like staged drama to an audience of jurors, coroners and investigators as a legion of passengers, divers, undertakers, former crew members, musicians, boat-maintenance workers, past and present steamboat pilots, captains and a bartender were all subpoenaed to appear at one or both of the inquest hearings.

Clary requested the largest circuit courtroom in the Tazewell County courthouse. He ordered extra chairs for the back of the room on the apparent assumption that the people of Pekin would come out in droves. He was wrong. When the courthouse doors opened and the hearings began most of the extra seats were empty. "Less than a half-dozen spectators appeared," the *Peoria Journal-Transcript* reported. The witnesses, on the other hand, promptly showed up as ordered by law.

The room was comfortable despite the warm July weather. Several large metallic fans helped circulate the stale air. A plain chair was set up in the front where the witness sat. A table was directly in front where Clary and the other investigators faced the witness chair. The jury sat off to the side. "State your name and address, please," Clary politely asked the conservatively dressed woman who had just been sworn in.

"Mrs. Pearl Harvey, 346 Ann Eliza Street," the first witness said.

Clary asked if she was on board the *Columbia* the night it sank.

"Yes. I was on the lower deck at the time when the steamer ran into the trees and stumps," she responded.

"Please, tell us what you saw."

"I saw large willow branches come through the windows and brush glasses off tables."

Clary asked if she had noticed anything unusual on the trip, prior to that event.

"Yes. On the trip downriver it appeared to me that the steamer was going from one side to the other."

"And that was unusual?"

"Yes, at the time I thought it was very peculiar."

"How did you get out?" Clary asked.

"After the boat rammed the trees, I started up the back stairs and heard Captain Mehl shouting at me. The stairs were covered with glass and debris. I went down the stairs and ran toward the women's rest room. The boat was so close to shore I thought it was making a landing. That's when it sunk."

Clary stopped her. He wanted to clarify one comment. He was a bit taken aback. "The captain was shouting at you. Is that right?"

"Yes, that's right"

"Well, what did he say?"

"'Stay down there you damn fool,'" she replied with downcast eyes. "That's what he said."

The hearings were off and running.

BEN MEINEN WAS NEXT. He was the president of the South Side Social Club, the group that had sponsored the event. Meinen and his brother Tom were on board the *Columbia* and helped with the rescue efforts. Ben was on the lower deck when the boat struck the willows. Ben said he saw a man down in the hull of the boat and that "he jumped out of the hole and said to another man standing there, 'Order all on top.'"

"Did you know the man who looked into the hull?" Clary asked.

"He was a member of the crew," said Meinen.

"Did you hear anyone say anything about investigating the hull or other parts of the boat?"

"I did not."

"Did you know who the man was who was standing next to the hole?"

"No, only that he was a short fellow."

"Did you see the captain?"

"No."

"Who was the man who hollered everybody upstairs?

"The short fellow."

"Was he in uniform?"

"Yes, I think he was."

The questioning turned to the shoreline. Ben Meinen testified that he felt a pretty stiff jar.

"Did you know, or do you now know what the boat struck?" Clary asked.

"No, sir," Meinem replied.

"In what direction was the boat going when it struck?"

"It seemed to me the boat was facing Peoria, but it's hard to tell when you are out on the river at night. I was facing the front of the boat when the bump came. As soon as I felt it I knew we hit something."

"You are unable to tell us which shore the boat rubbed up against?" Clary asked with some incredulousness.

"Yes."

"Could you feel the willows?"

"Yes. I stuck my hand out over the fence and grabbed hold of them."

Clary and the state investigators settled back in their chairs and prepared to call another witness.

Meinen got up. As he walked away, someone, possibly a juror, asked the witness if his brother got out safely. "Yes, he was thrown by the list into the water up to his neck on the lower side," Meinen responded, "but scrambled to a higher side and worked in water waist deep. He helped rescue others."

"Did *he* see any of the crew members?" the questioner continued.

"Yes. He ran into August Mehl, the boat's purser. My brother told Mr. Mehl that he thought the boat was sinking."

"What was Mr. Mehl's response?" the questioner prodded.

"He told my brother to shut up," Meinen said matter-of-factly.

THE QUESTION ON WHETHER there was any fog that night came up frequently. The answers were inconsistent. Some had seen fog or steam while others were just not sure. Some had seen no fog at all.

"I could see the stars and it looked bright," said Tom Miller, another fortunate Pekin resident. Miller testified that he was on the dance floor and heard the sound of willows scraping the boat. Then he heard a window break. He leaned over the railing and could see a log sticking out of the water, but no fog. "I could see both shores after the steam settled down."

"So you did not notice any fog?" Clary reiterated.

"No," said Miller, "only the steam rising and when it subsided I could see the trees. When we struck, the searchlight played on the Peoria shore and I could see them plainly...the trees."

"Did you hear any breaking of timbers?"

"No."

"Did you see the captain before or after the crash?"

"No."

"Hear him give any commands?"

"No."

NICHOLAS ISENMILLER testified that he was on the dance floor when the "shock" came and went to the window to look out.

"It was clear," he said. "We could see automobiles coming down the road and also the willows and trees on both shores."

"Are you positive there was no fog?"

"Yes, sir."

"Did you notice anything unusual about the boat on the trip upstream?"

"No."

"Did you hear anyone say there was something wrong with it?"

"No."

CLARY MUST HAVE BEEN told there was a passenger who refused to re-board the *Columbia* after it docked at the Al Fresco Amusement Park. Did that man know something the others did not? George Hyme, the navy veteran, was called to the stand.

"I've been on the water 30 years," Hyme told Clary and the jury. "I knew from the time the boat started that she was not running right." Hyme said that after he boarded the *Columbia* in Pekin he went to the top deck and the boat had just pulled away from the landing when he turned to his wife and said, "Allie, the boat is not running right."

"She said to me, 'What's the matter?' and I said, 'I don't know, I'm going down to see.'" Below Hyme ran into a woman named Mrs. Tinney. "I told her the boat was not working right. 'It's drawing too much water,' I said."

"Did you tell that to a crew member?" Hyme was asked.

"Yes, I went down to see an engineer who was busy, so I talked to a fireman instead. I asked him how much water the boat drew, and he said he didn't know. I asked him how long he had been a fireman, and he said he was just hired. I told him he really didn't know anything about the boat, and he said 'no.'"

"So you didn't get back on board after it landed in Peoria?"

"I told my wife that if this boat lands safely here [in Peoria], I am one who is not coming back on it. I've been on the water too long to be drowned now," he said.

CLARY CALLED MRS. TINNEY to the stand.

"Did you hear a conversation between George Hyme and the others on the boat?" he asked her.

"Yes," she replied. "He stated the boat was not going fast enough. I told him that it was probably light yet and that it was probably being run slowly on purpose and that there was no cause for alarm. Mr. Hyme then asked me the way downstairs and I directed him. I did not see him again."

"Did you hear him advise anyone not to return to the boat?" she was asked.

"No," she said.

CLARY'S NEXT WITNESS was John Chance, the coal miner from Wesley City who lived near the spot along the river where the boat went down.

"Was there any fog?" Clary asked.

"There was no fog, or I could not have seen the lights, which were distinct," he said. "The only thing that looked like fog was from the boilers."

Mansfield took the opportunity to ask a question pertaining to the river. "Is there a buoy about your cabin?" he asked Chance.

"Yes, a quarter-mile," Chance answered. "But no other within sight."

"How could you tell the boat was in distress?"

"The boat was going slow when it passed my cabin. There is a swift current at the bar. The boat was not in the swiftest current, more toward the Peoria side. The river is about 100 yards wide at the bar. The boat was nearer the Peoria side, and missed the bar by about 20 yards. The reason I thought the boat was in distress is because the stern was turned towards me."

"Do you know of any stumps on that side of the river?"

"There are stumps there, but know of no one in particular."

RUDOLPH 'CURLY' LOHMANN was called to the stand. Curly was a little skittish about boat rides and told his friend Leo MacDonald that he was staying near the top deck in case there was a problem.

"In your opinion was there fog on the Peoria shore?" Clary asked.

"It looked like white steam," he replied. "It seemed to be ahead of the boat."

"So was it the crash of the willows that first attracted your attention?"

"No."

"What was it?"

"The jolt."

"Could you tell us where the jolt struck the boat?

"No, I was riding backwards at the time."

"How soon after the jolt did you see the water?"

"Two or three minutes."

"How soon after the jar did the boat settle?"

"Not over five minutes."

JOSEPH RUPP TOLD CLARY and the jury that he was playing cards and drinking on the lower deck when the tree broke through the window. "It was a large branch," he said.

"Was it on the Peoria or Tazewell side of the river?

"On the Peoria County shore," he recalled.

"Did the boat come to a stop?"

"No. When we hit several bells were ringing, although I don't know what they meant. Someone said that the boat was sinking and we saw several women come back from the front of the boat. They said that the men would not allow them to go up the front stairs but sent them around to the back stairs."

Rupp was asked if the "men" the women referred to were members of the crew, and he told them "yes." He said they were forced to climb up the small stairs, and many were trapped in the wreckage before they had a chance to escape.

"Did you pay any attention to the weather that evening?"

"Yes, I could see lanterns and boats along the shore."

"Did you see any men with miner lamps on their heads?"

"Yes."

"Were they the first to arrive?"

"Yes. They reached the boat about 20 to 30 minutes after she sank."

"Was there any fog overhanging the river at the time?"

"No fog to amount to anything during the night, but it became awfully foggy along towards morning."

Since Rupp stated he was drinking at the time, Clary asked him about the sale of liquor on the boat. Rupp said his friend, James Blackburn, obtained a pint of whiskey from Captain Mehl's brother. "The sale of beer was general and sold at the bar," he said, "but the whiskey could be obtained on the quiet from boat officials."

FREDA SNYDER HAD BEEN waiting patiently. Now it was her turn to speak. She was sworn in and quickly took a seat. Her testimony was the "most sensational" so far the *Peoria Journal-Transcript* reported.

"Whatever struck the boat that night," she told the jury," it went right through the hull!"

"How do you know?" she was asked.

"I heard the water rushing into the hull with a sound like Niagara Falls. That's when the boat struck the Peoria shore. It sounded just like pushing a crowbar through a rotten board."

She continued, "No searchlight was on at the time. The willows came through the Peoria side of the boat, and the searchlight immediately commenced playing on the Pekin bank as if they were trying to make that. The bells [from the engine room] started ringing violently, and we started for the front of the boat when Captain Mehl told us, 'Go back and sit down. Don't be foolish. We only hit another sand bar.'"

The coroner and state investigators turned and looked at each other. Freda was a firecracker that was about to go off. Just then she did.

"I tell you what!" she continued, raising her voice to a shout. "I don't see what made the captain pull out into the middle of the river!" She paused and looked in the direction of the jury box, waving her fingers in anger. "It looked as if he tried to drown us like rats in a trap!" Her last words echoed off the nearly empty courtroom walls—*like rats in a trap!*

WITH THAT, CLARY adjourned the proceedings. It had been a productive couple of hours and an interesting first day. Everyone agreed. The hearings were off to a good start. Clary had hoped more people would have been in the courtroom to see the proceedings in person, but the papers, he would soon discover, covered it well.

In the following days, witness testimony was expected from more passengers, former steamboat men, a carpenter who repaired the *Columbia*'s hull and the two main characters in the unfolding drama, Captain Herman Mehl and pilot George Williams, who were both scheduled to appear. The state's appointed diver, Dunscombe, would testify too. He had arrived, gone under the wreckage and found something "significant," Clary was told.

WALTER FLUEGEL
TAZEWELL COUNTY GENEALOGICAL AND HISTORICAL SOCIETY (TCGHS)

33

THIS THEORY

THE STATE INVESTIGATION continued both inside and outside of the courtroom. At the wreck site, now that all the bodies had been removed, state workers, mostly hired engineers, swooped in. Soundings and measurements were taken to determine the river's depth and the boat's movement. The team mapped out a blueprint of the riverbed in the vicinity of the sinking and determined that every second the boat remained above water, after it hit the shoreline, it was moving into deeper water.

The engineers' report was the most damaging evidence yet against the pilot and captain of the *Columbia*. It surmised:

> *The water from the Peoria shore from a distance of 33 feet varies in depth from four to ten feet. Had the boat stopped when it struck shore while an investigation was made and it went down, no lives would have been lost. The water where the vessel went down is approximately 16 feet in depth. The surveys ahead of the boat and in the direction in which the nose was*

pointed and for which speeding as fast as the rapidly filling hole would let her was 18 and 19 feet deep. The Columbia *was plowing into deeper water all the time after it struck the Peoria shore and a few seconds more would have put it into the deepest water in the section with a greater loss of life.*

The engineers determined the boat was taking in water, sinking rapidly and steered dangerously into deeper water. That was an indisputable fact. But the reason why the boat listed then collapsed on itself was still a mystery. It remained a nagging question for which everyone seemed to have a different explanation.

"The impact broke one of her hog chains," said Peoria Police Chief Rhodes, who was no expert on boats or physics, but was asked his opinion, and he answered. "The man at the wheel, instead of letting the boat lay on the bank until it was found whether she was injured, backed her into deep water. Then without the hog chain support on one side she buckled and sank."

Mehl had vehemently denied that the hog chains on his boat snapped. The tall wooden masts that held the taut chains broke in the fall and the chains slacked as a result, but the chains themselves did not break. Mehl was certain of it.

Federal inspector Downs supported Mehl's claims with facts: "This was not the case," Downs said when asked by a reporter from the *Peoria Journal-Transcript* if the hog chains broke. "The salvage workers and investigators aboard the *U.S.S. Comanche* pulled the hog chains out intact.

"In the face of this," he added, "hardly any theory remains but that the hull crumpled like paper."

Another explanation for the boat's sudden collapse came from the area's Harbor Master, A.T. Griffith. "If the hog chains held as reported, then the *Columbia* hit a log which stove a hole in her hull," Griffith concluded. "My theory of the cause is that the log probably rolled along under her and ripped open a long gash. The weight of the water made her list to one side and the crowd ran to that side, making her list more. Then she buckled in the middle.

"She hits the banks every time she lands," added Griffith. "That, I don't believe, is what happened. I think the submerged log ripped the hole and the weight made her buckle. Maybe the fastenings of the deck to the hog chains came loose and the decks fell."

Ora Barnewolt, the local man who was supervising the removal of wreckage, advanced his own theory, telling the *Peoria Evening Star,* "I don't believe a single abrasion or puncture of the hull was the cause. The steamer grounded on a sand bar and the contact with the flat keel opened seams of the boat to such an extreme that it loosened the hog chains and caused the supports to give way, thereby letting the decks crash together. The seams between the planking split wide open and allowed the water to rush in with terrific weight."

"This new explanation," the *Star* reported, "that 'the steamer sprung her seams,' would seem to support the findings of the authorities, who discovered the peculiarly regular broken windows on one side. If the steamer was running on a slow bell as was stated, the action of scraping for a full length over the sand bar might produce sufficient jar to break the windows."

There was no question that the boat had sprung a leak, but the bigger question remained unanswered. If the *Columbia* had struck something, likely a log, would the obstruction be large enough to pierce the hull and fill it with water? The job of the diver was to find the hole in the hull. If so, that would cement the theory.

The proof lay in the river itself. It was time to find the log.

AT THIS POINT Walter Fluegel was called. Fluegel was the man, authorities were told, who claimed to have seen "the log" that struck the boat.

The 24-year-old Fluegel, a grocer, was on the *Columbia* with his wife Goldie and another couple, Walter and Hattie Koch. As his family told the story, Fluegel lost sight of his wife after the boat sank. He was a good swimmer, and he was besieged by panicked passengers who were trying desperately to tread water. They reached for him and ripped off a portion of his clothing and glasses.

"He would bring someone to shore," his daughter Mary Alice

later recalled, "and ask if anyone had seen Goldie."

After several trips back and forth, each time bringing another passenger to safety, Fluegel collapsed from exhaustion.

"He had no hope his wife or unborn child were alive," Mary Alice said—Goldie was nine months pregnant and due in just a matter of weeks.

Fluegel was gasping with exhaustion on the riverbank when a friend delivered the good news: his wife and their companions, the Kochs, were all safe and resting on the hillside. As it turned out, when the boat tipped Walter Koch grabbed Goldie's and Hattie's wrists and pulled them both out at the same time. "They didn't even get their feet wet," Mary Alice explained.

Hattie Koch was also pregnant and expecting later that year.

The two *Columbia* babies would eventually come into the world safe and sound. Mary Alice Fluegel was born on July 20 and Marcello Koch at the end of October. The two women who survived the wreck while protected inside their mother's wombs would remain lifelong friends.

"Dad never let me near the water," Mary Alice said, "unless he was with me." Each year on the anniversary of the wreck the family would pray together. Grandfather Fluegel would bow his head and say, "By the Grace of God, [the family] was spared."

Walter Fluegel had a lot to be thankful for that night—he and his pregnant wife survived. He also had something to tell reporters. He had seen the log that struck the boat. When the state investigators heard about his story, they wanted to see Fluegel.

"You are going on another boat ride," they told him, "to find the log."

In a crowded small launch—Sackett, Mansfield, Greene and even federal inspector Downs were aboard—Fluegel was taken back on the river.

"It was almost against the shore," Fluegel directed the oarsman. "It was projecting from the bank."

The boat made several passes along the Peoria shoreline while Fluegel shaded his eyes and concentrated, but it was fruitless. Due to heavy rains the river was nearly a foot higher than the night of the tragedy. The log, along with anything else that might have been sticking out of the water at the time of the wreck, was now submerged. The state investigators thanked Walter Fluegel for his time.

FORTUNATELY, BENEATH the surface, the state's expert diver had better luck.

In his diving suit tethered by a long air hose, Dunscombe dropped beneath the murky river and began searching the hull of the ship. He wasn't down there for very long. When he surfaced he had something in his hands. Commissioner Sackett, who had just returned from the search on the river, was back overseeing the operation on the boat. He ran to the diver. Dunscombe showed Sackett what he had found.

Later that evening at the posh Jefferson Hotel in Peoria, Sackett, Mansfield and Dunscombe discussed the finding further. "At that time," the *Peoria Journal-Transcript* reported, "exclusively to the ears of the state officials, diver Dunscombe told what his trip into the hull had developed." Sackett then went in front of reporters. "The real story of how the *Columbia* sank has never been told," he said, "Of course why she sank is more or less obvious—there was a hole in her hull. But the story of how the hole got there and why she sank as she did is still a mystery." He paused dramatically. "When we get through with our investigation," he concluded, "I think the truth of the matter will be apparent to all."

Mansfield spoke next. "We want to get in absolutely first-class shape before we begin the public investigations. There's no use shooting the gun until it's fully loaded and we know exactly what we are talking about."

Sackett also praised the federal government, specifically the men on the *Comanche,* the derrick steamer, for "aiding in the work of the recovering bodies and dismantling the wreck for purposes of the state probe."

"Of course it is a government boat," he added, "but the promptness of the government's action is indicative of the manner in which the federal officials are usually ready to aid in a case of this kind."

Nearby, Dunscombe took his treasure, a large board, nearly four feet in length and four inches thick, and tucked it away. Nobody would see what he had found until the next day in the courtroom and he was ready to explain it.

WILLIAM C. REDFIELD
LIBRARY OF CONGRESS

34

ADMIRALTY LAW

ON THURSDAY, JULY 10, Supervising Inspector General of the Fourth District Captain George Greene sent a telegram to Washington, D.C., and the office of the Steamboat Inspection Service at the Department of Commerce. The message read:

> CONCLUDED INVESTIGATION *COLUMBIA* DISASTER. CHARG-
> ES WILL BE IMMEDIATELY PREFERRED AGAINST BOTH
> MASTER AND PILOT FOR NEGLIGENCE INATTENTION TO
> DUTIES AND UNSKILLFULLNESS. DETAILED REPORT WILL
> FOLLOW. LEAVE FOR ST. LOUIS TONIGHT.
> GREENE, SUPERVISING INSPECTOR

In the letter that followed, dated July 12, Greene was more specific.

> *I am thoroughly satisfied, from the depositions taken in my presence that the responsibility of the disaster rests entirely on the Master and Pilot of the steamer. According to the depositions of the pilots, having license on*

the Illinois River, that part of the river passing Wesley's Bar, where the accident occurred, is the most treacherous part of the Illinois River. I made two trips over this part of the river, while there, in a gasoline launch, and in my observation, I am satisfied that it is a difficult piece of river to navigate with a steamer the size of the steamer COLUMBIA *under most favorable conditions.*

Greene further explained that inspectors Downs and Bower had arrived early Saturday morning and immediately went to the wreck site and "made considerable progress" in their investigations, taking several depositions of the captain, pilot and crew before Greene arrived on Sunday. Greene wrote:

We continued to take depositions at Peoria on Monday and Tuesday, July 8 and 9, and went to Pekin Wednesday, July 10, and took several depositions. While the depositions taken at Peoria were sufficient, in my opinion, to fix responsibility for the disaster, I deemed it advisable, for the good of this service, for us to go to Pekin and take depositions of some of the survivors who resided there, as they were informed that the City and County authorities there, as well as the public generally, were very much disturbed on account of the disaster, and several rumors were afloat to the effect that the steamer was not in good condition, etc.

Greene had some backtracking to do, however. In a letter written by his two inspectors to Steamboat Inspector General Uhler in the capital, Bower and Downs addressed some concerns they had about the "local press" and reports in the "Peoria papers" that statements about the Steamboat Inspection Service were "very severe in their criticism." They wrote:

While most of the statements were too ridiculous for any consideration, we know from personal knowledge that the public in general have given these stories some credence, they feeling the Board of Local Inspectors have been negligent in their duties in permitting this steamer to navigate. For the interest of the Service in general, we would welcome an investigation by a practical, experienced, disinterested party or parties chosen by the Department.

Bower and Downs had set themselves up for more scrutiny, but they appeared to be showing their bosses that their actions were 'just' and were not afraid to be judged or criticized, if warranted. In the meantime, they had a job to do and were doing that to the best of their capabilities. They continued:

We could have closed this investigation earlier, having sufficient evidence in testimony by officers and crew of said steamer to warrant us in making the charges we have this day preferred, but owing to the enormous loss of life, grief and wrought up condition of the public in that vicinity, we wished to show that we were desirous of obtaining all the information possible by taking testimony from a great many passengers (which testimony only bore out that which we had already received from the crew of the steamer) in order to appease the public feeling as much as possible.

Redfield must have personally read the letter about the media's criticism of the inspectors, because he immediately sent a message to General Uhler. In an expression of support and encouragement, Redfield defended Uhler and his men:

Referring to the newspaper charges, it appears to be the case that in the matters of this kind commonly done without any inquiry is to damn the inspectors. The facts elicited, however, and such facts as have been definitely stated in the press seem thus far to warrant no criticism whatever on the part of the officers of your Service.

The letter was written July 16 and postmarked July 17, although Redfield could just as easily have delivered it by hand, since Uhler's office was also in the same building, maybe even on the same floor. His letter was mailed.

At the same time, Redfield was receiving all sorts of suggestions, criticisms, and crackpot ideas via incoming mail. One of the most entertaining episodes involved a man in Milton, Pennsylvania— a small borough north of Harrisburg and located on the snaky Susquehanna River.

In a modest envelope, the one-page letter, written on ruled note paper in cursive handwriting, was addressed directly to Mr. Redfield. It read:

> *Dear Sir,*
> *I have a very simple and effective way of doing away with such disasters caused by drowning. The government is responsible for all drownings in the nation today much more so than the Captain and Pilot of the* Columbia. *They had nothing to do with the* Eastland *sinking. If you really wish to wipe out drownings in the nation I would be delighted to explain how easy it can be done and will meet you at your request any place in the country.*
> *Respectively yours,*
> *Wm. L. Hartnett*
> *501 Walnut Street, East*
> *Milton, Pennsylvania*

It's hard to imagine Redfield's initial reaction to the eccentric letter, but it clearly intrigued him for some reason. He called on his Deputy Supervising Inspector General, D.N. Hoover, to write back to Mr. William Hartnett of Milton, Pennsylvania. "Find out what this is all about," ordered Redfield.

Hoover wrote:

> *Sir:*
> *This Bureau is in receipt, by reference, of your letter of the 19ᵗʰ instant, addressed to the Secretary of Commerce, Washington, D.C., in regard to your method for*

doing away with such disasters as that of the steamer
Columbia, *and in reply you are informed that if you
will submit a description of your plan to this Bureau
it will be carefully considered and you will be further
advised.*
    Respectfully,
    D.N. Hoover

In just four days, another letter arrived from Milton, Pennsylvania. This time there were two full pages of handwritten notes with a photo included:

Dear Sir,
    *In response to your reply to my letter of July 19th on
file #75639 will say I fear to endeavor to explain on
paper as I cannot do justice to it. I cannot (sic) water
in steamships' boilers or stop it from running on rocks.
But I can place it within the power of the government
to teach every school child in the nation to swim.*
    *I have invented a machine (photo enclosed) that
teaches swimming on land so that all that is necessary is an earnest try in the water. The machine places
a person on equal with a four-footed animal the first
time in the water, one lesson of from one to two minutes is enough.*
    *I have taught six boys in 9½ minutes total time for
the six including time taken for tests in the water. It is
my idea to place one machine in each school District
and teach every child to swim at the age of six years.
Other machines could be used for older children.*
    *I understand that about 7,000 people in the U.S. are
drowned every year. That is more than the losses of life
in the war to date. If this does not include a thorough
investigation, please ask questions, I can explain better. Hoping to hear from you soon. I remain,*
    William J. Hartnett
    Milton, Pa.

Hoover read the letter and showed it to Redfield before writing back to Mr. Hartnett:

> *Sir:*
>
> *Receipt is acknowledged of your letter of the 24th instant, enclosing photograph of a device invented by you to teach persons to swim, and the comments made in your letter have been carefully noted.*
>
> *In reply you are informed that when writing its letter to you of the 22nd instant, the Bureau was of the opinion that you had some device such as a life preserver or life raft, which devices are subject to the approval of the Service. However, the Bureau has no jurisdiction whatever in the matter of the approval of a device such as yours, and therefore the Bureau can take no action in the matter.*
>
> *Respectfully,*
> *D.N. Hoover*

After Hoover's rejection letter, there are no more records of correspondence between the Department of Commerce and William Hartnett. Perhaps the Pennsylvania correspondent took the government's dismissive attitude in stride, perhaps not. Regardless, the swimming machine stayed in Milton, Pennsylvania, where one can only hope very few people drowned.

ON JULY 12, Captain George Greene finished his letter to General Uhler with these damaging charges against the operator and the pilot of the *Columbia*:

> *We therefore have this day preferred charges against Herman F. Mehl, Master and George T. Williams, pilot on watch as follows:*
>
> *Herman F. Mehl, master, Violation Section 4439 R.S.U.S. Inattention to his duties and incapacity.*
>
> *INATTENTION. In his duties in permitting pilot to navigate Steamer* COLUMBIA *during smoky and foggy*

weather, especially when approaching a very danger-
ous place in the river.

INCAPACITY. In failing to grasp the situation instant-
ly after the steamer got in the willows on a rough shore,
thereby permitting pilot to proceed and not hold along
the bank and willows until an examination of the hull
has been made, and until the fog cleared away, instead
of proceeding down and out in midstream, the Steam-
er thereby sinking in deep instead of shallow water,
resulting in great loss of life.

George T. Williams, Pilot, Violation Section, R.S.U.S.
Unskillfulness and negligence.

UNSKILLFULNESS. In navigating Steamer COLUMBIA
on a slow bell ahead for a distance of at least two and
a half miles while descending river towards a danger-
ous place with a strong current in the fog and smoky
weather, thereby permitting said steamer to come in
contact with a rough and dangerous shore with too
great headway.

NEGLIGENCE. In neglecting to entirely check Steam-
er COLUMBIA*'s headway when said steamer was in on*
and scraping willows, thus holding her alongside of
bank until an examination of hull had been made and
fog cleared away, instead of going slow bell proceed-
ing down and out in mid-stream, the Steamer thereby
sinking in deep instead of shallow water, resulting in
great loss of life.

The first charges in the case of the wreck of the *Columbia* had
been brought just six days after the steamer sank. The captain
and pilot were charged with negligence and unlawfulness by the
federal government. A trial would follow with federal inspectors
Downs and Bower acting as judge and jury. Captain Mehl and pilot
George 'Tom' Williams would have a chance to defend themselves
in a more public forum. At stake would be the privilege of continuing to own and operate a steamboat, for Mehl, and to earn a living

as a riverboat pilot, for Williams.

Greene officially ordered the actions of the Department to commence with the trial. In his letter to General Uhler, perhaps foreshadowing the fate of the captain and pilot of the *Columbia,* his final words were ominous: "I have directed the Local Inspectors at St. Louis, Missouri, to hold the trials and dispose of them, as speedily as possible," Greene wrote.

CAPTAIN MEHL IMMEDIATELY sought legal consul. He had a wrecked boat on his hands, no insurance, and the potential for a slew of lawsuits. He was also responsible for salvage of the ship, which could cost thousands. He sought legal advice and under the admiralty law would eventually find a safety net.

The admiralty law was designed to protect the owner and operator of a floating vessel from liability in case of great loss of life. Mehl's attorney, Charles E. Kremer, a maritime law expert from Chicago, asked a federal judge to limit the captain's liability to the value of the boat after the wreck and receipts from the excursion that fateful night.

The value of the boat, Kremer estimated, was about $1,500 to $2,000. "Do the math," he must have told the judge in his best lawyer speak, there were 87 lives lost and under state law the maximum liability allowed by each victim would be $10,000 for a grand total of $870,000. "The court is bound to do by precedent of the admiralty law," Kremer said, "that administrators and relatives of persons who lost their lives on the *Columbia* will be restrained from bringing suit for damages in any other court." Kremer cited that the limitation on liability of a boat owner was fixed by a federal statute enacted in 1851 and amended twice, in 1884 and 1886. "Action in today's proceeding was brought under rule 54, the same law that applied to the *Eastland* disaster in Chicago, the *Christopher Columbus* in Milwaukee and the *Titanic,*" he argued.

Judge Louis FitzHenry agreed. FitzHenry, an educated lawyer and former newspaperman from Bloomington, was in his first day on the federal bench of the Southern Illinois Seventh District that served several counties in Central Illinois. He had been appointed by President Wilson and sworn in on July 6, just a day after the *Columbia* wreck. FitzHenry signed the order stating that Mehl, the owner of the boat, had no prior knowledge of any defect in the *Columbia* and was entitled to the benefit of the admiralty law. Under the provision, Mehl was ordered to turn the wreck of the *Columbia* over to U.S. Marshals, who were then authorized to sell the salvable parts, and "later a commissioner will be appointed to receive claims and apportion damages from the revenue derived from the sale." Mehl would also turn over $100 dollars, the cash he received from the excursionists that night. With that order, the government now owned what was left of Mehl's 'old tub.'

Mehl wasn't off the hook, at least not personally, but since he had no insurance on the boat, his financial strain was lifted a bit. He was also absolved from being directly sued by victims' families who had already placed blame on the captain for their loss. That legal juggernaut could have been an ugly and costly one for Mehl.

Assistant Attorney General Mansfield, appearing on behalf of the state, asked the judge for permission to raise the hull in order that "the question of criminal liability might be ascertained."

Kremer objected. "The state properly could not be a party to the proceeding in admiralty law," he argued.

Judge FitzHenry overruled. "Mr. Mansfield has a right to be heard," he told the attorney.

The civil motion settled, FitzHenry added some flair to the proceedings by telling Kremer directly, "I am not sure that the federal grand jury should not investigate this case."

A federal grand jury! Mehl was likely startled by the judge's unusually frank opinion. So far the federal government had only threatened to take away his operator's license. Up until that point, the criminal portion of the case was in the hands of the state and local jurisdictions only. A federal grand jury could mean serious indictments that carried lengthy potential prison sentences. Similar circumstances surrounded the *Eastland* disaster when the boat's owners, captain and crew were all indicted by a federal grand jury. They went to trial and were eventually found not guilty. (It helped that the original charges of negligence and manslaughter were later changed by a judge to a lesser charge of conspiracy to operate an unsafe ship. Since it was determined that no one conspired to cause the accident, they were all acquitted.)

Mehl and his legal team left the courtroom and prepared their next move. As expected, the captain had been called to appear before both of the coroner's inquests. Even if the captain was ready to tell his side of the story, his high-priced lawyers were advising him otherwise.

Meanwhile, in a couple of stuffy hearing rooms, Coroner Clary and his counterpart on the other side of the river, Peoria County Coroner Elliott, continued to issue witness subpoenas. They each called in a mix of past and present employees of the *Columbia* to testify.

The witnesses had a lot to say, and as it turned out, not all of it would be bad news for the embattled Captain Mehl and his soon-to-be-scapegoated pilot.

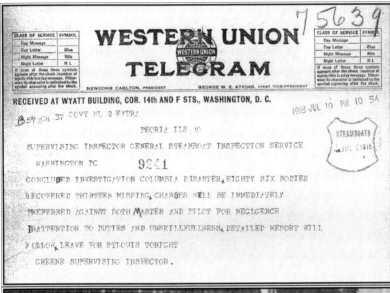

TOP: TELEGRAM ANNOUNCING CHARGES AGAINST COLUMBIA CAPTAIN
AND PILOT; BOTTOM: WILLIAM HARTNETT AND THE SWIMMING MACHINE
U.S. NATIONAL ARCHIVES AND RECORDS ADMINISTRATION
WASHINGTON, D.C.

35

FLANKING IN

IN 1911, STEAMBOAT MAN and author Fred Way Jr. described what it was like to meet a riverboat pilot face-to-face for the first time:

> We turned to gaze upon the countenance of a slight-built man with a long white beard; the hand which lay upon my shoulder was clothed in a white glove. The man was wearing a black swallowtail suit. He had on a white stiff shirt with a turnover collar and a derby hat. There was a hint of Santa Claus in the twinkle of his light blue eyes, and there seemed no harm in him, yet we were struck speechless because we could not be sure whether he was a preacher or not.

Way was only ten years old when he and a friend sneaked up to the pilothouse door of the steamer *Queen City* to marvel at its wonders and "drink in its details." The door was locked. "We shoved our noses against the small pane and ogled inside," he recalls. Just then the white-bearded, well-dressed man appeared. "It would not do to have a preacher catch us red-handed in the act of sinning, and trespassing and violating the written laws," Way wrote. The man, of course, was the pilot of the *Queen City:*

> The white-bearded one went in, took off his hat, hung it on a peg, and walked around as though he owned the place: for the first time it commenced to dawn upon my feeble brain of this huge steamboat; he guided it; he was the person who stepped up to that enormous wheel and took the superhuman responsibility of making decisions while this vast tonnage of decks, freight, passengers, machinery and all was at the mercy of the rivers currents.

Way could have been describing any steamboat pilot (or captain, for on many boats they usually carried the dual role). In reading Way's and Twain's books, it's clear that steamboat men, especially pilots, considered themselves a privileged lot who bravely endured the rigors of training on the river to master the art of piloting. They were often very proud men who wouldn't mind sharing with anyone who was listening just how important they were.

For years, during the height of the steamboat's popularity, the captain and pilot were treated like celebrities in river towns. The pilot would be especially revered as he sat high above the ship, a mysterious figure shrouded by the glass windows and fancy trimming of the pilothouse. To a young boy like Way, who loved the river and its fanciful tales, the pilot of a steamboat must have been as admired and seemingly unapproachable to him as a favorite major league baseball player is to a young sports fan.

So honored were the men who guided the striking ships through the swift river currents that after retiring many captains would have their homes built in the same architectural style as their boats. Some took it even a step further. Captain Fred Dippold, as Way recalls in his book, had the pilothouse of the old towboat *Dick Fulton* removed and placed in the front yard of his summer home along the banks of the Ohio River.

By the early 1900s, it was not uncommon for men who piloted the excursion steamboats on the Mississippi and Illinois Rivers to say they had been working on the river for many years, and they were quick to regale a willing listener with stories about low tides, soft groundings and near misses. Mark Twain had made a comfortable living doing just that.

The *Columbia*'s pilot, George 'Tom' Williams, had an especially impressive resumé. Williams was a veteran river man who had piloted and served as captain and pilot on many boats, including one called the *Reindeer.* He even worked for the state in the newly formed Illinois Fish Commission which regulated fishermen on the river who were illegally using nets that were so large they hampered riverboat travel. Who better to spy on law-breaking fishermen than steamboat pilots?

It was no ordinary circumstance then, that Clary, Elliott and even the federal inspectors called on the old river men to testify in the investigation of the *Columbia* disaster. They not only wanted to know the make-up of the men who were being held responsible, their reputations and character, but also use their expertise of the river, especially the Wesley City sand bar, to figure out how and why the boat ended up where it did, when it did. Many of the witnesses they summoned had previously worked on the *Columbia* and had first-hand knowledge of the crew, captain and pilot.

"I know Tom Williams well," said Charles Spicknell, a former engineer on the *Columbia,* who appeared before Clary and the jury. "He is considered one of the best pilots on the river and knows every eddy."

The words reverberated around the near-empty Tazewell County courtroom as the second day of testimonies got underway.

"You say the pilot knows the eddies well?" Spicknell was asked. "Does that include Sand Bar 11?"

Spicknell replied, "Tom has been with the Eagle Packet Company for years and has negotiated that dangerous place hundreds of times with the Eagle boats and the *Columbia.*"

"If Williams is such a good pilot, then what is your explanation of the cause of the accident?"

Spicknell told the jury that the boat evidently made a flank movement and was cast up on the stump by the river. "That is the only way I can account for it. The pilot probably saw he had swung pretty far down in Wesley bend and threw her over hard. When the boat got out in midstream the current caught the rudders and reversed them on him. The boat then undoubtedly flanked up on the willows out of her course."

"What do you mean exactly by the boat being 'flanked up'?"

"By flanking I mean that the boat slid over sideways onto a stump. Like something sliding on a slippery pavement."

Clary knew Spicknell had worked on the *Columbia* when it was overhauled over the winter. He asked about repairs to the hull.

"Some spots were bad in her last year," Spicknell replied. "The instructions were to start tearing off [boards] and wherever we found something bad to replace it." Spicknell said that Captain Mehl wanted the job to last six or seven years before having to do it again.

"You say there were some bad spots that were replaced?"

"Yes, we started tearing off and replacing. We kept at it eight weeks steady."

"So, there were rotten timbers, is that what you are saying, Mr. Spicknell?"

"I didn't say they were rotten. If there were any rotten floor timbers, I did not see them. The same with the ribs. We started in at the bow and went back on both sides to past midship. Then steel was put on the outside of the new material."

Spicknell paused and thought for a moment.

"About the timbers," he continued, reverting back to his previous answer, "I don't say there are no rotten ones, but I want to see them first."

Clary asked Spicknell if he was present when the federal inspectors checked the hull.

Spicknell replied, "Inspectors Downs and Bower spent the day on the job in Chillicothe [the *Columbia*'s dry dock in the winter]. They put on overalls and went over everything. Downs went down in the hull with Captain Mehl. They were gone for two hours. Inspector Greene stayed with me and passed on the machinery and boilers."

"So in your opinion the boat was sound?"

"I would say the boat was a good one. She had more cross ribs in than any boat I know of, and I have worked on many. I inspected the 50 engine plates often and they were in good shape. I saw the other ribs in passing along, but did not specifically notice them well enough to say what condition they were in while working on the boat."

"Did you ever see water in the hull?" Clary asked.

"I never saw water in a noticeable quantity in the hull," Spicknell replied. "There is always a little, but the siphon pump would be working if there were any quantity. This is the duty of the fireman. If there were any considerable amount of water in the hull, the duty of the watchman would be to tell the engineer to start the pumps."

"What would happen if water ever did get in the hull, say three feet of water?"

"The hull is only four feet deep," Spicknell said. "If three feet of water ever got in the hull she would have gone to the bottom just like she did. It is not unusual for the boat to get low in the Wesley bend. It has happened many times. Invariably the pilot has trouble getting her under control again. The 'flanking in' theory is the only one I can give. The boat made the bend. The pilot was paying attention, otherwise he would have never made the turn. The night was clear and the 'flank in' threw him out of the channel and into the stump.

"I know the boat. I know the pilot," Spicknell added. "I cannot fit any other theory to the facts other than she flanked in as the current hit the rudders broadside."

"Does the pilot drink?" Spicknell was asked.

"Tom Williams does not drink," he answered without hesitation. "He is a temperate and competent man."

Spicknell was asked an obvious question and answered it directly.

"I resigned my position on the *Columbia* ten days ago," he told the jury.

"Is there any particular reason why?" he was asked.

Spicknell had a rather unusual response: "The poor grub," was his short answer.

"Come again?" Clary said surprised.

"I worked on the boat two seasons and would still have been in the employ of the captain had the meals been more to my liking," Spicknell replied.

He was asked to step down.

ROY JONES, A FIREMAN on the *Columbia,* took the stand next. As a fireman, Jones did the grunt work, working the boilers, shoveling the coal and keeping the fires burning. He said he noticed the boat traveling near the willows, "but I did not think anything of it. I didn't know there was anything wrong until she tipped and I heard timbers crack."

"Did you feel a jar?" he was asked.

"No. I didn't feel a jar nor notice willows scraping against the hull."

"How fast was the boat going at the time?"

"We were running under a slow bell between the McKinley and Peoria and Pekin Union bridge. After we passed through the last bridge, the pilot ordered full speed ahead. Later on he slowed down again."

Jones explained that while rounding the bend, the pilot turned the searchlight on. "The boat was backing up when she struck the willows. She had stopped then backed up trying to keep from hitting the willows. Then the pilot gave a bell to go slow ahead."

"Do you think the pilot lost control?"

"It may be that he lost control after he rounded the curve in trying to catch her up she flanked on him." Jones paused and looked at the jury members. "I know that Tom Williams is a good pilot," he said.

"Did you think the boat was running low in the water?" Jones was asked.

"The *Columbia* had been coaled just before the trip and I know she was setting low in the water."

"So in your opinion it was the weight of the coal and not any abnormalities in the hull that caused the boat to sag?"

"The hull was in splendid condition. I never knew of the boat leaking."

"So you considered the *Columbia* a safe boat?

"I felt as safe on the *Columbia* as I did at my own home," Jones answered.

THE LIST OF PRESENT and former men who worked on the *Columbia* continued with the man who piloted the boat during the 1917 excursion season.

Albert Edwards declared the *Columbia* was a seaworthy steamer during the 1917 season, but it was his "general belief at that time that she would have to undergo repairs soon." Edwards showed the jury several photographs of the *Columbia* while in dry dock. The steamer had been stripped, he explained, and repairs were being made on the hull. Steel reinforcement had been placed on the exterior.

"At least 75 percent of the timber in the boat this year was new," declared Edwards. "I thoroughly inspected it at Chillicothe last February and found her to be in first-class condition.

"Money could not have put the *Columbia* in better shape than she was this season," Edwards continued. "The one thing about Mehl, whenever he made any improvements he spared no money. Captain Wisher of Quincy had a steamer in dry dock at the same time as the *Columbia* was being repaired. He told me it was a crime to remove timbers from a steamer like Mehl took from the *Columbia*."

"Then what do you think caused the accident?" he was asked.

"The sand bar curve at Wesley City is the most dangerous on the Illinois River," he said. "Although a pilot used extreme precaution in rounding the bar he was likely to be carried over towards the Peoria shore at any time.

"The current makes in at the bend," Edwards continued. "It takes you broadside and makes it rather difficult to handle a boat. It is a fight to keep off the sand bar and also miss the Peoria County shore, especially when weather conditions are against you."

"So a boat would normally go slow around the bend?"

"The speed of the boat going around the bend depends largely upon the weather. In clear weather, they generally proceed at full speed and have no difficulty, but in cloudy or heavy weather conditions, they generally travel under a slow bell."

Edwards was asked what a pilot would be thinking at that point.

"Possibly the pilot did not feel the jar," he explained, "and consequently did not stop the boat, but proceeded into mid-stream."

"Is that what you would do?"

"There is no law which compels a pilot to stop his boat after hitting something, but most pilots do when they encounter an accident."

"Would you say that feeling a jar or scraping the willows constitute encountering an accident?"

"The willows along the Peoria county shoreline are considered soft willows. I have been close to the willows many times with the boat myself. Williams is a man whom I would consider the best pilot on the Illinois River. It may be that he just lost control of the boat. It is possible he did not feel the jar."

AUGUST MEHL, THE COLUMBIA'S purser and brother of Captain Mehl, was called. "The boat never leaked," he said. "I've been in the hull hundreds of times but never saw any water in it. Henry the watchman was always calling to my attention how clean he kept the hull."

"Did you personally inspect the boat after the winter repairs?"

"I went through with the inspectors and the watchman. I saw the new ribs and planks. There was not a cracked rib on the boat. The inspectors Downs and Bower came by around May 6. The task consumed practically a day. Downs spent two hours in the hull with the watchman. When he came up he said, 'You have the best boat on western waters. You have one [good] steamer.' The inspection papers are carried in the boat. They must be displayed at all times or else the boat could be tied up by the government and could not leave dock.

"The boat was inspected while tied up at the Al Fresco Amusement Park," he finished. "Henry declared then that there was no water in it."

The purser was asked about weather conditions. He was reminded that the federal inspectors recently submitted a report to the Department of Commerce that stated at the time of the wreck that conditions were "foggy."

That would have come from the closed-door testimonies of both the captain and pilot, Mehl was reminded. "Would that be your assessment, also?" he was asked.

Mehl's answer was a bit of a surprise. "I could see both shores, the boats carrying the passengers to safety and also the stars shining above."

DELL SIVLEY WAS THE assistant pilot on the *Columbia* the night of the wreck. Sivley told the jury he was not on duty when the wreck occurred but was sleeping in his room on the dance deck. He had been asleep since leaving the Al Fresco Amusement Park and was scheduled to go on duty at 1 o'clock and relieve Williams. Presumably, Sivley would have piloted the *Columbia* back upstream to Peoria after the last passengers disembarked at Kingston Mines.

"The first I knew of the accident was when my wife came and called for me," Sivley testified. "She told me there was something wrong with the boat. Just then [the boat] listed and I got out as quickly as possible. I never felt the jar or jolt, unless that is what woke me up."

"Have you talked to pilot Williams since the accident?" Sivley was asked.

"Yes, Williams told me he encountered considerable trouble rounding the sand bar at Wesley City and the boat swung around too far and he had trouble straightening her around.

"It's all he could do before striking the willows," he added.

"Is that what you would have done?"

"If I was at the wheel I would have tried for the Tazewell County shore. The water along that shore is very shallow and Williams and Mehl knew that. After an accident a river pilot always tries to reach shallow water."

"Would you have done anything different if you had felt a jolt?"

"I probably would have stopped the boat and waited for a report from below, if I had felt the jar," he responded. "It's possible Williams did not feel the jolt."

HENRY SOPER, A FORMER special officer on the *Columbia*, told the jury that he always considered the boat to be in first-class condition and one of the safest on the river.

"I never made a personal inspection of the hull," he added, referring to that night, "but had been in [the hull] 15 to 20 different times."

"Do you remember the boat ever striking the shore before?" he was asked.

"The boat struck some piling at LaSalle last summer, but the damage was immediately repaired. The injury to the hull was on the port side. The boat also rammed some rocks at Camperville three years ago."

Soper was asked about the exits on the boat. During repairs, Mehl had removed the second deck promenade—including two doorways—and extended the wall of the dance floor to the deck rails. Soper declared that in his opinion there should have been more exits on the steamer.

"There was only one double door and two small doors on the sides, which were eliminated this spring when the dance-floor improvements were made."

Soper told the jury that while he was an officer on the *Columbia* he was in charge of life preservers. "Captain Mehl was always very careful to exercise every precaution in handling them. The breaking of a cord would release 300 life preservers on the upper deck." Soper also said that there were a large number of life vests hidden under seats on the dance floor.

"Who was in charge of those?" he was asked.

"The man working the candy counter," was Soper's response.

TWO FORMER MATES on the *Columbia*, James Lord and James Castelle, testified in the Peoria County inquest. Lord had been working on the boat for six weeks and was in the boiler room during the fatal trip. Coroner Elliott had been told that Lord, perhaps in jest, had made some incriminating comments about the condition of the boat to another family member. Lord denied it.

"We are giving you a chance here, Mr. Lord," Elliott said raising his voice. "We want the truth and nothing but the truth. Did you or did you not make a statement in reference to the presence of water in the boat's hull or to the condition of the hull?"

Lord waited a moment then replied that he had not.

"And if your own brother-in-law states that you made reference to the [poor] condition of the hull, how do you respond?" Elliott demanded.

"If he said that," Lord responded, "then he did not tell the truth."

Castelle was also asked his opinion of the boat's condition.

"First-class condition all season," was his response.

Castelle told the jury that he resigned his post on July 2, just three days before the wreck, when he and Captain Mehl's wife got "into a wrangle over affairs on the boat." Whether he was asked to be more specific about what type of argument he had with the captain's wife, the newspapers didn't report it.

PERHAPS THE MOST DAMAGING testimony came from a former pilot, Charles Spear, who commanded the government steamer *Comanche*. Spear told federal investigators that he would put the blame squarely on the shoulders of the pilot of the *Columbia*, but refused to elaborate when asked to explain.

"Spear was conservative in his replies," the newspapers reported, "and said that many conditions should be taken into consideration in arriving at an opinion."

In an effort to get an explanation, Spear was asked a hypothetical question: "Could evidence of bad judgment and unskillfulness be determined if a steamer carrying passengers in a fog ran into a bank?"

"If I was the pilot and ran into the bank," Spears replied, "it would be my fault."

Spear tapped himself on the chest, the papers reported, when he said that last line, *it would be my fault.*

The papers also reported that Tom Williams, the pilot of the *Columbia,* "was present and heard the statement."

Unlike Captain Mehl, who had spent considerable time talking to reporters, Williams remained relatively quiet and out of sight after the wreck. His one brief rendezvous with the press occurred on the Sunday following the accident, when he politely answered reporters' questions before testifying in front of investigators at the federal building in Peoria. In the following days no newspaper reports suggest that Williams was at the wreck site, watched any of the rescue efforts, sought out any undue attention or hired a big-city lawyer like Mehl.

He appeared at the hearings and seemed willing to tell his side of the story, plain and simple.

He did not have to wait long for his chance.

JOE WEIL
PEORIA PUBLIC LIBRARY

36

SENSATIONAL ORDER

THERE WAS A SHORT BREAK in the testimonies that lasted several days, although the reason is not clear from the newspaper coverage. It was reported Mehl had made a trip to Chicago, likely to get his law-yer or seek legal advice, and perhaps both coroners were waiting for him to return. The state investigators had asked for permission to raise the hull in order to determine its condition first-hand, but that was a slow process, both physically and legally. The *Columbia,* piece upon broken piece, sat dormant in the Illinois River for weeks.

Walter Williams, the Deputy of the U.S. Marshall's Office, was in charge of the wreckage. His job was to secure the site and oversee the removal of 'equipment' from the sunken boat, which, reported the papers, consisted of "chairs, tables, piles of life pre-servers, the bell and other nautical supplies." Basically, anything that was still intact was considered 'equipment' to be removed. Under orders from a federal judge, the salvageable goods would be converted into cash and put into a claims fund to be paid out to victims' families. Earlier in court, Mehl had waived his financial title to the boat in order to avoid multiple lawsuits.

Deputy Williams placed a Wesley City resident named Andrew Blessing in charge of the boat's remains. Blessing lived across the river from the wreck site and could "put out the lights each night and care for them," according to a newspaper description of his role.

"Nothing will be touched," it was reported, "until the coroner juries of Peoria and Tazewell Counties have gained all the evidence to place responsibility. Following this, the hull, machinery and the rest of the salvage will be disposed of to the best advantage."

To be eligible for compensation from the fund, victims' families were asked to file a claim on behalf of themselves or a lost loved one. The public notice would be published "once each week," the judge ordered, "until the return day of said motion." Although several days had passed since the claims fund was first announced, the man in charge, Commissioner I.R. Wasson, told a reporter that "no claims" had yet come into his office.

In the meantime, Peoria County Coroner Elliott was losing patience. There were only a few witnesses left to question, including the captain and pilot, and while some recent delays were unavoidable, Elliott was obviously annoyed. "I expect to start taking evidence again unless something new is developed to present," he told reporters. In stark contrast to Coroner Clary, who was taking his time with the investigation and carefully putting emphasis on each and every witness' testimony, Elliott was eager to wrap it up. Heretofore both men had been respectful and patient with each other, often waiting without complaint for witnesses who were called to testify in both hearings. Still it was clear Elliott was not pleased with the pace of the hearings so far. "The practice of hearing one witness and adjourning will be abandoned," he said. "I want to rush the testimony through without stop. The matter has dragged on for too long now."

For Clary, complete and considered testimony was worth the wait. In many respects, he was right.

When the inquiries finally resumed, the two undertakers from Pekin—H.C. Wilmot and Orville W. Noell—were called to Clary's courtroom. Both had personally attended to victims of the *Columbia*.

Wilmot surprised the jury by testifying that several of the 55 bodies he handled may not have died by drowning as suspected.

"Did any of the bodies show any marks of violence?" Clary asked.

Wilmot didn't hesitate to describe the victims' conditions and mention them by name. In describing Martha Sapp, wife of Jeff Sapp, he said, "the right cheek was broken and crushed in." Both the Capoots, Mr. and Mrs. Capoot, he said, "must have had some heavy object across their head and forehead that left a dent. No bones were broken, but we were unable to remake the face from the half-way up."

"So in your opinion they did not drown?"

"I do believe that a considerable percentage of the bodies handled by us were not drowned. That would be correct. This is what the embalmers told me as well."

"What exactly did the embalmers say?" Clary asked.

Wilmot explained that several of the embalmers had asked him to come over to where they were working. "Previously I had found fault with the way they were injecting the fluid," he said, motioning with his hands to show how it would be done. "If you hold the heads too high, you see, you let the water drain off."

Wilmot continued, this time actually answering the question. "A couple of them told me this party was never drowned. There was no water in the lungs. The neck was broken, I believe."

He tried to expand on the evidence that there were many causes of death other than drowning. "Some of the bodies were badly bruised and clothing on some of the women victims was literally torn off them.

"There was one man," Wilmot continued, "the body of Harry Neavar, which was badly bruised and indicated that he had been attempting to hold up a big piece of timber. It must have been too much for his great strength and it fell on him and several women nearby.

"I would judge," he concluded, "that as I hurriedly looked over the work and the excellent embalming results obtained, that at least eight to ten of my cases were never drowned. They might have died from either violence [being struck by an object] or fright. In some cases there were no signs of bruising or no water in the lungs."

Whether the coroner or jury wanted to hear it or not, Wilmot gave them another lesson in good embalming. "The body of Mabel Stout, aged eleven years, was found five days after the accident. It was in excellent shape and you can never prove to me that she was drowned. There was not a scar on her. The case was so beautiful that I granted the request of the father for another look at the body at the cemetery."

With that, Wilmot proudly stepped off the stand.

Orville Noell, the other local undertaker, told the jury his firm handled 23 bodies from the wreck.

"Did any of them show evidence of bruises?" Clary asked.

"One in particular," Noell said. "He was bruised about the head and there was a wound on his temple."

Clary was convinced after hearing the undertakers' testimonies that many of the victims had been struck by falling timbers and were either knocked out or killed by the strike.

Still, Clary had more questions than answers.

Had the investigations up until this point been focusing more on the condition of the hull rather than the aging upper structure? Could it be that the boat's woodwork was so old and badly rotted that it simply broke apart on impact? Was it possible there would have been fewer victims if the boat itself had stayed in one piece with only the hull and a portion of the boiler deck submerged?

Unfortunately, the condition of the boat's woodwork, even the condition of the hull, was only speculative so far. One witness had told the jury that when she reached for the deck railing, it crumbled in her hands "like rotting wood." And several broken boards that had drifted downstream and washed ashore in Pekin were said to be badly aged and worn.

IF CLARY WAS LOOKING for proof that either the hull was weak or the boat's structure was unstable, collaborative support came from his next witness. The testimony of John Hillyer, a carpenter, "was of sensational order," the papers reported.

The 60-year-old Hillyer had been building and repairing boat hulls for 14 years, he told the jury, and for three years up until 1917, he had worked for Captain Mehl. Clary asked him what kind of repairs he did.

"Well, that would be hard to answer," he said. "If anything was broke, I repaired it. If any ribs were cracked or there was any leakage, I repaired it."

"And you did all these things on the *Columbia*?"

"Some parts of the hull were worn, worse than others, and some of the ribs were decayed," Hillyer said. He also didn't waste any time offering up a theory as to why she sank. "If the boat was in the same condition when I left it [last season], a sudden jar might have a tendency to make a hole."

"Did you notice any dry rot?" Hillyer was asked.

"Yes, in different places, from the boiler to the dance floor."

Hillyer went on to explain that at the close of the 1917 season, he repaired the hull with several cement patches. The cement patches, he explained, were placed between the ribs and headers on each side of the boat and securely fastened by planks at the top of the ribs. "If there was a break in a plank," he said. "I would put cross pieces between the old ribs to make a box, fill the box with cement, push it into place with jack screws till the cement became hard, and then nail the pieces over the cement to hold it."

"Would you consider this to be a permanent or temporary hold?" Clary asked.

"Very, very temporary," Hillyer replied.

"Were these cement patches ever replaced by permanent ones?"

Hillyer stated that federal inspectors came to the boat once during the 1917 season and never went into the hull and never asked him any questions about the patches. So without directly answering the question, it was clearly, 'no.'

Clary continued the questioning. "Did Mehl continue to advertise for passengers and carry excursions after these patches were put on?"

"Yes," replied Hillyer.

Later in the year, Hillyer testified, Mehl had made plans for some extensive remodeling and called in a contractor to figure an estimate on the job. "This contractor," Hillyer said, "went through the vessel and made an inspection of the timbers by boring into them."

"In what condition did you find the timbers?"

"Some of them were good and some of them were very poor."

With that answer, Clary must have thought, he was finally getting somewhere. The coroner's suspicions that wear of the aging structure may have been a factor in the wreck were being expounded by a man who actually worked on the ship.

"Did you tell Mr. Mehl of the rotten timbers?"

"Yes, sir."

"What did he say?"

"Well, I'll answer it this way," Hillyer said. "You couldn't tell Mr. Mehl anything because he would tell you, you was a fool.

"He didn't know anything about a boat," Hillyer continued. "I told him there should be a lot of repairs and he would tell me I was a fool."

Hillyer stated he made alterations to the dance floor, directed by Mehl, in spite of his objections. "The promenade deck was removed," said Hillyer, "and the dance floor was widened by eight feet, four on either side."

Hillyer was asked to describe the change.

"The bulkheads [side walls] were originally built four feet inside the vertical line of the hull," he told the jury. "This was to maintain equilibrium. By widening the floor, these bulkheads were set out four feet on either side to the deck rail, doing away entirely with the promenade deck and the side exits."

"You stated you objected to these changes, is that right?" Clary asked.

"Yes. I told [Mehl] I thought it would make the boat top-heavy and he said I didn't know what I was talking about."

"So do you think changing that dance floor made the boat top-heavy or damaged in any way?"

"In my judgment, I would think that it did."

"Did you ever tell anyone you thought the boat was not safe?"

"Yes, different ones. I told the watchman when we have been in the hull that I thought she would go down some day."

Hillyer stated that the boat had siphons in the hull, but never saw any pumps.

"What was the condition of the hull when you last saw it?" he was asked.

"The condition of the hull the last I saw it was not safe," Hillyer answered.

"Did you ever see any water in the hull?"

"Oh, yes. There were lots of times when she had six or seven or eight inches of water in her, and we had to siphon her out."

"Was there ever any other time when there was more water in the hull?"

Hillyer nervously shifted in his seat. "Well, I wouldn't like to answer that if I could."

Clary admonished him. "We want the truth, Mr. Hillyer, and all the truth! Don't keep anything back that will shed light on this matter! There were 87 lives lost. It's a serious affair!"

Hillyer nodded and continued. "Well, I was in the boat once last summer at Main Street with the clerk's excursion on board. The water in the hull was this deep."

The papers reported that Hillyer stood up and held his hand across his body a little over his waist. "She had come in from Beard-stown," he added, "and there was one man down there with me, a member of the crew, who will corroborate it. I keep pretty quiet about it since, but others knew it was true when they denied it."

Hillyer was asked by a member of the jury if there was as much as three feet of water in the hull at the time.

"At least three feet," he said.

"Did you report that to Captain Mehl?"

"Yes."

"What did he say?"

"He said that it was not enough water to hurt."

CLARY MUST HAVE BEEN very pleased. The coroner had been looking for tough questions to ask Captain Mehl, and now he had witness testimony to back them up. Mehl was due in court the next day. Clary would finally get his chance to question him.

The captain of the *Columbia* never showed up. Mehl's defense lawyer Joesph Weil made it clear in a message sent to Clary and state investigators that the captain would not be testifying in front of either coroner's inquest. "The statements he made in front of federal investigators after the wreck should be sufficient enough," the message read.

The decision to refrain from testimony likely surprised Clary, since Mehl had been cooperative up to that point. But the influential Weil, the local boy who worked for a law firm shortly after graduating high school and became a lawyer at the tender age of 20, had flexed his legal muscles right from the outset of the investigation.

Known for his fancy 'dollar' cigars, hair slicked-back with pomade, and a bushy carpet of a mustache that completely covered his upper lip, Weil was a force both inside and outside the courtroom. His late night freewheeling exploits were the talk of the town.

One night while attending a vaudeville send-up at Peoria's Orpheum Theater, Weil was so impressed by one performer that he went backstage to offer his congratulations. The rising star was Sophie Tucker, the buxom singer who would later become known as one of the 'Red Hot Mammas' and find success by exploiting her large size, formidable presence and playful teasing stage manner. An act she perfected over the years. "Give me a song," she would shout out across the packed theater. *"If I Had One at Home Like You,"* a fellow replied. Tucker fired back, "What would you do with her?" before breaking into the suggestive tune. The crowd went wild. It was just silly and salacious enough to make her a star.

Tucker also gladly indulged in a pastime that gave her both pleasure and grief throughout the rest of her life. It all started with a backstage visit from a prominent Peoria lawyer who gushed over her performance and invited Tucker to a party he was throwing in her honor. Quite taken by the man's kindness and praise, she accepted. Years later, while performing in San Francisco, Tucker was approached by a man who said he was from Peoria. "Peoria?" Tucker said, surprised. "Joe Weil of Peoria taught me how to play poker."

By 1918, if there was a high-profile case in Peoria County, Weil's name was usually attached to it. In March of 1915, along with famous Chicago attorney Clarence Darrow, Weil played peacemaker by convincing then Illinois Governor Edward Dunne to pardon Newton C. Dougherty, a Peoria school superintendent who was convicted of forgery.

Several years later, Weil represented one of Peoria's wealthiest citizens, Jesse Barker, in a scandalous trial that involved money, a nasty divorce, a newborn baby and murder or suicide, although at first no one was quite sure which. Barker was a successful grocer turned bank owner who was also one Peoria's first residents to have—read, be able to afford—a fancy new automobile. But Barker's ostentatious wealth was more a curse than a blessing. In 1907 he was sued by a local woman who claimed he frightened a horse and left her disabled with a bad kidney and curvature of the spine. Her case was tossed out when a doctor testified that a spinal deformity like she was experiencing took years to develop.

The spurious suit as it turned out was the least of Barker's problems. A few years later Barker married a woman named Chamie, a pretty divorcee with a seven-year-old daughter, but she didn't stick around for long. Soon after she gave birth to another girl, this one named Jessie after her father, Chamie left her husband and ran off to Chicago with her first daughter. Distraught, Barker took his newborn and mother to California, only to return to Peoria a year later, in 1917. Despondent and too often alone, according to his friends, one Sunday Barker shut the massive double doors of his bathroom, rolled up some throw rugs, and shot himself in the head.

Jesse's family insisted it was murder, and they hired Joseph Weil, who had been one of Jesse's friends. Weil immediately claimed foul play in the case. The fatal bullet was never found in the bathroom, he argued. Someone must have removed it. But the case fell apart when the bullet was discovered in the bathtub where it ended up after ricocheting off the walls. Weil conceded that Barker had committed suicide, but he still fought against Chamie for the grandmother's right of custody for the baby Jessie.

With that kind of resume and notoriety, how could Mehl choose anyone other than Weil? Now 48, the prickly lawyer had a little less hair and a little more girth but an impressive list of argued cases and correspondence that added to his allure as an influential attorney. He was also very busy, which, as it turned out, would be a good thing for the captain. Weil's first order of business was letting the coroner know his client would not testify.

CLARY WASN'T THE ONLY one surprised by the sudden change of heart. Federal inspector Bower was infuriated by the precipitous lack of cooperation. He had expected to re-examine Mehl for negligence and incapacity, the charges brought against the captain and pilot by the Department of Commerce and Steamboat Inspection Service. "That testimony [the questioning behind closed doors] could not be used in this trial," Bower explained. "If Mehl has a defense to make against the charges, he must testify again."

"If he refuses to take the stand again," Bower added, "his license *will* be revoked." Bower asked to confer with Mehl in "reference to the situation" and clear up the matter.

Clary was torn. The star witness had bowed out, but the hearings so far had been more than illuminating. From survivors to former steamboat pilots to past and present crewmembers of the *Columbia*, the testimonies had been full of expressive descriptions and opinions about how the boat went down, the weather conditions, the condition of the boat and ultimately the character and worthiness of the pilot and captain. And however well concluding testimony from Mehl might have suited the dramatic structure of the story, it was the first testimony heard by the jury that had been the most damning.

Dunscombe, the state's appointed diver, had asked that a special session be called a day before the inquest was scheduled to begin. He had done the work he was asked to do and wanted to testify so he could return to St. Louis and move on to another government job. Clary granted his request and quickly gathered the jury a day early. Dunscombe had arrived in the courtroom with a slab of wood that was splintered and damaged at both ends.

Dunscombe's object was a piece of the sunken *Columbia*.

ORIGINAL SHEET MUSIC FOUND IN THE COLUMBIA'S WRECKAGE
PEORIA PUBLIC LIBRARY

37

DEAD WOOD

LONG BEFORE MEHL was scheduled to appear, Dunscombe took the stand and was sworn in. He set the long board beside his chair and settled in.

Clary stood up and approached the bench.

"How long have you been a professional diver?" Clary asked.

"For the past 17 years," Dunscombe replied.

"Were you called to Peoria to make an investigation of the sinking of the *Columbia*?"

"Yes, sir. I received a telegram on Tuesday evening and left Wednesday, arriving in Peoria Wednesday evening."

"When did you get to the scene of the disaster?"

"Thursday morning."

"Did you examine the boat at that time?"

"Yes, I cleared away the stuff from the hatchway and went into the hull and found the hole."

At that point, Dunscombe may have given a blow-by-blow description of his examination of the hull to the jurors. Just a day before, an article in the *Peoria Journal-Transcript* did the same, describing the diver's actions with detailed clarity:

> Hours of preparatory work preceded Dunscombe's descent
> into the ill-fated wreck. It was necessary to remove a great
> quantity of debris before the hatchway was exposed. He
> instructed the master of the government boat *Comanche*
> to tie the huge hawser to the wreck and "stand-off with
> a taut line" before he descended. This was to prevent the
> hull from rolling as he worked in the interior. The wreck-
> ing crew had been instructed not to touch the hull and the
> first thing Dunscombe did after donning his diving suit
> and padding his numerous scars—sustained in the course of
> his perilous career—was to descend just back of the wheel
> of the wreck and attach a tow line to the *Columbia*'s rud-
> der shaft. Much of the exposed wreckage was then cleared
> away and the real work of the examination began.

The paper went on to describe Dunscombe's descent to the boiler
room which took about an hour. "He carefully examined the 'wha-
len' [top of the hull] and sent up refuse and debris which blocked
entrance to the hull through the stern blockways."

The article continued, "Pieces of machinery, clothing, slot
machines, sacks of nickels, bar fixtures, beer cases, tables, wick-
er chairs, and much of the many jumbled articles which instructed or impeded progress along the top of the hull were sent up to
watchers above.

"Occasionally the diver's helmet, visible through the muddy
water, disturbed the surface as he climbed over chairs in the café."

With most of the debris cleared, the diver rested for about a half
hour then went back under. This time he was set to explore the hull.

> After a breathing spell and respite, the air pump was put
> in motion again. Diver Dunscombe let himself down to the
> boiler deck, the life line unwound and a trail of bubbles
> from his helmet valve were all that was visible as he low-
> ered down into the hold. Back and forth the life line ran
> as he worked to and fro along the hull's bottom. Finally a

long stretch of line ran out, and became very still. He had found the hole.

"So you found a hole?" Clary asked Dunscombe under oath. "Can you describe it?"

"Actually I found two holes in the hull of the *Columbia*," the diver responded, "one was eleven-foot one-inch by two-feet. The other was a caved in section three-feet by six-feet."

"Do you think the *Columbia* could have received such an injury by striking a sand bar or a floating log?"

"I do not."

Dunscombe explained that the planking in the hull had been "renewed" but that the upright timbers, or ribs, were much older, and those that he examined were "dead." He had taken a saw underwater with him to remove sections around the biggest part of the hull but realized he didn't need the tool. "I pulled away the boards with my hands," he said. Dunscombe then showed the jury the board he had brought to the courtroom. "The pieces show plainly," he said, "that the wood in all but one of them was 'dead.' In one of them it was partly 'alive.'"

Dunscombe explained that he found the first and larger hole near the stern and the second hole several feet forward from the first. "It was not a clean-cut hole," he said, "but was stove-in."

"Do you consider a boat that had timbers like that a safe boat to carry passengers?" Clary asked.

"No," was Dunscombe's reply.

Another juror asked him "substantially" the same question but in another form.

"Absolutely, no," was his assertion.

Clary asked if a steamer going down a river at the rate of two miles an hour with a current of three miles an hour and carrying 500 passengers hits a projection, would it ram through the hull?

Dunscombe replied, "It would take a strong hull to stand such a blow from a solid projection, such as a stump. But a sand bar or floating log would not knock such a hole in a hull under such conditions."

After his appearance in Tazewell County, the papers reported that Dunscombe "privatively expressed" the opinion that the
Columbia went into the shore and that in swinging her off the
shore her stern went up against a stump or other projection. If
he made those comments to reporters, it was when he was on his
way out. Dunscombe grabbed his 'dead' wood plank and hurried
back across the river—he was due in coroner Elliott's courtroom in
Peoria County that afternoon. As he had done earlier in Tazewell
County, the diver took the stand and read the oath.

"As an experienced diver and boat builder," Elliott asked, "what
do you think caused the *Columbia* to sink?"

"It would have had to have struck some solid obstruction...and
hit hard."

Elliott then asked, "In your opinion, had the hull been leaking
prior to when the boat struck the obstruction, would the pilot have
a hard time managing the steamer?"

"Yes, it would have become 'loggy' and very hard to handle."

"The accident happened just below a turn in the river," Elliott
continued. "In that case, would it have been hard to turn the boat?"

"A boat with lots of water in the hull is hard to handle, yes," Dunscombe answered.

Elloitt asked him if he was familiar with the navigation laws
with reference to running a boat on a foggy night.

Dunscombe became a bit defensive. Elliott was asking questions
that went beyond his expertise as a diver. "I am not a pilot," he
said, "and consequently would not desire to express an opinion on
that question."

Elliott persisted. "Do you know the law in reference to the boat
ramming into something which states that the officers should
make an examination of the steamer before proceeding?"

Again Dunscombe reminded the coroner that he was not a pilot.
Elliott moved on. He asked the diver if he was able to extract any
parts of the boat. Dunscombe showed Elliott the timber he had
pulled off with his bare hands.

"What condition were the timbers in reference to 'soundness'?"
Elliott asked.

"They would not pass as good timbers for a boat. One is good, but the others are bad. One piece is absolutely rotten. It is cracked clear down and shows signs of having been in the boat more than ten years."

"So the condition of the timbers show they have been in use for a long time, don't they, and in your judgment should have been removed?"

"Yes, sir."

"Did you make any further examination of the other timbers while they were in place?"

"I just felt them, but could not see them."

"From the examination you made could you tell whether any work had been done on the hull?"

"The outside planks felt good."

"In making your examination of the boat were you able to tell whether there was a covering, say a sheet of iron on the hull?"

"I couldn't feel any sheet of iron at all."

"Would you consider it safe to allow a boat with timbers of that character to run and carry passengers?"

The diver's reply came quickly.

"No," was his response.

IN ONE NEWSPAPER in particular, the *Peoria Evening Star*, witness testimonies were printed verbatim every day with little or no commentary. But the diver's testimony was treated differently. Ever since local auto mechanic and diver Earl Barnewolt arrived at the wreck site the morning after the disaster and Chicago celebrity Harry Halvorsen stepped off the train in Peoria, the reporters from the *Star* made it a point to follow their every move and report their actions in detail. The divers quickly became the face of the investigation, and Dunscombe's testimony was given the attention it deserved. But the *Peoria Evening Star* took it even further. The day after Dunscombe testified, this editorial ran:

> In the minds of many who heard the story of W.E. Dunscombe, professional diver, Saturday in Peoria and Pekin,

it was settled that the responsibility of the accident lies
upon the owners of the boat and the inspectors who made
the alleged inspection last spring. The diver's testimony
was startling and it showed the boat criminally unsafe for
carrying human beings.

With that biting commentary, the paper had apparently 'settled
the case' and brought the gavel down. The only thing the writer
failed to mention is how to punish the men responsible. If Pekin
was like the Old West, a rendered verdict like the one editorialized
in the paper that day may have stirred the townspeople into a lath-
er and sent an angry mob out into the dust-filled streets calling for
the captain, pilot and inspectors to be hanged from the nearest tree.

Luckily, cooler heads prevailed. The diver had appeared as the
first witness, so the bulk of the hearings had not even begun at the
time of the inflammatory editorial. Captain Mehl and pilot Williams were scheduled to be given a chance to speak, and Elliott
had planned to interview both the federal inspectors.

However, the diver's testimony would continue to resonate
throughout the rest of the hearings. And the paper's comments,
as it turned out, were almost prophetic.

COLUMBIA POSTER FOR AN EXCURSION THAT
WAS SCHEDULED THE DAY AFTER THE WRECK

38

TAKING THE STAND

AFTER A WEEK OF TESTIMONY there was another recess. Both Assistant Attorney General Mansfield and Waterways Commissioner Sackett asked Governor Lowden for permission to leave. They had been exhaustively pouring through the evidence and listening to testimony at both coroner's inquests, and they wanted a break. Mansfield's stay in the area had been even lengthier than Sackett's because he was attending to murder hearings in Peoria. But he was needed a bit longer.

The Governor allowed Sackett to leave but asked Mansfield to stay until the hearings were completed. The absence of Illinois' second highest law-enforcement officer, and the state's most visible and prominent figure on the case, would not be acceptable, the Governor explained. Mansfield graciously agreed. Even the newspapers recognized the importance of having Mansfield at the hearings. "It is hoped that the Governor and the Attorney General will allow Mr. Mansfield to stay," reported the *Pekin Daily Times*, "until the real cause is determined and responsibility is fixed." Mansfield stayed for another week.

However, the Attorney General's office had also requested that the inquest be delayed by several days in order that "more evidence be gathered to present to the jury." Plans were being made for the hull to be raised, they were told, and many involved with the case, including Clary and the jurors, wanted a look.

Mansfield went to Judge FitzHenry. "The diver went down with a saw to bring up portions of the hull," he implored. "[Dunscombe] broke off pieces with his hands and pieces of the rib were so nailed into that I could stick my fingers in the hole." FitzHenry granted the order and "directed the trustees of the vessel to give the state's attorneys and coroners of Peoria and Tazewell Counties an opportunity to measure and photograph the hull."

In addition, a special committee was formed made up of several of the state's top men—including Mansfield, Tazewell County State's Attorney Black, Clary, Sackett (who would remain in close contact while away) and several local committeemen including a Pekin judge, W.R. Curran, who would act as an assistant on all legal matters. According to the papers, the job of the committee was to "look up various threads of evidence connected with the tragedy, clear up disputed legal points, and prepare briefs."

The committee faced tough decisions. They loosely agreed that the question of jurisdictions in the case and resulting action lay in Tazewell County. It was reported in the *Times* that "while the *Columbia* rubbed the shore or hit the shore on the Peoria side of the Illinois, the alleged criminal carelessness of the pilot and master of the vessel resulted in the death of Tazewell citizens, in great numbers, on the Tazewell side of the river." While no one faulted Peoria County Coroner Elliott for conducting inquest hearings on behalf of Harry Brown, Tazewell County would likely have final say on criminal charges against the pilot and captain, and, if warranted, a trial against the accused men would take place in a Tazewell County courtroom.

And the issue of cost was not insignificant. The men who were called and worked on the *Columbia,* including diver Barnewolt with his brother Ora and helpers Herbert Fitch, William Parker and Pete Sansone, were expected to be compensated for their efforts. Sansone, who owned a small barge that was used to dump salvage, was granted a check for $12. Dunscombe was eventually paid $193.90, according to the *Peoria Evening Star.* The paper also reported that "the claim of the Chicago Dock Company, growing out of sending to Pekin the diver Harry Halvorsen, Hero of the *Eastland,* by the Chicago Police at the request of Coroner Clary, was held up. It is said that this claim is too large in proportion to services rendered." The amount was never disclosed.

The committee was generous to services that benefited the safety of its citizens. "In order to show appreciation of the valuable assistance rendered Tazewell County during the recent boat disaster by the Home Guards," the *Pekin Daily Times* reported, "the board voted the organization $50 and also donated to them the ammunition for the rifles which they are using and which belong to the county. The ammunition has been on hand for the past three years."

CLARY HAD NO CHOICE but to accept the short hiatus and prepare for the next batch of witnesses. "I have no idea when the hull will be raised," he said. "That matter is entirely up to the federal authorities, and we are willing to wait until they get around to it." He told reporters that twelve witnesses remained to be heard, but more might be called when the "conditions of the boat's timbers are learned."

Deputy U.S. Marshall Walter Williams, who was in charge of the wreckage, had earlier testified to Coroner Elliott that no action had been taken, to his knowledge, to raise the hull. Nor did he know when it might happen. For now, the wrecked boat would stay in its watery grave. One observer noted that the remains of the boat, shrouded by fog in the morning and cast by moonlit shadows at night, resembled a "ghost ship."

WHEN FEDERAL INSPECTOR Bower got word that Mehl was refusing to testify in both the federal trial and the coroners' hearings, he furiously called Weil. After a short discussion, it was agreed that Mehl would appear in the federal trial–but only the federal trial. Mehl's counsel also asked Bower that his client be tried separately from pilot Williams. Bower said that testimony during the trial would be considered in both cases, and that witnesses already heard would be recalled and their examination repeated for the record in Williams' case. Williams, perhaps putting too much trust in his captain's loyalty or hoping to avoid multiple questioning, said he was willing to go ahead and let the testimony taken in Mehl's case stand as testimony in his case. Bower balked. "It would not be proper," he said and ordered both men to appear.

MEANWHILE BOWER AND Downs had a court date of their own. Coroner Elliott subpoenaed both men to appear in Peoria County and defend their inspection of the sunken steamer just months before she went down. With the governor's approval and fearing a public reprisal if they refused, they had reluctantly agreed.

Downs took the stand first and testified as to the condition of the *Columbia*'s hull. "There were minor defects in the hull last year," he said, "at which time the certificate [to issue an operating license] was held up. Mehl immediately repaired them and accepted our recommendations for a thorough overhauling in the fall."

Bower testified that the initial inquiry did not lead officials to believe there was anything wrong with the boat before it struck the willows. "They did not use good judgment," Bower said. "The master or supreme officer on the steamer should have ordered the boat stopped until an investigation was made."

"Any experienced steamboat man would know when there were four or five inches [of water] in the hull," he said.

Bower told Elliott that he tried to secure a statement from the dry dock in Mounds City where the *Columbia*'s repairs took place, but they "absolutely refused to comply with the request." In a letter, Bower said, "they declared that they would probably be called upon to give testimony and that they did not desire to make any statements previous to that time."

THE BRIEF PROCEDURAL delay was over. A new committee was in place and the question of legal authority between the two counties was settled, at least initially. The witness testimony could continue.

When the coroner hearings finally resumed, both Clary and Elliott focused on the one witness they were able to call without provocation: the pilot of the *Columbia,* George 'Tom' Williams. Considering Mehl's decision not to testify in any other investigation other than the federal trial, Williams was warned that any statement he made to the jury might be used against him if further charges should result from the other inquires. Williams said that he had but one story to tell and that he was not afraid to tell it.

"I was in the pilothouse with Captain Mehl when the steamer struck," Williams told the jury. "There was a slight mist, or a fog in various spots along the river, but they did not interfere with my vision. The boat was weighted down with a hundred tons of coal, and when she rounded the Wesley City sand bar she became very hard to handle. The coal was in the forward part of the main deck and the crowd was light and did not weigh down the stern.

"When we reached the Wesley sand bar I threw her over toward the Peoria shore in order to avoid striking the bar. I saw that the boat was going over too far and I stopped the engines and signaled the engineer to back up.

"That halted the boat's headway, but then the stern swung around, being higher in the water than the bow. There was a slight jar and Captain Mehl told me to hold her and that he would go down and see if everything was alright.

"The blow was very light, and I did not think it would have any effect on the hull as I knew she had been reinforced with steel last fall. We drifted into the willows and the tree branches crashed through the windows and made considerable noise.

"Captain Mehl returned to the hurricane deck and yelled at me to take the boat ashore as quickly as possible. I ordered full speed ahead and started for the sand flat about 200 yards ahead toward the Tazewell County shore."

Williams was asked why he made the decision to steer the *Columbia* to the Tazewell County side of the river.

"The Tazewell County shore was the closest because of the manner in which the steamer was setting. The bow was headed straight to the other side while it was impossible to turn the boat around in the spot where she was lying." Williams said that he had been a pilot in several instances when another boat struck the shore and water had entered the hull. Each time he was able to return the boat safely.

"An examination would be made and water would be found in the hull," he continued. "It was the same that night. I thought we had just slid in on the shore and she was working her way off when I tried to get out of the willows. I would have run her right on [to the Peoria shore] if I thought the hull had been pierced."

Williams was then asked to identify several pieces of planking taken from the boat's hull by the diver. "Do you recognize these boards as coming from the *Columbia*'s hull?" he was asked.

"Yes," answered Williams.

BACK AT THE RIVER, state engineers continued to make soundings in the raised river and hit the jackpot. Along the shoreline they had found several large tree stumps and logs hidden under the water. The obstructions were large enough to cause damage to the bottom of a ship.

'GHOST SHIP' COLUMBIA STUCK IN ITS OWN MUD
MURPHY LIBRARY UNIVERSITY OF WISCONSIN-LA CROSSE

39

THE
PLEA

IN THE OFFICE OF the collector of customs at the federal building in downtown Peoria, Captain Downs and Bower prepared to hear the testimonies of both the pilot and captain of the *Columbia*. Williams had already testified at the coroners' hearings, but Mehl had not. Mehl would be under oath at a public trial for the first time. His lawyers conceded his participation only after federal officials threatened to revoke his license without deliberation. Both Mehl and Williams were told they were not being criminally charged. They were simply defending their right to own, operate and pilot a steamboat. Williams, who was accused of "unskillfulness and negligence," was asked to speak first. Mehl would listen and wait.

"Did the captain give you any orders?" Bower asked the pilot.

Williams testified that Mehl said, "Tom, we are going into the bank." He then told Bower that Mehl said he would go down to the hull and see if everything was alright. "When he came up he told me to get to the bank as quickly as I could."

"So he did not give you orders to back up?"

"We were too close to that shore."

In a response to a question about weather conditions, Williams testified that just below Peoria "it was misty and smoky."

"Could you see the shoreline?" he was asked.

"Yes, sir."

Williams added that it was "awful dark," but he could see the bank when the searchlight was on it. He was asked if he had conferred with Mehl about the fog. "We talked about going slow when we passed through the bridges. We were running on a slow bell," Williams said.

"Did you feel a jar?"

"I felt a little rub, just like she slid on the bank. I did not feel a jar."

"So you ran on a slow bell after the bridges, is that right?

"Yes, it was very, very dark."

"And you were running on a slow bell when you hit, is that right?"

"No," said Williams, "we were backing [up]."

Bower pointed out that at the closed-door hearings held shortly after the wreck, Williams testified that the fog bank was five to six feet high. He asked an obvious question: "If the fog bank was five or six feet high, would you be able to see a bank that's only one-foot high?"

"No, sir, but we had the searchlight burning."

"Do you consider it safe to navigate on a night like that?"

"We were seeing all the bridges," said Williams. "The fog was more like a mist."

"Then if there was no fog," said Bower, "what caused you to hit?"

"The boat must have taken a little run from that bar on Wesley City."

Bower was getting frustrated. "If it had been daylight," he asked stubbornly, "do you think you would have hit the bank?"

"No, sir."

"So the weather conditions did have something to do with you hitting the bank?"

"Yes, sir."

Bower had only one more question for the pilot. "Did the captain ever tell you to tie up the boat on account of the weather conditions?"

"No, sir," was Williams response.

Mehl was in the room and listening to his pilot's testimony. A newspaper report claimed the captain's attorney (not named) "examined" Williams after that final question and asked the pilot if he had ever navigated under worse conditions. Williams replied that he had, according to the papers.

AT LAST MEHL TOOK the stand. He faced the two inspectors and was sworn in.

"Not guilty," replied the captain when Bower asked him to enter a plea regarding charges of "incapacity and inattention to duty" brought by the federal government.

The two inspectors wasted no time getting to the point. They asked the captain directly how his boat ended up on the shore. Mehl responded quickly. He placed the blame on the pilot, telling Bower and Downs that in his opinion, "Tom Williams did not operate the boat skillfully."

Downs pressed, "So do you think a man like Williams used good skill and judgment when he can see a shoreline and still lets the boat get too close to the shore?"

"I don't think so," Mehl replied.

Mehl's counsel then stepped in and asked the captain if he could have done anything to prevent the accident.

"I do not think that there is any human in the world, no matter what he is and what he knows, could have done more than I done," was the captain's response.

The papers reported that after Mehl made that statement he "put his handkerchief to his eyes and wiped away some moisture." He then asked to be excused for a moment and walked over to the water cooler for a drink. When he returned, the captain described his actions at the time the steamer got into trouble. His testimony, the papers reported, repeated many details told by other witnesses.

Mehl would not admit the weather conditions were bad or that there was any fog. He called it a "little mist."

"How do you explain the boat getting so close to shore?" Downs asked.

"Well, I have thought of that many times," Mehl said. "It has come to my mind that [Williams] might have pulled the boat too far. I advised him that the boat was getting too close to shore."

"You advised him no further than that?" Downs inquired.

"No, sir," was Mehl's reply.

"Why didn't you?" Downs quickly shot back.

"As I stated before," said Mehl, "I did not think there was any danger."

Mehl added that as master of the *Columbia*, "I did everything any man could have done to prevent the disaster."

With that the trial was over. Bower and Downs had heard enough. If their minds were not made up already, the testimony of the captain and pilot did little to sway their opinion. They immediately sent a telegram to Redfield at the Department of Commerce office and Steamboat Inspection Service. It read:

> LICENSE REVOKED OF BOTH MASTER AND PILOT STEAM-
> ER *COLUMBIA*.

75639

STEAMBOATS
AUG 17 1918

1918 AUG 17 AM 10 4

2wuhx 16 collect govt

St.Louis Mo. 828am Aug 17,1918.
Steamboat Inspection Service,
                    Washington

License revoked of both master and pilot steamer Columbia .

                Local Inspectors.

1031am

TELEGRAM ANNOUNCING LICENSES REVOKED
U.S. NATIONAL ARCHIVES AND RECORDS ADMINISTRATION
WASHINGTON, D.C.

40

STICKY ISSUES

WITH THE ANNOUNCEMENT of the revocation of licenses against the captain and pilot of the *Columbia* and for the first time since the accident itself, the national media became intensely interested. From newspapers as influential as the *New York Times* to dailies as diverse as the *El Paso Herald* and as remote as the *Idaho Plains Statesman*, headlines blared: FEDS PULL LICENSES OF CAPTAIN AND PILOT OF SUNKEN STEAMER.

There was good reason for the national attention the ruling received. William Redfield was a prominent government official whose work on the *Eastland* disaster, while controversial, was still fresh in the national consciousness. Another steamboat wreck under Redfield and the banner of the Department of Commerce made the national news.

The federal government's decision to abolish the rights of Herman Mehl and Tom Williams from ever owning or operating a steamboat under U.S. jurisdiction was as meaningful a punishment to fellow rivermen as any criminal action would be. To Mehl and Williams, personally, the government's ruling was a devastating blow: They could no longer earn a living doing what they knew how to do. For Mehl, the excursion business he helped nurture for nearly a decade—and was finally paying off in big numbers—was yanked away. Even if he felt in his heart that he was personally not responsible for the tragic circumstances of the wreck, he would never get a chance to repair the damage or restore and reclaim his prominence on the river. This was above and beyond the thousands of dollars he lost on the boat itself. Likewise, Williams had been a steamboat man for more than 20 years and was a well-known and respected pilot on the Illinois and Mississippi Rivers. No matter how many of his colleagues defended him as a good and competent man, his career and reputation now lay in ruins.

However, the government's decision to revoke the licenses was unsurprising to anyone who had followed the investigation from the very beginning. Since they had arrived in Peoria, just a day after the wreck, inspectors Bower and Downs had openly criticized the captain and pilot for what they called "poor seamanship" and "bad judgments." The accusations started almost immediately after Mehl and Williams first testified privately before the inspectors.

The indictment that ultimately led to the ruling was clearly defined and extensive. The charges of neglect, incapacity, inattention to duty and unskillfulness were not difficult to prove, since the ruling was a subjective judgment made by the inspectors and not placed in the hands of a jury. It seemed evident that Downs and Bower had their minds made up from the minute they toured the wreck site. They also had the support of their superior Captain Greene, who just weeks before sent a letter to his boss, Steamboat Inspector General Uhler in Washington, D.C., stating that he expected his two inspectors to "dispose of them speedily," meaning the captain and pilot.

In a three-page typed final report submitted to General Uhler and Redfield, and listed under the headline REMARKS, Bower and Downs included a 400-word summary of how they determined the boat sank and the pivotal role of the captain, pilot, crew and passengers in the disaster. Beginning with the words, "According to the testimony taken in this case," the two inspectors went on to describe how the spot in the river where the boat went down is known for its "thickness and density of the fog in unfavorable weather" and that "for reason of high bluffs on the left hand of shore, a pocket of fog and smoke from manufacturing plants [appears] on the low, flat, right-hand shore."

They explain that the river is very difficult to navigate and very narrow at the Wesley City sand bar. The right hand shore, they reported, is "lined with submerged stumps."

"In navigating a steamer," they continued, "should the pilot get too low on the Wesley Bar, and have to make an abrupt turn with the current on the upper side, it would be necessary to stop and flank steamer instead of backing up and throwing head out of shore and stern in, as current setting in, together with rudders, would throw stern on above mentioned snags and stumps.

"In this particular instance, the testimony shows that the steamer's head pointed for this right hand shore just above a dead tree, diagonally across from Wesley Bar. The pilot then reversed to back full head, throwing head out, and stern in. Marks on the snags out from shore in the water above the dead tree and ahead of the willows below substantiate this testimony."

The report was not entirely critical. "The officers and crew of the steamer," they wrote, "and surviving passengers, lent all possible assistance in saving life after the disaster and looking after women and children first. The crews were commended by all survivors for their heroic action. All lifesaving equipment was ready and available for immediate use, and in good condition."

If the report was designed to put the government in the best possible light, it succeeded. Conspicuously absent was any mention of the inspection from May 7, 1918, just months before the wreck, when Bower and Downs proclaimed the *Columbia* was the "safest boat on western waters." Nor was there any mention of the condition of the boat, especially the hull, before the boat went down. The only place the hull or any problem with the boat itself comes up is when Mehl arrives on the main deck and notices that the steamer is "taking in water" and is told there is "two feet of water in the hold." Even then there is no mention of any structural problems with the boat before it strikes the shore.

Mehl and Williams had no recourse. They were expected to accept their punishment and move on. The best the government could do for the two men at that point was to let it end there, without putting the case before a federal grand jury. They spared Mehl and Williams federal criminal charges.

Bower and Downs returned home to St. Louis. Their names would surface again in the coroner's jury verdict, but the local jurisdictions were unlikely to prosecute the two inspectors for incompetence. After all, Bower and Downs had the protection of the federal government *and* the head of the Department of Commerce.

Redfield was more than pleased with the work of his two officers. Shortly after receiving the news of their decision, he sent a telegram addressed to Captain Greene, but referencing Bower and Downs, acknowledging their work in the case, and asking them all to "accept the thanks of the Bureau."

MEANWHILE, CLARY AND Elliott continued to wait. The matter of raising the hull had become a sticky issue between the government and local authorities. Both coroners had asked to see the hull and were told it was "being worked out." They had since called multiple witnesses to the stand and heard revealing testimony from survivors, steamboat inspectors, river pilots, past and present crewmembers and "mute evidence of rotted ribs and timbers taken from the hold by an expert diver," the *Peoria Journal-Transcript* remarked. But the questions about the hull continued to nag the investigations. It was already partly to blame for the week-long delay in the case.

Clary felt the testimony heard so far was sufficient. Rather than risk another long break in the proceedings, he asked the jury to convene and see if they could come up with a verdict. They could not. The determination of the hull's condition was too important. The diver and several other men, including a former carpenter who worked on the *Columbia* the previous year, had all testified that the hull was in a weakened state before striking the shore. But that wasn't proof enough for the jury. They wanted to see the hull for themselves. Clary understood. He conferred with Elliott, and they both agreed that the coroner inquiries would wait until the hull was raised and all parties could get a first-hand look at the damaged boat. "The inquest is adjourned until further notice," Clary announced. "I cannot say exactly when it will be resumed but it will not be this week. Probably we will get around to it about the beginning of the week."

Clary's announcement was just a good guess, of course. No one knew exactly when the hull would—or could—be raised. Even the newspapers ventured an optimistic guess: "It may not be until next week or later," the *Peoria Evening Star* reported. They were all hopelessly wrong. The length of time would be much greater, they would soon find out. In the meantime, the *Columbia* remained stuck in the mud in the middle of the Illinois River.

Away from theoretical conceptualizing in a courtroom, the men who could actually do the work estimated that it would take several months, maybe more, to raise the boat's hull from the bottom of the river. And that would be only after they were given the green light to do so. In the interim, the boat itself was being watched by a Wesley City resident who was hired by the U.S. Marshall's office to keep an eye on the wreckage from his front window. Just in case any poachers wanted a closer look, a sign was placed on the *Columbia* that read:

THIS VESSEL IS IN THE POSSESSION OF V.Y. DALLMAN
UNITED STATES MARSHALL AND ANY PERSON OR PERSONS
TRESPASSING HERE OR MOLESTING THIS PROPERTY IN
ANY WAY WILL BE SUBJECT TO ARREST

For now, the captain and pilot of the *Columbia* were free to go where they pleased. Mehl and Williams were under no arrest, and neither charged with any crime. Even the coroner's ruling, if and when it eventually was handed down, would not mean that the two men would be rounded up in the middle of the night and carted off to jail. The inquest by design was meant to determine cause and manner of death only and was considered merely a "fact finding mission in nature and statistical in purpose." There was no civil or criminal significance in the ruling.

The jury could implicate a person as the 'unlawful slayer' of the deceased and in some instances, for example the case of an obvious homicide victim, an arrest would follow. But typically, the verdict would be passed along to the State's Attorney's office as a recommendation for arrest only. The State's Attorney, in this case likely Tazewell County's E.E. Black, would then decide whether or not any charges would be filed and an indictment sought from a grand jury. The testimony itself had been documented and recorded and could be used in future trials.

In Tazewell County, the inquest had been in session for six full days (although few had been consecutive), demanding far more time and effort than Clary had anticipated.

Evidence of public frustration can be seen in a small debate regarding pay for jurors and the coroner. "The statute is reasonably clear," the papers remarked, "that the jury be paid only one dollar per day, no matter how many bodies there are in the investigation." There was no indication that any of the jurors demanded more.

"It is probable," the papers went on to report, "that the coroner can collect his fee of $10 for each body if he is so disposed." Yet Clary had never said he would seek full restitution in the *Columbia* case. He was, by law, entitled for pay in each and every death case along with compensation for his time. Until the hearings began, Clary had been at the wreck site every day and spent many hours collecting evidence. "That he will be compensated for his time is reasonably certain," the papers reported. In the end, for his weeks of labor Clary would request only the $10 fee for a single death certificate.

In Pekin and Peoria, life returned to normal for most people. In Pekin, the street cars were filled again, and businesses along Court Street were flourishing. The theaters were showing the latest silent 'flickers,' and the factories along the river belched out the 'round-the-clock plumes of soot, ash and smoke. Mark Twain's description of a "town that works" certainly applied to Pekin.

In Peoria, the bustle of big-city life carried on with little break. The night life especially continued to thrive. The latest theater productions were drawing in big crowds, and the dance halls were packed as usual. At the Hippodrome Theater on Jefferson Street a special movie was being offered. "For three days," an article in the *Peoria Journal-Transcript* declared, "moving pictures showing the recovery of bodies and the clearing away of wreckage of the steamer *Columbia* will be shown." The manager of the Hippodrome, H.J. Weisbruch, reportedly had received a telegram noting that his "tireless efforts to get the pictures had finally been crowned with success." The papers explained, "The pictures are said to contain many 'close-ups.'"

ON TUESDAY, JULY 23, the same week the coroner hearings were delayed, thousands of out-of-town conventioneers who knew a little something about 'dragging their feet' were filling Peoria's downtown hotels. Despite the unfavorable attention the Peoria area was getting at the time in regards to the wreck and overall safety of its citizens, The Annual Convention of the Illinois Shoe Retailers Association had come to town as scheduled.

"The 'Great Shoe Exhibit' would be well attended and full of pep," the papers excitedly reported, perhaps hoping to bring some semblance of balance and stability back to an unhinged community. The event was described as one of the biggest in the state:

> At least 50 of the largest manufacturers in the United States will be represented. Each firm will have an individual exhibit. A most interesting one will be that of ancient shoes and the evolution of styles from the sandal to the modern boot. Another feature well worthwhile is the display of fall style shoes worn by eight of Peoria's most beautiful models. Since the ruling on the restriction of leather, the Illinois shoe men have not met. And this will make the convention a most important one. The height and shades of shoes will be an important topic.

Also important would be how to entertain the nearly 800 visitors who were present for the three-day event. A grand entertainment itinerary was planned that included fancy banquets and balls, sporting events and theater trips. The first night's activities were booked:

For the men, a stag dinner at the Ye Olde Tavern will be followed by a four-round bout between George McFadden and 'Chu Chu' Emmett. Both weigh 122 pounds. Then there will be a four-round fight between T.P. McGuire and 'Fighting Dob.' Last there will be a battle royal for the championship of the city. The winner will be rewarded a gold watch.

As the gentlemen shoemakers cheered and stomped their feet at the fights, the ladies were treated to a more delicate night out on the town. "While the men are being entertained," the *Peoria Journal-Transcript* reported, "the wives and daughters will go to the Apollo Theater and afterwards to the Sugar Bowl for refreshments."

The city was buzzing and the conventioneers were enjoying their stay. It was the first big event in the Peoria area since the *Columbia* disaster and it went off without a hitch. But noticeably absent from the list of entertainment activities scheduled that week was one attraction that was always a staple for convention-goers in town and a popular selling point for the city of Peoria: there would be no steamboat excursion rides on the Illinois River.

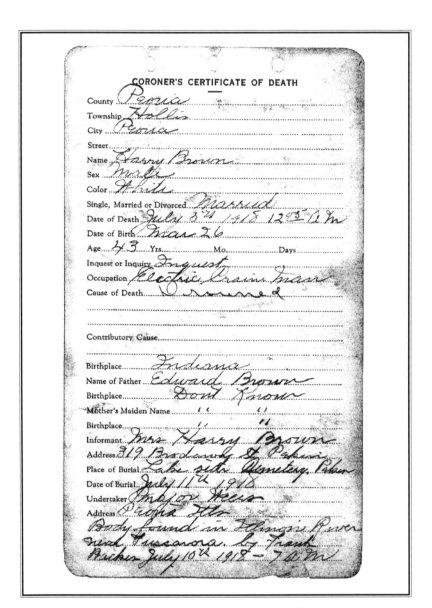

CORONER'S CERTIFICATE OF DEATH

County *Peoria*

Township *Hollis*

City *Peoria*

Street ....

Name *Harry Brown*

Sex *Male*

Color *White*

Single, Married or Divorced *Married*

Date of Death *July 3rd 1918 12:35 A.M.*

Date of Birth *Mar 26*

Age *43* Yrs. .... Mo. .... Days ....

Inquest or Inquiry *Inquest*

Occupation *Electric Crane Man*

Cause of Death *Drowned*

Contributory Cause ....

Birthplace *Indiana*

Name of Father *Edward Brown*

Birthplace *Dont Know*

Mother's Maiden Name *" "*

Birthplace *" "*

Informant *Mrs Harry Brown*

Address *319 Broadway St Pekin*

Place of Burial *Lake side Cemetery, Pekin*

Date of Burial *July 11th 1918*

Undertaker *Major Weis*

Address *Peoria Ill*

Body found in Illinois River near Tuscarora by Frank Becker July 10th 1918 - 7 A.M.

DEATH CERTIFICATE FOR HARRY BROWN
PEORIA COUNTY OFFICE OF CORONER

41

PEGGED AHEAD

AT THE END OF JULY, nearly a month after the *Columbia* sank in the Illinois River, and the inquests were still incomplete. Clary had hoped the raising of the hull would only take a couple of weeks at the most. Now he was forced to inform the six jurors that the delay might stretch into months.

July turned into August and August into September while the hull still sat in the water. Armistice Day came at hour eleven on November 11, but the *Columbia* was unmoved. Then Christmas arrived with a glimmer of hope—the government had sold the wreckage to a local junkman named Ruben Bruce for $900, considerably less than the $2,000 the boat was estimated to be worth. The government had one stipulation upon sale of the wreckage: The hull needed to be raised within 30 days of receipt. The scrapper agreed, signed the contract and paid in cash. Ruben Bruce was the new—and final—owner of the steamboat *Columbia*.

Bruce went right to work. He had a plan. He thought that by removing the six tons of coal from the front of the boat and reducing the weight in the bow, the hull would simply float to the surface. "But she didn't," Bruce later testified. He left the hull alone for the time being and concentrated on the upper part of the boat. He removed most of the machinery and some of the superstructure until only the hull and the first deck floor remained in the water. "I have had several inquiries from prospective purchasers who probably expect to use it in construction of a new boat," he said. But the question of raising the hull was still a sticking point. Bruce was ready to give it another try. Then he met with Captain Mehl.

"What?" Coroner Elliott must have shouted in surprise.

Bruce went on to tell the coroner and the Peoria County jury that Mehl had visited him at the wreck site just weeks after he bought the boat. "We had a difference [in opinion] on how to raise the hull," Bruce said, "and the idea was abandoned."

After a nearly five-month delay, Elliott had had enough. In an unexpected move, he hastily called back the Peoria County jury to the courtroom. The case against the pilot and captain of the *Columbia* was to be settled with or without the raising of the hull, he ordered. He called Bruce to the stand. The junkman testified that Mehl's unexpected visit to the wreck site wasn't the only reason the hull was still in the water. Bruce said that it was impossible at the present time to lift the hull because he was unable to secure necessary equipment to do it. "I need two barges," he said, "one on each side, and heavy cables under the hull to lift her." He also stated that he could not drag the hull to shore because of the steep banks along the river.

"When the proper equipment is secured," Elliott asked, "how long do you think it will take to raise the hull?"

"Might be a year," Bruce answered.

The jury, the papers noted, decided at that point to close the investigation and return a verdict on evidence that had already been submitted. On New Year's Day, 1919, nearly a full five months after the *Columbia* sank and 87 people perished, the federal government was exhorted to do a better job of inspecting excursion and passenger boats. And Captain Herman F. Mehl and pilot George 'Tom' Williams were charged with manslaughter.

After the verdict was announced, Peoria County Sherriff Lewis

M. Hines was "present with warrants," the papers reported. It was an order from the Peoria County State's Attorney's office. Hines told the *Peoria Evening Star* that he thought both men would come in the next day upon being notified by him and that "they would not await personal service." That was a kind way of giving both men a chance to turn themselves in rather than have county officers go and get them.

"Both Mehl and Williams were out of the city," the *Peoria Evening Star* went on to report. "Mehl was in Chillicothe where he is engaged in the operation of the fish market. Williams is either in Meredosia [his hometown] or Beardstown."

Mehl appeared as ordered the following day, posted a sheriff's bond and was released. Although there is no record of what transpired upon his arrest, it's safe to assume that the captain was briefly detained, signed the proper paperwork, paid the bail amount and walked back out the door. This was Peoria, after all, where police likely had more than a passing acquaintance with business leaders in town. Mehl probably personally knew many of the men who were booking him. Perhaps they shared a laugh or two before the captain was freed to go about his business selling fish and cigars. They gave him only one order: stay close to town and wait for instructions following the Tazewell County verdict, since it was probable that any trial would be held on that side of the river.

Mehl had misgivings about going to Pekin. At one point, a newspaper reporter wrote that Mehl, fearing for his life, asked to be jailed instead of making an appearance there. Considering the furor that erupted in Pekin just days after the wreck, if Mehl felt threatened, he had cause. Whether he actually made the statement about being incarcerated is unknown. But for the first time since his boat went down, the captain of the *Columbia* was about to find out what was in store for him in Tazewell County.

Upon hearing the verdict in Peoria County, Clary immediately called his jury to meet at the courthouse in Pekin. Inspired by his counterpart's decisive action, and realizing it could take another year before the hull was raised, Clary was determined to wrap up his side of the case. He told reporters that a verdict would be rendered within the week.

In the meantime, the coroners, local authorities and the sheriffs of Peoria and Tazewell counties received some disturbing news. George 'Tom' Williams was very ill and could not travel. Yet he also could not evade arrest, if warranted. The authorities knew where he was and how to reach him. Williams would remain at home in Meredosia until he was physically able to appear.

As Clary prepared the jury to conclude hearings and announce a verdict, he had a few final requests. Just like Elliott, he wanted to question the junkman who had bought the wreckage from the government. The matter of that chance meeting with Mehl at the wreck site was "curious." Clary also asked to speak to another man, a diver, who assisted in the removal of salvage. Clary was told that the man had made some remarks about the hull's condition. Since Clary and the jurors would never get the chance to view the hull themselves, the diver would have to be their eyes. He was the last person to view the hull up close. Both men were called to testify.

Clary had also recently learned a few other details from the wreck site. When the engine of the boat was brought to the surface the throttle was said to be in the neutral position and not 'pegged ahead' as expected. The finding seemed to contradict statements by Mehl that he ordered "full steam ahead" after the boat struck the willows. Clary must have thought this new information sent mixed signals, if anything. If the captain never shouted "full ahead," and the pilot never acted out the 'ghost' order, wouldn't that benefit both of their cases? The consensus was that if the boat had stayed near the Peoria shore and had not steamed back into deeper water, many lives would have been saved. Unfortunately, it was too late to ask any more questions. Williams was incapacitated, and Mehl refused to testify. Clary let it go. "This fact," the *Peoria Journal-Transcript* reported, "never was touched upon in the testimony."

On Sunday, January 5, 1919, Clary called together the Tazewell County coroner's jury and refreshed them on recent facts brought to his attention. He also called two witnesses.

Clary asked Ruben Bruce why he had not raised the steamer's hull and permitted the coroner's jury to inspect it. Unlike his answer to coroner Elliott–that it "might be a year" before the hull would be raised–Bruce indicated to Clary that the hull might not be raised at all, according to the *Pekin Daily Times.*

"Practically all the salvage, save the hull, has been raised," he told the jury.

Next Clary called a diver named John Hancock, who helped Bruce with the removal of wreckage and was the last man to see the hull up close. "What is your opinion of the hull's condition?" Clary asked.

Hancock did not mince words. "The timbers were rotten and unsafe," he said. "I wouldn't want them in any boat of mine."

Clary was through. He thanked the witnesses for their time and for reasons unclear told the jury to return in three days. At that time, Clary told reporters, he expected a verdict that would "somewhat" follow that which had been returned by the Peoria County jury.

The news of the forthcoming verdict, Clary must have thought, would finally appease the residents of Pekin who had been waiting patiently for justice to be done. But things worked out somewhat differently from Clary's plan. The next day, Monday, January 6, in large bold headlines across the front page of virtually every newspaper in the country were these three words: THEODORE ROOSEVELT DEAD! The beloved, jovial 26th president of the United States and the country's most ardent supporter of river travel, navigation and safety–especially on the greater inland waters–was gone at the age of 60.

Roosevelt's death shocked the nation. Even though he had been out of the White House for nearly a decade, and mostly out of politics, the former president's exploits never left the papers, including his unabashedly biased opinion on the question of war. To no one's surprise, Roosevelt was a strong proponent of U.S. involvement overseas. Roosevelt saw the issue as a question of honor and blamed Wilson for the 'Chinification' of America, referring to China's policy of regarding peace as an alternative to war in any circumstance. Even in 1918, the last full year of his life as it turned out, the former president's words had an influence on the nation.

In that year's 'off year' elections, the Republicans took back control of Congress and Roosevelt's attacks on Wilson were widely considered the reason why.

With renewed vigor and freedom, the naturalist with the toothy grin was still full of life, spending the previous years exploring wild and dangerous locales collecting hundreds of specimens and trophies and bringing them back to museums. But Roosevelt's adventurous spirit was finally taking its toll. With politics finally behind him, in 1914, Roosevelt went to Brazil to explore the mysterious River of Doubt. Roosevelt's family, especially his wife Edith, begged him not to go. Roosevelt would hear none of it. His son Kermit went along in part to keep an eye on him. The mission was rewarding, but Roosevelt came back weary and damaged. He contracted jungle fever, almost lost his leg to injury, suffered a tooth infection and dropped nearly 60 pounds. He was 56.

Five years later, on Sunday, January 5, 1919, at his hillside home in scenic Oyster Bay, New York, Roosevelt was busy writing letters and going through papers. He was feeling well despite a nagging case of rheumatism in his right wrist. He went to bed that night after receiving a sedative, likely morphine, from the family doctor, and everything seemed normal. The night air was still, and the large house up on the sleepy hillside seemed empty. Most of the family was out of town—only his wife, Edith, was there. At Edith's request, a black servant named James Amos stayed by her husband's side. Roosevelt fell quietly asleep, and Edith retired to another room. Several hours later she was awakened by a nurse. Amos had noticed the colonel's breathing had become heavy and rough. Edith ran down the hall calling "Theodore, Theodore, darling," but by the time she reached the room, Roosevelt had stopped breathing. A blood clot had found its way to the former president's lung.

THEODORE ROOSEVELT DEAD! the front-page headlines screamed the next day. The nation was in mourning.

In the back of that day's *Pekin Daily Times* there was a somewhat smaller headline: CORONER JURY TO RENDER VERDICT ON *COLUMBIA* NEXT THURSDAY.

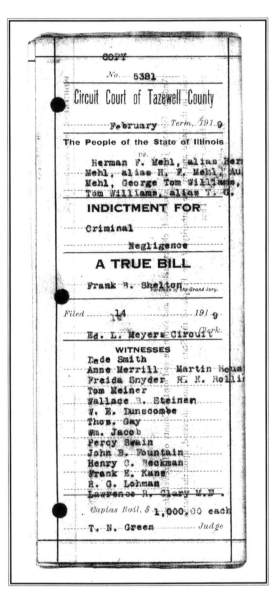

No. 5381

Circuit Court of Tazewell County

February Term, 191 9

The People of the State of Illinois

vs.

Herman F. Mehl, alias Her
Mehl, alias H. F. Mehl, Au
Mehl, George Tom Williams,
Tom Williams, alias T. W.

INDICTMENT FOR

Criminal

Negligence

A TRUE BILL

Frank B. Shelton
Foreman of the Grand Jury.

Filed 14 191 9

Ed. L. Meyers Circuit *Clerk.*

WITNESSES

Dade Smith
Anne Merrill Martin Hous
Freida Snyder R. E. Rolli
Tom Meiner
Wallace R. Steiner
W. E. Dunscombe
Thos. Gay
Wm. Jacob
Percy Swain
John B. Fountain
Henry C. Beckman
Frank E. Kang
R. G. Lohman
Lawrence R. Clary M.D.

Capias Bail, $ 1,000.00 each

T. N. Green Judge

TAZEWELL COUNTY GRAND JURY
TRUE BILL INDICTMENT OF CAPTAIN AND PILOT
U.S. NATIONAL ARCHIVES AND RECORDS ADMINISTRATION
WASHINGTON, D.C.

42

LEGAL BATTLE

THE TRAINS ARRIVED LATE due to a heavy snow storm, the *New York Times* noted, "but soon friends and opponents gathered to pay their last respects to Col. Roosevelt." On a steep hillside overlooking Long Island Sound the former president was laid to rest in a spot he had picked out for himself. The pallbearers with Roosevelt's casket on their shoulders slipped and slid on the muddy snow. "Former President Taft was deeply moved and wept as the casket sank slowly into the final resting place," read the papers.

It was easy to see why Roosevelt picked this land to be his final resting place. "Many birds dwell in the trees and round the house or in the pastures and the woods nearby," he wrote in his autobiography about the beloved family home and property on Sagamore Hill. "We love all the seasons...the spray of spring; the yellow grain, the ripening fruits and tasseled corn...the deep, leafy shades that are heralded by the green dance of summer...the winter gulls, loons and wildfowl that frequent the waters of the bay and Sound... and the sharp fall winds that tear the brilliant banners with which the trees greet the dying year."

For a man who was so full of energy and pomp while alive, Roosevelt's funeral was rather subdued and plain in its ceremony. "There was an absolute lack of any military touch," the *Times* noted, "nothing to indicate that an ex-president and former commander of the armies and navies of the United States had been buried here." Roosevelt was a man who appreciated the country's natural resources, especially the forests and rivers, and did everything in his power to preserve and protect them. His final bow was an indication that a man was no bigger than the land that consumes him. "It was like a funeral of a country gentleman well beloved of his neighbors," the paper read. The neighbors—the nation—bowed their heads for a day and paid their last respects.

It seemed only fitting that on Thursday, January 9, 1919, a day after the former president was buried, and exactly four months and 22 days after the *Columbia* sank in the middle of the Illinois River, the six-man jury of the Tazewell County coroner's inquest met for the eighth and final time to render a verdict. The decision took no one by surprise.

"From evidence as offered," it read, "we find Captain Herman Mehl; George Williams, pilot; and August Mehl, purser of the steamer *Columbia* guilty of criminal negligence [and manslaughter] in not asserting damage done to hull of boat after it struck an obstruction along Peoria shore west of the river channel before allowing boat to proceed."

The ruling was similar to that rendered in Peoria County with one difference, the addition of August Mehl, the purser of the *Columbia*. "It is understood," the *Pekin Daily Times* reported, "that evidence tended to show that August Mehl told some of the passengers of the boat not to go up the stairs after the boat had struck and there was danger." August Mehl's name never appeared in the Peoria County verdict.

The Tazewell County jury recommended that all three men be held for manslaughter charges until discharged by the due process of law. The jury also went a step further than Peoria County by recommending the United States government also prefer charges against the "inspector or inspectors" for failing to properly inspect the hull that, according to the jurors, "showed signs of decay and defect which made the boat unseaworthy."

The Peoria County jury had only recommended that the government make changes in policy and the inspectors themselves were never mentioned by name or charged. There was also no public record of the two inspectors, Bower and Downs, testifying in the Tazewell County court as they had under oath in Peoria County. But in the end, the amount of testimony in the Tazewell County case was too damaging. Juror Ed Nickel would tell reporters that the jury determined that "evidence at the inquest showed that the inspection [of last May] was lax and done in such a manner that would not reveal the defects afterward."

The charges against the federal inspectors, of course, were mostly pointless—more a gesture than anything else. The bigwigs in Washington could be expected to ignore them. At the very least, Clary must have thought, the awareness of such action, whether it was ruled "lax" or not, was satisfying enough. The jury had done its job.

Although they signed the verdict for each of the 86 victims assigned to the county, the final ruling was represented in the name of just one person, William Gordon Gay, a 33-year-old unmarried pipe fitter from Pekin. Why Gay was chosen to represent the case over any of the other victims is not known.

> *We the jury sworn to inquire into the death of William Gordon Gay find that he came to his death about midnight, July 6, 1918, as a result of the steamer Columbia upon which he was a passenger, sinking in the Illinois River about one-quarter mile or more, below the river bend south of Wesley City, Tazewell County Illinois, said body being recovered from the Tazewell side of mid-stream.*

As soon as both jury rulings were on paper, the question of jurisdiction had to be settled. Earlier, an informal agreement had been reached that Tazewell County would likely handle the lion's share of any trial's time and expense. It just made sense. All but one victim in the disaster was assigned to Tazewell County, and the county's State's Attorney, E.E. Black, had attended every hearing, heard every witness, and seemed eager to proceed. Also, due to the large number of cases, the testimony taken in Pekin was considerably more complex than what was heard in Peoria.

There was also the matter of who wanted it more, or in this case, who wanted it less. On Monday, when the Peoria County verdict was announced, State's Attorney C.E. McNemar, who had kept a low profile during the proceedings, made it clear that he was ready to export the matter across river to Tazewell County and be done with it. He respectfully stood by the law and accepted the jurors' decision, but in a brazen act of defiance, he criticized the process and mocked the results. "This case is not in shape to present," he said. "There is not sufficient evidence of a crime to warrant action yet."

McNemar also seemed wary of spending the nearly $20,000 he estimated it would cost the county to put on such a high-profile trial. That prompted the *Pekin Daliy Times* to remark that perhaps "the attorney was thinking more of the possible expenses in the case than he was the evidence."

Earlier that week, when Mehl appeared in Peoria County, and before he posted bond, McNemar tried to convince the circuit court judge to dismiss the case altogether, claiming jurisdiction would likely by handled in Tazewell County. The appearance of the captain in the Peoria court, he must have thought, was just for show. The judge disagreed and told McNemar to be patient and wait until the Pekin jury returned a verdict. Soon thereafter, it was announced that the venue in the case, if any exists, would be in the Tazewell County courts and *not* in Peoria. The matter was settled.

Even though he was committed to justice and had made that point clear from the very beginning, Tazewell County State's Attorney Black had reservations of his own. The trial would be costly, as his counterpart from across the river surmised, and the county would have to assume the burden for expenses. Still, Black thundered, "The parties charged with responsibility for the catastrophe will be made to answer for the negligence that cost 87 lives."

Black assembled a legal team and prepared for battle. He had hoped the large amount of testimony in the coroner's hearings would be sufficient for a grand jury to return an indictment. Even the newspapermen remarked on the volume of testimony to be presented to the grand jury, using, of all things, the court reporter's handiwork—piles of transcribed notes—as an example.

Black also knew that criminal charges against a ship's captain and pilot, just as had been the case with the *Eastland* disaster, were extremely difficult to prosecute. Still he was determined. "There need be no fear that the matter will not be prosecuted to the end," the *Pekin Daily Times* confidently reported. "For the Tazewell County's board of supervisors have employed able counsel to assist in the matter and volumes of testimony have already been gathered. The case will be presented to the grand jury in this county, regardless of what is being done by our neighbors up the river."

The January term of the circuit court was already under way with its usual full docket of petty theft, forgeries, land disputes and divorce cases. The case of the *Columbia* would have to wait a month or longer. The criminal case against the pilot and captain was delayed from the outset.

Not much had changed.

ON FEBRUARY 14, 1919, a full month and five days after the Tazewell County coroner's jury verdict, the grand jury of the Tazewell County circuit court issued a True Bill of Indictment for criminal negligence and manslaughter charges against Herman Mehl, August Mehl and George 'Tom' Williams.

A lengthy indictment report was written and signed by State's Attorney Edward E. Black. It contained some of the harshest language yet about the three men, who now faced serious charges that could force them to endure lengthy prison terms if convicted. The indictment blamed the men for "gross carelessness and neglect" and accused them of "unlawfully, feloniously and with culpable negligence" causing the wreck of the *Columbia* and contributing to the great loss of life. The legalese is almost a self-parody, as this sample shows:

*Herman Mehl, alias Herman Mehl, alias H.F. Mehl
was then and there what is commonly called Captain
of certain steamboat, commonly called 'Columbia'
and one August Mehl was then and there commonly
called purser of said steamboat 'Columbia' and one
George 'Tom' Williams alias Thomas Williams, alias
Tom Williams, alias T.G. Williams was then and there
and for a long time prior thereto, as such captain, purser and pilot respectively had personal management
and control of said steamboat 'Columbia' and said
steamboat 'Columbia' was then and there and for a
long time prior thereto used as a public conveyance
for the common carriage of passengers while upon the
waters of the Illinois River and while said steamboat
was damaged and while a great amount of water from
said Illinois River was coming into hull of said steamboat and while said steamboat had on board a large
number of passengers to-wit, 500...manage and control said steamboat with gross carelessness and neglect
where by the safety said was endangered by then and
there unlawfully, feloniously and with culpable negligence, failing, neglecting and refusing to cause said
steamboat to be guided, propelled and driven to and
against the Peoria County shore of said Illinois River
and failing and neglecting then and there to cause
passengers to remove themselves from on board of said
steamboat 'Columbia' to the Peoria County shore of
said river which said steamboat was then and there in
shallow water of depth of to-wit, three feet and which
said steamboat was then and there, to wit, 20 feet
from the Peoria County shore...failing, neglecting and
refusing to then and there manage, control said steamboat which were of the depth of to-wit, 20 feet while
said steamboat was then and there in damaged condition and about to sink in the water of the Illinois River
aforesaid and the passengers then on said steamboat*

were then and there forced, hurled, threw and sub-
merged into and upon the waters and the safety of said
passengers were endangered...

With the 'true bill' now signed, the case was ready for trial. Typically, when the county circuit court was in session over the last
three weeks of each month, the final or third week was reserved
for the more complex and serious criminal cases, such as the one
involving the *Columbia* tragedy. The first two weeks were usually
loaded down with civil matters like bankruptcies and marital splits.

During the civil portion of the circuit court's term, one day was
always set aside as 'Divorce Day,' when only spousal cases were
heard. That day, for some reason, was usually a Friday. 'Divorce
Day' received special attention from the press, mostly because of
its sensational, newspaper-selling material: "It was a sad series of
stories to which the court listened and made the casual listener
wonder if marriage after all is not a failure in a larger proportion
of cases," a correspondent wrote.

Getting a divorce was no walk in the park. The divorce rate in
the early 1900s was still low, about eight percent, but ending a
legal marriage was widely looked upon as a sign of weakness for
a woman. A divorced woman was stigmatized, mostly by other
women. "I have gone down the aisle of the church when women I
have known from childhood drew back in their pews and refused
to speak to me," wrote one socialite in 1895, who claimed she was
the "first woman in America to dare to get a divorce from an influential man."

But changes were underway that would continue throughout the
20th century. The shifting social attitudes that occurred during the
war and greater responsibilities for women outside of the home
began to unlock the chains. Some woman no longer thought of
marriage as an 'ultimate destiny' or an economic necessity. Others
chose careers over marriage. And some decided to live in homes
shared with other women. Yet, despite its trials, getting married
and having children was still the goal for most women at the time.

Men too, the ones who wanted to change, were reshaping their attitudes about traditional marriage, realizing that the path to a happy relationship was to consider the wife as an equal rather than a subordinate. And women became more comfortable with the idea of a lifelong commitment once they were independently choosing when and who they were marrying rather than what society demanded. Marriages were lasting mostly because of shared responsibilities and joys. But even if the marriage was unstable, the process of getting a divorce was demanding, legally tricky, and often not worth the trouble or the potential ridicule that accompanied it.

In 1918, if a divorce case got as far as the circuit court, it was usually granted, but not without the embarrassment of the matter being put on public display and printed in black and white the following day:

> Ethel P. Hines of East Peoria carried coal she had borrowed
> from the neighbors while her [husband] Harold toasted his
> shins in front of the fire; and she did not complain about
> that. But when he playfully blackened her eyes and broke
> her jaw she thought that was carrying a joke too far.

In the middle of February, shortly after the grand jury returned an indictment against the three men in the *Columbia* case, the papers reported that quite a number of marital cases were pending. Apparently, there had been several slow months with only a few divorces on the docket. "February cases," the papers sarcastically reported, "could bring the average back up."

It was apparent the February term of the circuit court was too crowded. "It is not likely," the *Peoria Evening Star* reported, "that any of the [*Columbia*] cases will be tried at this term of court."

The *Columbia* case would not be brought up again until May. The reason for the three-month delay was the absence of Mehl's lawyer, Joseph Weil, who was busy in Springfield arguing the appeal of Edgar Strause, the man convicted of murder just a year before and whose trial in Peoria was the reason Illinois Assistant Attorney General Mansfield was already in the city when he received the call from Governor Lowden to investigate the *Columbia* wreck.

Captain Mehl, his brother August and pilot Williams remained free men, if pariahs. The papers listed bond at $5,000 apiece for each manslaughter charge and $1,000 each for the charge of criminal carelessness. Captain Mehl's bond posted in Peoria at the beginning of January was said to be sufficient. August Mehl, who was only charged in Tazewell County, appeared in Pekin, paid his share and was released. Williams, still too sick to travel, was given a special dispensation.

On Sunday, May 4, 1919, before that month's circuit court hearings were scheduled to begin, the papers reported that in the case of the *Columbia,* "it was considered unlikely that charges would be brought up during this term." Although no concrete reason was given why, it was believed Mehl's lawyer was still tied up in Springfield. "When the cases are brought up in trial," the *Peoria Journal-Transcript* reported, "it is certain that the attorney for the indicted men will put up a strong legal battle to prevent the conviction of their clients."

The month of May went by, and so did June. Then July passed without a trial. In the first week of July there was no mention of the *Columbia* on the one-year anniversary of the wreck in the newspapers, not even in the hometown *Pekin Daily Times.* There were no plans for a memorial service—no event or commemoration was scheduled to honor the victims. Apparently the city of Pekin—along with the rest of the nation—was too busy celebrating the end of World War I.

If the previous Fourth of July holiday was noted for its honor, patriotism and unity among allied nations, July 4, 1919 was filled with flag waving, cheers and smiles as the boys from overseas were finally returning home. In Tazewell County, a circuit court judge canceled several days' proceedings that month so jurors could join the joyous celebrations in the streets as local troops marched back into town.

This was no time to bring up the ghosts of the past, even the very recent past.

Whatever the reason for the absence of any official notice of the one-year anniversary of the *Columbia* disaster and its victims, for the three men accused of contributing to their deaths, the town's apathy was almost a Godsend. Time was on their side too. The longer the delay, the more interest in the case waned.

Even the immense grief that a year earlier had consumed nearly the entire community had been supplanted by a greater urgency, a more widespread tragedy. The town's anguish over the *Columbia* disaster lasted only a few short months. In the late summer and early fall of 1918 the Spanish Flu came to town.

INFLUENZA

Spread by Droplets sprayed from Nose and Throat

Cover each COUGH and SNEEZE with handkerchief.

Spread by contact.

AVOID CROWDS.

If possible, WALK TO WORK.

Do not spit on floor or sidewalk.

Do not use common drinking cups and common towels.

Avoid excessive fatigue.

If taken ill, go to bed and send for a doctor.

The above applies also to colds, bronchitis, pneumonia, and tuberculosis.

NATIONAL SPANISH FLU POSTER, 1918

43

BEYOND CONTROL

THE FIRST STRAIN of the flu-like virus actually appeared in the spring of 1918. It was a mild strain and quickly went away. "At first it seemed like nothing to worry about," writes John Barry in the book *The Great Influenza*. But a mutated strain came back with a vengeance several months later. By October of 1918, nearly every town in America was dealing with the Spanish Flu. Pekin was no exception.

"Pekin today is holding a tight rein on the ravages of influenza through the community," the *Pekin Daily Times* reported on October 19, 1918. "The public hospital is filled. The emergency hospital, manned by volunteers, is caring for as many as possible." Many volunteers were likely those who got sick when the first wave of the virus hit, then recovered and were immune to the second strain.

The arrival of the second wave was greeted with panic. Newspapers admonished the public to keep children off the streets, not to burn leaves, not to spit on the sidewalks, and on and on. Schools and businesses closed for a week.

"She sneezed and I felt the spray over my face and hands," said one woman, describing how she picked up the lethal virus. For some victims of the virus, death came quickly, almost overnight, and in some cases in just a few hours.

"You might notice a dull headache," writes Gina Kolata in the book *Flu: The Story of the Great Influenza Pandemic of 1918.* "Your eyes might start to burn. You start to shiver and you will take to your bed, curling up in a ball. But no amount of blankets can keep you warm. You fall into a restless sleep, dreaming distorted nightmares of delirium as your fever climbs. And when you drift out of sleep, into a sort of semi-consciousness, your muscles will ache and your head will throb and you will somehow know that, step-by-step, as your body feebly cries out 'no,' you are moving steadily towards death."

The pandemic baffled scientists at the time. "The path curves were w-shaped," writes Kolata, "with peaks for babies and toddlers under age five, the elderly who were aged 70 to 74 and people aged 20 to 40."

Even today it's difficult to prove where the germ originated. By virtue of its name most people think it came from Spain. The flu had certainly come to Spain. In fact some believe a sunlit northern coastal town called San Sebastian was one of the first in the country to contract the disease. The touristy town was hit hard, most of its residents became sick, and the busy vacation season was threatened. Town officials panicked. They thought about keeping it hushed up, but the word started to spread as quickly as the disease. San Sebastian was not the place to be.

Spain was neutral during the war, so there were no restrictions on the press as there were in France, Germany and Great Britain, all of which kept a tight rein on their writers and closely monitored what news was filtering out. In an effort to protect troop morale, the other European papers ignored coverage of the killer bug. Since the Spanish press was filled with unfettered reports of the outbreak, the name 'Spanish Flu' may have resulted from other countries picking up on their coverage. Much to Spain's chagrin, however, the moniker stuck.

The most recent theory on where the germ originated centers on the prairie state of Kansas, of all places. As the story goes, a "severe influenza" was said to be raging through Haskell County, Kansas when three unidentified men left the ravaged town and arrived at Camp Funston, an encampment just outside of present-day Fort Riley. Around the beginning of March, army doctors began receiving the first cases of soldiers with influenza-like symptoms. Within three weeks, hundreds were sick. As troops moved about, the flu spread quickly to bases in the U.S. and overseas. This was the first strain, the mild one. Troops were debilitated, but most recovered. By the beginning of August, the disease appeared to be gone. The flu had not become as widespread in the U.S. as it had other countries. "But the virus did not disappear," writes Barry. "It had only gone underground, like a forest fire left burning in its roots, swarming and mutating, adapting, honing itself, watching and waiting, waiting to burst into flames." When the flu returned, it was far more lethal. By the end of October thousands of American citizens and millions of people worldwide were overcome.

In Pekin, the hospitals were overrun and understaffed; saloons and pool rooms were ordered shut. Public gatherings of any kind, both indoor and outdoor, were banned. Once again the town was under a sort of martial law. The Home Guards worked in squads, on six-hour tours of duty, to enforce the laws.

The police force was decimated. "Three police constitute the night force," the *Pekin Daily Times* reported, "and one, Billy Kumpf, is the entire day force." William 'Billy' Kumpf was the father of Joe Kumpf, the 'Hero of the *Columbia*,' who witnesses said died trying to save others. The elder Kumpf was also on the *Columbia* that night. Now in October of 1918, as a member of the Pekin police department, or what was left of it, he was trying to save lives, just like his son had done on the *Columbia* several months before. Even Kumpf's boss was laid out by the bug. "[Police] Chief Harm Smith," the papers reported with some assurance, "is slightly improved today."

On October 22, there were 1,000 cases of the flu reported in Pekin. The papers tried to run a death tally like they had for the *Columbia*: "Total deaths up to midnight, October 20: 56 with eight more reported Monday, October 21." It seemed to get worse each day. On October 25 it was reported that Pekin had seen 18 deaths in one day and 20 more on another. In many instances, doctors were too busy treating the sick to count the dead. "The victims were buried quickly," the papers reported, "in an attempt to retard the spread of the contagion."

Even in the face of such death and sadness, there was a war of words between the two neighboring cities across the river and their respective newspapers. When the Peoria paper first reported that the situation in Pekin was "almost beyond control" the *Pekin Daily Times* fired back: "Such is not the case. The local situation is kept well in hand." But it was difficult to see any silver lining in the outcomes.

Like he had done after the *Columbia* disaster, Coroner Clary helped coordinate many of the local efforts. This time, in addition to his duties as coroner, Clary kept a close watch on the public bans and precautions. He also worked directly with the State Board of Health to get an anti-influenza serum to Pekin from the Mayo Brothers Clinic in Rochester, Minnesota. "When the serum arrives," the *Pekin Daily Times* reported, "it will be administered at once by physicians to persons exposed and in the earlier stages of the malady."

Whether a citywide inoculation statistically helped is unclear in all aspects regarding the disease, not just in Pekin, but nationwide. The death tolls were so staggering that vaccination experiments were mostly dismissed as test-tube fodder for scientists and in the end only proved the original theory that contracting the virus was avoidable only by strict prevention. Still at the time, Clary, like other doctors faced with such insurmountable odds, must have felt they had no other choice.

By the time the virus slowed in November, hundreds had been stricken and many had died. In Pekin, the exact number of deaths is hard to determine. Nationally and internationally the numbers are staggering. More Americans were killed in a single year, it was later reported, than died in battle in World War I, World War II, the Korean War and the Vietnam War combined. Globally, the number was in the millions. In 2002, studies conducted using better methods to record data and statistics estimated a mind-numbing 50 million Spanish Flu deaths worldwide during the 1918-20 pandemic—and debate about the figure is only that it may be too low. Some researchers believe as much as five percent of the world's human population perished in those two years.

For Clary it was another deadly crisis in a busy year. At the time the virus struck, he was in the middle of hearing witness testimony in the *Columbia* case. Fortunately in October, when the flu was at its deadliest, the jury was in recess, waiting for the hull to be raised before rendering a verdict. Clary had time to concentrate on the latest calamity.

Now a community that had just months earlier mourned the loss of dozens of its citizens in a tragic and possibly preventable boat accident was devastated again by sudden loss of life, this time to an unstoppable force of nature. Clary's job was simple this go-around. There was no one to blame and no investigation to conduct.

Still, he had hoped the latest heartbreak would not lesson the bitter feelings initially expressed over the *Columbia* disaster. He and local officials like State's Attorney Black needed the support of the community to continue the case against the men accused of contributing to the death of 87 lives on the Illinois River. It would prove to be a difficult task. "The flu roused people from the summer shock," explained one writer.

"It gave them something else to worry about," said Agnes Smith, who at the time of the outbreak would have certainly been busy working at the town's drug store.

DAVID SWAIN
S&D REFLECTOR

44

LOCK AND DAMS

BY OCTOBER OF 1918, as the Spanish Flu was raging, all was quiet on the river. The steamboat excursion season was over. Most of the Swain steamboats that lined Peoria's shore were gone to dry dock for the winter.

If there was one name that was synonymous with riverboats in Peoria, it was David Swain. Born in Garden Prairie, Illinois, in 1841, Swain became interested in machinery and steamboats after moving to Stillwater, Minnesota while in his mid-20s. In Stillwater he opened a foundry and started building boats. In the late 1800s, he sent his first boat to Peoria, the *Borealis Rex*. For decades after that, Swain would dominate the Illinois River, building and operating elaborate steamboats named after his children and grandchildren. The *Percy Swain, Verne Swain, Fred Swain* and *Julia Belle Swain* all did good business in the Peoria area. But after the *Columbia* wreck, things changed.

David's son, Captain Percy Swain, who ran the family business at the time of the *Columbia* disaster, remained optimistic. "Although business may be smaller," he announced on July 10, just five days after the accident, "we do not expect an actual cessation." It was wishful thinking. Despite the Swains' best efforts, the boats were noticeably less crowded than before, and many never even left the dock. "That is the way they have excursions now," one Pekin man wrote to his son in the service. "Tied up at the landing, they have dancing."

On July 19, an advertisement for a steamboat excursion on the *Julia Belle Swain* appeared in the *Chillicothe Bulletin:*

> A real excursion steamer...side wheeler...safest type. Built like a ship...No remolded freighter...Handled by officers with ability and years of experience.

Another steamboat ad extolled the "water-tight compartments" and "non-sinkable superior service." Still another ad proclaimed its boat was "a real excursion steamer" and one that was "not rebuilt or made over." A steamboat ride was "as safe as your Davenport," another advertisement boasted.

It was a last-ditch effort to save an industry that had taken a hard hit on the night of July 5, 1918. But it was too late. The next month, on August 12, it was announced that the beloved *Julia Belle Swain* was leaving Peoria. The Swain family had leased it to the Eagle Packet Company to carry freight on the Mississippi from Alton to St. Louis. Another boat in Peoria, the *East St. Louis,* also left the river at the end of the excursion season to carry freight to New Orleans. The passenger trade was dead, it was reported.

William H. Martin of the Eagle Packet Company said in August 1918, "The people seem to have curtailed their holiday trips especially as far as the river is concerned." One writer's wry reaction was, "That may qualify as the understatement for the year."

Was the *Columbia* wreck the only reason the steamboat business on the Illinois River ended so abruptly? It certainly seems to be. At the time of the accident, the men who ran the boats in Peoria were making good money. For Mehl, business had been so good that he had planned to sell the *Columbia* the following year and get a larger boat to accommodate the overflow crowds. Oftentimes, smaller one-deck, narrow flat-bed boats called 'dance barges' were towed by the main boats to make room for more passengers—and bigger purses. Before the *Columbia* wreck, there was never any mention of the larger boats moving on. In fact, there was talk of expanding the Peoria dock to make room for more boats. According to the papers, construction was already underway.

Of course, times were changing. As roads improved, especially after the war, and more and more automobiles were manufactured and sold, many people enjoyed the convenience of simply driving to attractions. The river was also becoming more crowded. Massive barges carrying tons of freight clogged the already narrow passages of the river, and the river itself was always considered dangerous, full of hidden sand bars and tree stumps. The unpredictable weather was always a hazard. But all of these factors would have had a gradual effect—and the excursion business on the Illinois ended abruptly. It's hard to argue that anything other than the *Columbia* wreck brought about the sudden end of the steamboat era on the Illinois River.

Post-catastrophe articles written about the men and women who had their hand in the steamboat excursion trade in Peoria, including David Swain, Garland and Josie Sivley (who was the first woman pilot on the Illinois River) and even earlier pioneers like Captain Sol York, consider the connection obvious: the *Columbia* wreck is the reason steamboats in the Peoria area were never the same.

Ironically, on July 3, 1918, just days before the *Columbia* sank, the founding father of the steamboat business in Peoria, David Swain, passed away in a Pittsburgh hospital. "Only a month ago he left with the *Verne Swain* on a cruise," the papers reported in his obituary, "and in May had finished a large contract with the government. After which he said that he would retire." David Swain was 77. The sudden news of Swain's death appeared in the Saturday editions on July 6, right beside the first articles about the wreck of the *Columbia*.

WHILE TAZEWELL COUNTY waited to try the men charged with manslaughter in the *Columbia* wreck, the state was doing its part to make the river safer. Shortly after the coroner's verdict, the highest state official at the investigations, Illinois Assistant State's Attorney Mansfield returned to his office in Springfield. Mansfield had spent several exhausting months in Peoria, first attending the Strause murder trial, then investigating the wreck. A planned summer vacation was cancelled. Mansfield was fine with letting the county courts handle the criminal case from this point forward and had confidence in State's Attorney Black. He gave him his blessing and went home to get some rest.

The boat itself was not Mansfield's concern, only the business of carrying passengers on excursion trips. The federal government had jurisdiction over the boat. Regarding the *Columbia,* inspectors Bower and Downs had determined that "no evidence of unseaworthiness was found...lifesaving equipment was found to be in good condition and available...improper seamanship and that alone was responsible for heavy loss of life."

Perhaps the two inspectors turned investigators were protecting themselves as well. But in many instances regarding safety, it was determined that the *Columbia* met all federal requirements: it had the mandated number of life boats, life vests and emergency exits. On top of that, Captain Mehl was no coward. Except for some vocal outbursts of anger, most witnesses praised the captain for helping others get off the ship safely. He did not abandon ship. The captain must take responsibility for the lives lost—that was a fact—but there were nearly 500 on board the *Columbia* that night, and thanks in part to the efforts of the captain and crew after the boat sank, more people were able to go home than not. The praise went that far at least. Mansfield had no objections.

THE QUESTION OF THE river's safety was now in the hands of the governor. Shortly after the accident, Lowden sent a team of engineers to do soundings and inspections on the river's depth, current and bottom. They were to report directly back to the Springfield, not just what they found, but more importantly, any recommendations.

They found plenty.

In layman's terms, at the spot where the *Columbia* went down, they determined the Wesley City sand bar was too large, the river level at the bend was too low, and the current too swift and dangerous.

Lowden had heard enough. Changes were on the way, but it would take some time. By the end of the 1930s, after some careful planning, the U.S. Army Corps of Engineers completed construction on five major locks and dams along the Illinois River, including the Peoria dam. The dams assured a constant nine-foot channel in the river, even during low-water seasons.

The 600-foot-wide Peoria dam, built in 1938 and located just south of Peoria, was an engineering marvel at the time that still stands today. It has a wicket-style gate that is lowered to the bottom and allows unimpeded travel during high river stages. During the low seasons, the gate is raised, a pool is created behind the dam, and travel is restricted through the locks only. Although it took nearly two decades to complete, the project itself was approved in 1919, shortly after the *Columbia* wreck. According to an Illinois Waterway engineer, in an article that appeared in 1991, "Things like the [*Columbia*] accident prompted people to seriously begin working to improve the waterways."

At some point, the Wesley City sand bar was dredged too. Today, there are a total of eight navigation locks and dams along the waterway—three have been added since 1938. Since the system of locks and dams was built, there hasn't been a serious commercial boating accident with a loss of life like the *Columbia*.

With the federal and state investigations complete, the only thing left to settle in the *Columbia* case was who should be held responsible for the accident, or in this case, criminally responsible. The months passed with little or no progress. In September of 1919, as noted, there was a brief mention about the *Columbia* at the beginning of that month's circuit court term. It was possible, the papers reported, that the trial of the three men accused in the *Columbia* case would finally be brought up. The word 'possible' was even replaced days later by the word 'probable.' But when the third week of criminal trials began, there was no mention of the *Columbia* or any explanation for the omission.

Another full year had passed without action. On July 5, 1920, the two-year anniversary of the wreck, the *Peoria Evening Star* ran a brief write-up about the *Columbia* in that day's edition. In it they mentioned the milestone date and described the wreck, the great loss of life, and the three defendants, Herman Mehl, August Mehl and George Williams who were "indicted by a Tazewell County Jury after a coroner's jury had fixed the blame on the crew." A brief history was apparently needed after two years had passed. "The cases against them for manslaughter and criminal negligence," the paper said, "were still standing on the docket."

In September 1920, while the *Columbia* case remained in limbo, a landmark decision was reached in Washington, D.C., that reverberated through every court in America. In Tazewell County, when the jury was drawn for that month's county court, in addition to Frank Riese, Edward Conathan and John Shade, there were also Belle Smallwood, Ida Smith and Emma Richmond. For the first time, women were called to sit as jurors.

It was a victory that took decades to achieve, just like a woman's right to vote that preceded and initiated it. The prevailing sense that women should have a say in matters of politics and law went all the way back to the Revolutionary War and the birth of the country, when the U.S. Constitution was argued, drawn up and signed by a roomful of men. "If women are not represented," Abigail Adams sternly wrote her husband, John Adams, "there will be another revolution." Women's groups were formed, petitions were signed and meetings were held. But not much was done. By the mid-1800s, Susan B. Anthony led the charge, spearheading an effort to have state laws altered to include the right for a woman to vote. She drafted a federal amendment in 1878 that up until 1919 was voted on five times in the Senate and three times in the House. The Senate kept voting it down, but in subsequent years the number of dissenting votes declined.

Sensing a shift in attitudes, the heat was turned up, and women groups became more aggressive in their tactics. Woodrow Wilson was a target from the day he took office. A day before his inauguration on March 3, 1913, in an immense show of force and support, an estimated 10,000 women marched down Pennsylvania Avenue. Parades and pageants were organized and well attended. Wilson was hounded by hecklers at every speaking event.

The president was a staunch opponent of the movement at the time, and his views were shared by many powerful and mostly married men. "Ellen Wilson was his ideal for all women," a Wilson biographer wrote of the president's respect for his first wife, "gracious, gentle, gifted, and devoted, willing to let him cast one vote for the entire family."

In 1917, a group of angry suffragettes—including the movement's leader, Alice Paul—stood at the gates of the White House holding up banners protesting the Wilson administration and proclaiming "Mr. President, how long must women wait for liberty?" and "What will you do for woman suffrage?" The group compared the opposition to the oppression of the German people. KAISER WILSON, the signs read. The protests were too much for Wilson, who was annoyed by the commotion and forced to apologize to invited guests, including a Russian delegation whose motorcade was nearly suffocated by the unfurling banners. Despite warnings, the group continued to obstruct traffic and resist fines. Wilson had no choice, he thought—he ordered them all arrested. But as soon as a group of four women were carted off to the jail, four more women replaced them. Paul, who coincidently had a bachelor's, master's and doctorate degree in sociology, spent seven months behind bars. Wilson's views on suffrage later changed during the war. It gave the movement a needed boost.

Now in 1919, with Wilson's support rather than hindrance, the House passed a bill with 14 votes more than the necessary two-thirds, and the amendment—the 19th Amendment, often called the Susan B. Anthony Amendment—was on its way to the Senate. The key vote took place on June 4. After four hours of debate, it passed 56 to 25. But the bill only allowed states the right to make their own laws regarding women's suffrage. It was ratified by most states the following year. Illinois was the first, where it passed in the state house by a vote of 132 to three.

The right for woman to serve on a jury should have been cemented with the ratification of the 19th Amendment, but the process was sticky. Many state courts interpreted a woman's right to vote with blinders on, refusing to give in until states mandated a separate law. The arguments against seating a woman in a man's courtroom were superficial at best. Those who were opposed worried that a woman who served on a jury would be away from her home too long. They argued that no one would look after the children. Additionally, they claimed, the courtroom was filled with all sorts of seedy characters and stories not fit for a woman, especially a mother, who was supposed to be the moral anchor of the family. And wouldn't a woman just vote as her husband instructed her to? Finally, it was brought up, if a jury was sequestered, where would a female juror sleep? It all seems absurd in hindsight, but these were urgent debates in 1920. Eventually, all states got on board. There simply was no logical reason why a woman who could vote shouldn't be able to sit in a jury box too. Besides, proponents said, thanks to the war, women were already spending more time away from home. The civic duty, they explained, would be a good lesson in teaching matters of the law and becoming better citizens.

In Tazewell County, on Wednesday, September 8, 1920, twelve jurors were seated, six of them women. The first case they heard was a simple one involving a petition from a Mrs. Elizabeth Lily of Little Mackinaw for the discharge of a conservator (guardian). The verdict, including the 'nay' vote of four women, was in favor of retaining the conservator.

With the precedent set, it was clear that if and when the *Columbia* case was brought to trial, there would now be a mix of men and women in the jury box. But unfortunately the only news regarding the *Columbia* the summer of 1920 was a tragic one. "George 'Tom' Williams, the pilot of the *Columbia*," the newspaper announced in July of that year, "died a few months ago."

That news may not have been a total shock to readers. Williams had been reported very ill and could not travel to Peoria. His sickly condition may have been partly to blame for the delay in the trial. Now the man who had been singled out by his own captain as the reason why the *Columbia* went down was dead.

Or was he?

As it turned out the papers had it wrong. As was once the case with Mark Twain, the reports of George 'Tom' Williams' death were exaggerated—although some people certainly thought he would just as well have been dead.

Months before, in Jacksonville, Illinois, near his home in Meredosia, a feeble Williams was escorted through the double doors of a five-and-half-story, lavish, Victorian building just off of Main Street. The solid stone structure, bulky in the middle, featured two long ells from its sides that, if viewed from above, resembled outstretched bat wings. It was a massive, eerie-looking place from any angle. Once inside, Williams joined nearly 3,000 other residents who called the Jacksonville State Hospital home.

The facility had been in operation since 1837, one of the first ever of its kind, and at the time of its opening was listed under a different name. That changed shortly after the turn of the century thanks to a man named Clifford Beers. In 1908, Beers wrote a scathing autobiography detailing his "degrading, dehumanizing" experience at a Connecticut state hospital similar to the one in Jacksonville. The book prompted the name change of all state institutions across the country. There were too many misconceptions, health officials determined, about what the hospitals were providing and to whom they were providing services.

The building's name changed, but the purpose of the state hospital remained the same. For many, the Jacksonville State Hospital would always be known by its original designation: The Illinois State Hospital for the Insane.

The pilot of the *Columbia* was now a permanent resident.

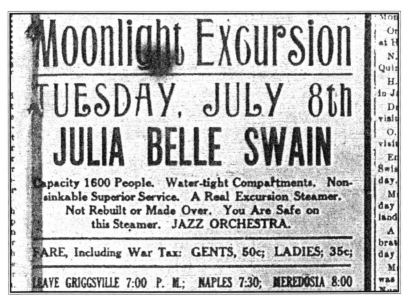

AD FOR EXCURSION ON JULIA BELLE SWAIN
A YEAR AFTER THE COLUMBIA WRECK

45

DEAD DOCKET

WHILE WILLIAMS LANGUISHED inside a massive mental institution, at some point, Herman and August Mehl were told that their cases would not be heard. Not just that month or that year, but never. There would be no trial. The charges stemming from the wreck of the *Columbia* were dropped. The accused men were cleared of any wrongdoing. They would not have to take the stand, testify in their own defense, or hear a judge ask the jury if they have reached a verdict.

It never happened.

But why?

Unfortunately, there is no solid answer. There are simply no official records stating when or why the decision to drop the case was made. Today, in the office of the Tazewell County Circuit Clerk there is a bundle of papers in an old frayed folder. The public is welcome to see it. They are the original and duplicate copies of the grand jury indictment. But that's all. There are no documents showing that the charges against the three men were dropped, nothing to say when the case ended. But at some point it did.

Not all legal decisions were recorded back then, so perhaps after a delay of two years or more, State's Attorney E.E. Black just had enough of waiting and discreetly wiped the case off the record.

Logic suggests that the accused men may simply have benefited from the process. According to the 6th Amendment, after the indictments, all three men had the right to a speedy trial after they had been "arrested, indicted, or otherwise formally accused." The government, however, was under no "constitutional or statutory" obligation to prosecute within a particular amount of time. The case could be 'on the docket' for years or considered a 'dead docket,' which is a procedural device by which the prosecution is postponed indefinitely but may be reinstated at any time at the pleasure of the court.

According to the law, a delay of a year from the date on which the 'speedy trial' was attached—in this case *the* day of the grand jury indictment—was considered, in legal terms, "presumptively prejudicial," or in other words, favorable to the defense. In this case, Mehl's counsel Joe Weil was previously disposed by another client, a man named Edgar Strause.

Strause, a prominent Peoria banker accused of murdering his wife, had been found guilty of manslaughter on July 3, 1918, just two days before the *Columbia* sank. The sensational trial and conviction was appealed due to jury bias, claimed the defense. "It was difficult to get a jury," they argued, "who were not in some way prejudiced or entertained opinions as to the merits of the case which disqualified them as jurors."

Perhaps the warning sign was in the process. "Some 425 men were called to report," the papers lamented, "which required seven weeks before a jury in the Peoria Court had been accepted."

The defense won. The appeal was heard before the Illinois Supreme Court and Strause was granted a new trial. This time to avoid any unnecessary procedural problems, all parties agreed that the case be held in a McLean County courtroom instead.

During the time Mehl's lawyer was tied up in the endless Strause case, the *Columbia* trial was on hold. While Mehl likely didn't have any objections to the delay—especially since it worked in his favor—he also couldn't later claim as a defendant that he had been "unduly delayed." It was a double-edged sword, but one that Mehl was forced to wield.

The reason for the prosecution to delay a criminal case is determined by many factors. It's stated that the prosecution may not "excessively delay the trial for its own advantages," but a trial may be delayed "to secure the presence of an absent witness or other practical consideration." This argument could be explained by the absence of pilot George Williams, who was ill. Did Black hope that at some point Williams would be well enough to return to Pekin and face the charges? Or did he conclude that Williams would never be able to stand trial?

It was obvious, due to the expected cost of the trial, that the three men would be tried together. Is this what Black had in mind—to wait for Williams so that all three men would face the jury as one body? Then came the sudden but erroneous news of the pilot's death. Did Black even know that Williams was still alive, and if so, did it make any difference? Williams was already incarcerated, so to speak, and in some people's minds serving a sentence worse than any jail time. Was this the reason Black abruptly ended the case?

There were other concerns. The more time passed, the less cooperation there would be from previous witnesses. Like the testimony in the coroner's inquest, which was used successfully to secure the grand jury indictment, the more witnesses called to the stand, the stronger the case. Now several years had passed. Could these same witnesses be asked to participate again? And, more importantly, could they be just as descriptive, passionate and resolute in their answers as they had been before? Would there still be any interest in the case? Unlike the coroner's hearings, where questions were asked only to gather facts and not to discriminate or demean, this time around a shrewd attorney like Joseph Weil could break down and expose weaknesses.

Black may have also viewed the continuing Strause case as a cautionary example. The task of finding an impartial jury could be a long and drawn out process, he must have thought. Would he also be facing a trial that, even after a conviction, could be successfully appealed, dragging on for years in different venues?

And did the state's attorney think he might lose the case? Joseph Weil had his hands full with the Strause case, but his influence and imprint on the *Columbia* proceedings was evident every legal side-step along the way. Black was up to the challenge, but he faced an insurmountable task. Weil was a dynamic lawyer with high-profile connections, including his friend and mentor, Clarence Darrow, the fiery and controversial attorney from Chicago.

Darrow was a national celebrity, known for standing up for the common man and defending the less-fortunate members of society. A staunch liberal, Darrow believed every man, no matter his background, had a right to be heard. The working class adored him. A block of a man whose frumpy appearance usually matched those he was defending, Darrow wasn't the flashiest lawyer in Chicago, but he knew how to work a courtroom and, better yet, he knew something instinctive about human nature. Even if a case seemed hopeless for the defendant, Darrow somehow pulled the emotions out of the jury with his long-winded but effective pleas for forgiveness and justice, often evoking tears from the jury box and later an outright acquittal or a guilty verdict that spared the accused from the hangman's noose (Darrow was a staunch opponent of the death penalty). The feisty lawyer frequently was fighting not for his client's innocence, but for his life.

At one point while the *Columbia* trial was delayed Mehl was reported to have traveled to Chicago. Was he there to meet Darrow? If anyone could have arranged it, Weil could. Darrow was at a lull in sensational trials and had spent most of 1918 doing speeches on behalf of fellow democrat Wilson and the decision to go to war (a stance he would later reverse when the government started accusing immigrants of being communists and traitors to America's cause, known as the 'Red Scare'). If Mehl tried to lure the celebrity lawyer from Chicago to take up his defense, it would have had Weil's blessing—Darrow and Weil had successfully worked an appeal case together, involving a man from Peoria. Would Darrow take up the captain's cause? It certainly fit the famous Chicago lawyer's resumé.

In 1915, Darrow had defended the chief engineer of the *Eastland*, Joseph Erickson, who was accused of criminal negligence. Erickson was reportedly the last crew member to abandon the wounded ship and bravely risked his own life trying to trim the boat by opening the faulty ballast. But someone needed to take the fall, and Erickson, the man who was responsible for the inner workings of the steamer, was an obvious choice. Of all things, Darrow's defense was that the ship had struck an unforeseen obstruction in the water. His argument gained credibility when Darrow's hired divers discovered some old pylons hidden beneath the *Eastland*'s mooring. But the evidence overwhelmingly favored a different theory, that the boat was overloaded and the trim was blocked by debris. Erickson was initially absolved just like the rest of the crew, but the case dragged on for nearly nine years before the chief engineer officially became the only person blamed directly for the accident. His conviction was posthumous—Erickson died of a heart attack in April of 1919, only four years after the *Eastland* tragedy.

Whether Darrow and Mehl actually met during the captain's trip to Chicago to "seek counsel," as the papers reported, is debatable. One thing is certain: Darrow never represented anyone in the case of the *Columbia*. Mehl would have to wait for Weil.

And did Black still have a case? None of the men charged was considered a menace to society or tried to shy away from his predicament. Both Herman and August Mehl turned themselves in, posted bond and were free by due process of the law. They lived their lives and ran their businesses in Peoria. They were family men who by all accounts felt remorse for the accident and owned up to their responsibilities. Those points alone any competent defense team could use to their advantage. Plus, Mehl and pilot Williams had already been punished. They lost their right to own and operate a steamboat. This likely had more of an impact on Williams, the veteran river man with a solid reputation, than on Mehl, but as a businessman, Mehl felt it in his pocketbook as well. In any event, Mehl was never a flight risk, and Williams certainly was no threat, especially now.

Perhaps Black felt at some point it was better to let the legal system do what it was designed to do: weed out the petty thieves and shifty cranks that normally clog up the courts. There were always enough cases to fill out a term each month, and a high profile, drawn-out trial like the *Columbia* might muck it all up by dragging out the other case loads over a month or two. The canny stiffs that filled the courtrooms every month were the true criminals, Black may have thought. They were the ones that deserved the ultimate penalty for their crimes if convicted, like Edgar Strause. Why make them wait?

Also, the men in charge of the *Columbia* did not set out to deliberately hurt anyone that night. The circumstances certainly warranted a thorough investigation, and no one could argue that a complete and thorough investigation had not been conducted. But even the federal government decided against taking any criminal action against the captain and pilot.

Whatever the reason, the wheels of justice ground to a screeching halt—there was no trial, no verdict and ultimately no closure for the victims of the *Columbia*. Black and both coroners, Clary and Elliott, had no one to blame for the outcome. They certainly couldn't blame each other. These were good, competent men who were asked to provide a public service and did their jobs admirably. They fixed responsibility based on evidence, heard witnesses, sought justice and let the legal process carry out.

Still, Black must have felt some sense of regret over the decision. No one would be held accountable for the 87 lives lost on July 5, 1918. His thoughts certainly must have been on the countless other victims of the tragedy that night, the families and relatives who hoped that their loved ones' deaths would not go unpunished. How would they react when told the men of the *Columbia* would never be brought to trial, face a jury and own up to their actions? In 1906, a similar trial against the captain of the *General Slocum* was delayed by nearly two years. The frustrating wait, noted the New York papers, eroded the public's faith in the legal system and caused it to lose interest. "Not only has indignation cooled," the paper reported, "but memories have grown dim in regard to the mute details of the affair." The captain of the *General Slocum* was eventually tried and found guilty of criminal negligence. He served three years of a ten-year sentence before being paroled.

There would be no such finality in the *Columbia* case. The three men accused of manslaughter and criminal negligence were free to live their lives as they pleased. Black would eventually move on too. If anyone objected to the decision to drop the case, the prosecutor soon learned, they were as silent as a nighttime grave.

Black continued as Tazewell County State's Attorney until 1924 and spent the rest of his life living and working in Pekin. On Tuesday, December 26, 1939, after a heavy snowstorm blanketed the town, Black spent the day shoveling snow off the walks at his home and retired for the night feeling ill. Later that week, on New Year's Eve, he died at age 71 from complications of a heart ailment.

A MAN IN THE COLUMBIA PILOTHOUSE
IS THIS THE ELUSIVE GEORGE 'TOM' WILLIAMS?
PEORIA HISTORICAL SOCIETY (PHS)

46

NO MORE GOOD MORNINGS

THE CAPTAIN AND THE PILOT of the *Columbia* followed very different paths after the disaster. Williams remained in Peoria only to testify in both coroner hearings and in front of federal investigators, and then he disappeared from sight. He returned to his home in Meredosia, where by all accounts he was welcomed back with usual hometown solicitude. "When the reports of the disaster first reached here," the *Meredosia Budget* reported the day after the wreck, "the thoughts of the community were turned toward fellow townsman, pilot Tom Williams, with the hope that he had safely escaped."

Meredosia comes from the French word 'marais d'osier' meaning 'willow swamps' or 'swamp of the basket reeds.' The hilly land formed by the glaciers sat at the mouth of Meredosia Lake, a five-mile stretch of water along the Illinois River known for its hunting and fishing. The rich, moist soil was a farmer's dream for planting fresh vegetables and duly delivered an abundance of watermelons and cantaloupe.

By the turn of the century, most shipping was by rail, and the steamboats had moved upriver to the larger metropolitan areas. A pilot like Tom Williams may have followed the boats north for work, but his roots and family remained in sleepy Meredosia. When word of the *Columbia* disaster was announced, the town held its collective breath. "It was not long before a message was received by his wife," the *Budget* continued, "that stated [Williams] was safe and uninjured, which was news of rejoicing to her and their host of friends here."

Williams found comfort at his quant riverside home, especially when he fell ill. His exact ailment was never disclosed. There were reports that he was taken sick shortly before the wreck, but it was never mentioned in the coroner's inquest. Whatever his illness was, it apparently did not affect his testimony or willingness to answer questions under oath. In addition, if Williams was even slightly disabled that night, any good steamboat captain would have excused him from duty. It's possible he may have suffered from a chronic condition that did not affect his duties as a pilot but may have worsened after the wreck; perhaps it was exacerbated by the wreck itself. The only news that made the papers in Peoria was that he was too sick to travel.

While the Peoria papers incorrectly reported his death several months before the two-year anniversary of the wreck, the local paper in Jacksonville got it right. On February 2, 1920, the *Jacksonville Daily Journal* reported, "Thomas Williams of Meredosia is now a patient at Jacksonville State Hospital, having been brought to the city [by his two sons and friends of the family]. The case is a peculiarly sad one as Williams lost his mind from brooding over the sinking of the Illinois River steamer *'Columbia'* of which he was a pilot."

Williams would never leave the Jacksonville State Hospital. He died on December 12, 1927, arguably another victim of the *Columbia* disaster. RIVER PILOT DIES HERE MONDAY was the headline in the next day's *Jacksonville Daily Journal*. There was no mention of the *Columbia* in the article announcing his passing. The Peoria and Pekin papers didn't even cover it.

Williams would eventually be tagged as the pilot who "lost his reason" over the *Columbia* wreck. Even the previous owner of the *Columbia,* Walter Blair, when asked, defended his former boat as sturdy and reliable and blamed the pilot for "losing his way" and causing the wreck. It was human error, plain and simple, Blair insinuated.

If true, steamboat history puts Williams in good company. Mark Twain and Fred Way wrote numerous stories of former steamboat captains and pilots who "lost their minds" after their careers on the river ended. Some brooded over an accident, of which there were plenty, others just cracked under the rigors of the job.

In *Pilotin' Comes Natural,* Way writes that the captain of the *Queen City,* the "white-bearded man" who playfully scolded him as a youth when Way tried to sneak into the pilothouse, "lost his reason" shortly after the incident and was "kept home nursed by a loving and gracious wife." That was in 1911. Way was only ten at the time. He never saw the pilot again or personally named him in the book. "I learned he was one of the most gentlemanly and agreeable of pilots who lived a scrupulous Christian life," Way recalled later. "He would not tolerate tobacco in the pilothouse, nor did he take a drink of anything stronger than tea, nor was he ever known to utter a profane word." That changed after he left the river. "Frequently he went into fits of temper in those sad days and swore bloody murder. He called his dear ones all the names in the catalogue." Way mentions that three or four prominent steamboat pilots "came to this horrible end."

"Every one of them had been brilliant and capable an extent far above the general average," Way noted.

Hardboiled veteran steamboat pilots tried to discourage others from joining their ranks. "I say any man is a damn fool and an idiot to learn to be a pilot," proclaimed Captain Ebenezer Cline, who was a "whopping big fellow who could roar like a bull."

"No woman ought to ever marry a man who says he is a pilot," the bull would roar. "There ought to be a law against it."

Cline would pace back and forth and pound his fist on the bench just to emphasize his points, telling some poor cub pilot who stood before him, "Get some sense boy and get away from this business while you are still young and have a chance."

And yet, as Way writes about men like Ebenezer Cline and others, "despite all this bluster, they wouldn't have traded places with the King of England."

Maybe there was too much pressure, too much risk, too much at stake. The burden of responsibility for the safety of others was great, particularly on such dangerous ships plying such dangerous waters. It was enough to keep a sane man up at night and nervously pacing during the day. Steamboat pilots were proud men who always felt like they did all the dangerous work and never got the credit for it—only the blame if something went wrong. The rivers were treacherous, swirling deathtraps, and their life-or-death obligations to passengers and crew must have weighed heavily on them.

Even today, it is the steamboats themselves, the glorious stern and side wheelers like the *Julia Belle* and *Dixie Queen,* that are noted and revered. The men who ran the boats are remembered mostly by their fierce, determined, bossy and sometimes downright crazy reputations. But those romanticized icons lived in the mid-1800s, when steamboats ruled the waters. George 'Tom' Williams lived in a different era.

By 1918, steamboats were big business, and the men who owned the business were making a living off of it rather than living for it. Maybe Williams was different. His reaction and eventual breakdown may be an indication that like the steamboat captains of the past, Williams also "lost his reason" on a foggy night in July when a steamboat named the *Columbia* ran too close to the shore, struck a hidden tree stump, and sank in the middle of the Illinois River. It was his hands on the wheel, his boat to steer, when a desperate shout came from below: "Run her ashore, Tom. Damn her, run her ashore!" Those very words may have haunted him until his last breath.

LIKE WILLIAMS, HERMAN MEHL had a loving family to turn to, but unlike the beleaguered pilot, he also had a life and career beyond the river to fall back on. The steamboat business had been a lucrative proposition for Mehl, and it was a shame to lose it, but there were other ventures that kept the former captain busy and his pockets full.

Ever since arriving in America from Jagersburg, Germany, as a teenager, Mehl and his two brothers Fred and August had been selling cigars in a shop in downtown Peoria and fish from a market along the river just north of Peoria, in Chillicothe. At one point Mehl lived in Chillicothe, where many of the boats from Peoria were dry-docked for the winter. He was involved in city government there too, as an alderman and chairman of the ferry committee. Later, after he had become a successful steamboat owner himself, Mehl would deliver his boat to its post each year with great fanfare and usually after some touch-up work had been completed to prepare the vessel for the long winter rest. "Freshly caulked with a painted hull," the *Chillicothe Bulletin* reported as the *Columbia* arrived in port on October 25, 1912. "Just minor repairs," were done, the paper boasted, as Mehl proclaimed the past excursion season an "exceptionally prosperous one."

From its very beginning, Mehl's fish market was a staple on Pine Street. Local fishermen would pull their rowboats right up to the landing and bring in the catch of the day. There was no middleman back then. From his riverside perch behind the shop's counter Mehl would also watch the grand steamboats go by, the Swain boats and the boats owned by his future father-in-law, Garland Sivley.

Whatever Mehl was witnessing while sharpening the filet knife, it must have made him long for a chance to be part of the more glamorous (to say nothing of more lucrative) steamboat business just outside the shop doors. He may have hungered for the day when he could trade in the ankle-length apron stained with bloody fish guts for a finely coifed captain's suit.

Maybe it was the tales of river life he would hear from the local fishermen who came to the shop to drop off their provisions. A local writer, Bob Burtnett, who for many years submitted articles about the history of the steamboats to the Chillicothe newspaper, recalled one such story about a fisherman named Johnny who was "rowing his big seine boat, loaded with fish" from the springs to

Mehl's fish market. "As he neared the point of the slough," Burt-nett writes, "one of the Swain boats, probably the *David Swain*, came boiling up the river for a flash landing at Chillicothe." John-ny got a good bath from the passing boat. The wash from the big wheel nearly knocked him and his catch back into the river. "Ye nearly swamped my boat, Capt'n," Johnny shouted. "Don't believe I'd do that again, cause if ye do, I'll put a stop to it." A week later, Burtnett writes, "Johnny was bringing in a load of fish to Herman Mehl's market when the same steamer went by again and once more Johnny's boat dipped and bobbed in the wake of the vessel. Johnny pulled the oars across his lap, reached back into a pile of nets and pulled out a big long-barreled gun. Turning toward the packet, he fired three shots, each one of them blasting out a win-dow of the pilothouse." Johnny laid the gun back down on the nets, went into Mehl's fish shop, sold his catch and quietly returned home to his cabin boat. "From then on," Burtnett wrote, "it was reported, steamboats in the vicinity gave respect and distance to any heavily laden small boat."

It's not clear whether Mehl heard the gunshots from the shop or Johnny told him the story—or even if the story is true. Burt-nett claims the fisherman didn't tell a soul until later. Regardless, Burtnett points out, "the little man proved his point that the river belongs to everyone, even at times it becomes necessary to remind some people to the contrary."

It was settled, the river would be Herman Mehl's next big busi-ness venture. After marrying Ethel Sivley in 1901 and working for his in-laws (he was only a year younger than his mother-in-law, Josie) Mehl eventually bought the *Columbia* from Walter Blair and started an operation of his own, separate from his two broth-ers. August would work the books for his brother's excursion busi-ness, and Fred, the youngest of them, continued to run the success-ful Mehl Leaf Tobacco Company. Herman focused his attention on the excursion business—until the boat sank.

After the accident Mehl stayed in Peoria, where he was known and where men in powerful positions, like the Peoria County State's Attorney, seemed to leave him alone, even after he was indicted.

(Other than the ruling by the coroner's jury, Peoria County never pursued any additional legal action against the captain.)

Mehl also received great support from his family. In the book *Josie*, a tribute to her grandmother Josie Sivley, author Nancy Cloud Loeschner writes that Mehl's wife Ethel sent a letter to her sister Daisy, who was living in Washington, D.C., at the time. The date was January 20, 1920, nearly two years after the wreck of the *Columbia*, and a seemingly tempestuous time for a wife and mother whose husband was awaiting trial on manslaughter charges. Yet there was still holiday cheer in Mehl's home. In the letter, Ethel thanked her sister for the Christmas gifts and excitedly announced, "Herman gave me a Singer sewing machine." Ethel explained to her sister that she was going to teach her daughters how to sew.

Daisy, the youngest of the four Sivley sisters (Ethel was the oldest) had been working in the D.C. area in early July 1918 when she heard a newsboy shouting something about a wreck of steamer. Daisy recalled that she thought at first it was another ship that went down in the Atlantic, like the *Titanic*, only to later learn it was her brother-in-law's boat in Illinois that sank.

The rest of Herman Mehl's life, especially after charges against him were dropped, seems to have been a quiet and peaceful one. By all accounts he was a good father and husband. His career on the river was over, but he continued to help his brothers with the fish market and run the tobacco shop. He even dabbled in real estate, owning property in Peoria and renting apartments. His trademark cigar stub was never far from his mouth.

In February 1928, Mehl's brother Fred died at age 61, after undergoing surgery in Philadelphia for complications brought on by a sinus condition. Fred owned and operated the successful Mehl Leaf Company, "the largest mail order house in the West." The plant was best known for speeding up the aging process of raw tobacco leaves artificially so the material could be ready for market in just a year rather than three to four years under natural aging. In the 1920s, The Mehl Leaf Company had 167 employees in both Peoria and Florida. When the cigar business slowed, thanks to the growing popularity of cigarettes, Fred Mehl discovered another business venture while on a tobacco-buying trip—on which he rode a bus. In his later years, he owned and operated a bus company, the next big thing, he reasoned.

Eleven years after Fred's death, in 1939, Herman's other brother August, purser of the *Columbia*, passed away. Nine years later, on April 19, 1947, at the age of 74, Herman Mehl died at home in his sleep. In the Peoria papers a short notice appeared that included an undated picture of the aged grandfather dressed in a suit and tie. "Mr. Mehl was in the steamboat business here," is all the papers reported about his life on the river and the long since departed excursion boats on the Illinois. There was no mention of the *Columbia*.

DR. LAWRENCE CLARY continued to serve as Tazewell County coroner until 1920, but the grind of running a large private practice and serving as a public official was too much. He left the post and served only as deputy coroner until 1924. He also served eight years as Pekin's health officer. Due to the increasing demand for his time as a doctor, and an ever-expanding patient list, Clary asked a friend, Dr. W.A. Balcke, to partner with him. The two men ran a successful medical practice for twelve years.

In 1931, Clary, now free from his civic duties and able to devote more time to his patients, opened up a new office on North Fifth Street. The proceeding years had been challenging for a man who spent nearly a decade helping others cope with grief and loss. But he was dedicated to his work as a doctor.

Shortly after his stint as county coroner ended, Clary experienced several tragedies of his own. In 1926, Clary's wife of 18 years, Bertha, died. Clary was suddenly left alone to raise a young daughter, Helen Marie, who was only a toddler when her mother fell ill. Clary's first child, Harmony Louise, passed away in 1915, just a day after she was born. Clary wasn't alone for long. A year after Bertha's death, he met another woman, Irene Sanders from Joliet, fell in love and remarried. Clary brought her to Pekin, but their union lasted little more than a year. Irene got sick and died on August 21, 1928. Despondent and still raising his young daughter on his own,

Clary found solace in another woman, Ruth Kettenring. They were married in Springfield on April 28, 1930. But they would spend only three years together.

In January 1933, after a long day at the office, Clary sat down for a late dinner and told Ruth he wasn't feeling well. "I could hardly make it home," he said. Clary was keeping a busy schedule as usual, working long hours, making house calls and taking business trips. That week, he had taken a train to a fair outside of town, came back and then drove to the fair again the following day. Clary remarked to a patient that the trips to the fair had tired him out. "I [worked] it pretty well while I was up there," he said, "but I've been paying for it ever since."

Ruth had good reason to be concerned. Three years before, Clary spent several weeks in a Peoria hospital recovering from what other doctors told him was a weakened heart. He was ordered to take it easy, advice that's difficult for another doctor to follow. After he got back home, Clary continued his grueling pace. There was always a line waiting for him every morning outside his office, he explained, and patients came first. "I wish I could get more life insurance," he would jokingly tell his loyal patrons, "but they won't take me on account of my heart."

Back at the supper table, a pale and weak Clary surprised Ruth by telling her he was going back to the office that night to do more work. She begged him not to go, but it was not up for debate. Despite his fatigue, Clary insisted. He went to his car, got in, but only sat there. Ruth stood on the porch and waited. After a few minutes, the doctor stepped out and walked back to the house. "I think I'll stay home," he told her. Ruth thought he would go right to bed, but instead Clary reached out to some friends and asked them over to talk about a "business matter." They came and left a little after nine, Ruth remembers, and Clary finally retired for the night.

Just an hour or so later, around ten, Clary's former partner and friend Dr. Balcke got an urgent phone call. It was Ruth. "Lawrence is very sick," she told him, and asked if he could come by. Balcke hung up, but before he could get dressed the phone rang again. This time Ruth was in "great fright," Balcke recalls. Clary was breathing very hard, she frantically explained. Balcke ran out the back door and down the half block to the Clary home. But it was too late. The good doctor's heart had given out. He was just 50.

"This morning the usual list of patients waited his call," the *Pekin Daily Times* reported the next day. "Some were very ill, some had broken bones—all were awaiting the tread of Dr. Clary's footstep and his cheerful 'good morning.'"

But that morning, the "cheerful" greeting never came.

"Instead the word spread," the *Times* continued, "by phone and by calls from neighbors that Dr. Clary would not be coming in—that he died during the night.

"He was gone," the paper sighed.

In the lengthy tribute that appeared in the paper the following day, Clary was honored for his accomplishments as a husband, father, church member and citizen. His achievements as coroner though were only suggested, not detailed. The *Columbia* disaster was never mentioned. Perhaps that chapter in history was too sad for many to relive.

For Dr. Clary, a humble and devoted public servant, actions spoke volumes. It was evident that night in July when he was awakened by a phone call and told a boat had gone down in the Illinois River. He set the phone down, put on his wrinkled blazer, placed a Panama hat on his head and went to work.

FOR THE TOWN OF PEKIN, the most disturbing reminder of the *Columbia* disaster remained in the churning waters of the Illinois River. Eventually the wreckage was removed, but exactly when and how is not precisely known. Several months after the coroner's inquests ended, there was no longer a need to raise the hull and save it for inspection. It could take a year or more, authorities were told, to carefully raise the ship's bottom without disturbing any evidence. Now without any restrictions the hull could be easily removed, bit by broken bit. And maybe it was.

The most fanciful report of how the ship's remains were finally purged from the river could have come right out of a Dickens novel.

A number of volunteers, as the story goes, were gathered up and went into the river to break apart and dispose of what was left of the once-mighty ship. We may never know, but perhaps they were so disgusted by the site of the boat's remains still lying in the river nearly a year after the accident that they took it upon themselves, as ordinary citizens, to remove it from sight. Instantly, one conjures up an image of a band of marauders with torches and axes in hand marching in line to the shoreline determined to take care of a problem no one else could or would. "There is prodigious strength in sorrow and despair," Dickens wrote in *A Tale of Two Cities*.

The paddlewheel, which remained mostly intact, was the final piece of the wreckage to be taken from the water, "the last grim symbol of the tragedy," one observer noted. Locals remembered the large paddlewheel sat dormant along the shore for a time, stuck in place, where kids played on its broken slats. It too was eventually ripped apart and burned.

THE ACTUAL SITE OF THE COLUMBIA WRECK TODAY

DO NOT FORGET

ON SUNDAY, AUGUST 13, 2006, several hundred people gathered at the foot of Court Street in Pekin for an arts celebration in the park. There were booths filled with oil paintings, photography, ceramics, jewelry and blown-glass sculptures. For the kids there was T-shirt dyeing and face painting. The festival was sponsored by the local historic society to honor the artists in the area. It was a perfect summer day, and the town came out to celebrate. In addition to the arts festival, the newly named Pekin Riverfront Park was finally reopening after being closed to the public nearly a full year for renovations. The wait was worth it. There was a new fountain, river walk and a shiny new playground that was constructed to look like a steamboat with tall black smoke stacks in the middle.

Shortly before the park was shut down, in 2003, a state historical marker was placed along a grassy area facing the Illinois River and just beside the span of the John T. McNaughton Bridge. A small ceremony was held to dedicate the marker. The marker read:

On July 5, 1918, the steamboat *Columbia* sank upstream from this spot near what was then Wesley City. What began as one of the season's premier social events ended in tragedy.

The Pekin South Side Social Club sponsored the ornate sternwheeler's ill-fated voyage. Beginning in Kingston Mines, some 500 passengers boarded it for a trip to Al Fresco Amusement Park in Peoria. On the return trip, as festivities were in full swing, a hole was torn in the *Columbia*'s hull and it sank. The deceased were brought to this riverfront for identification. Of the 87 who died, 57 were from Pekin.

Now that the new park was completed and reopening, several local dignitaries wanted to re-dedicate the marker and honor those who died on the *Columbia* just as the city had done each year for the preceding four years on the actual anniversary of the wreck. A small covered stage was set up, and a re-dedication ceremony was scheduled later that day during the arts festival. There would be a guest of honor, they were told.

The marker itself was placed in the exact spot where hundreds of passengers waited to embark on the *Columbia* that fateful night. There is a landing for small boats nearby, but the once sandy shore is replaced by concrete embankments on both sides and a long walking pier.

On the river itself, the grand steamboats are nowhere in sight. Now, hardly a boat goes by that's not much bigger than a speedy pleasure craft or much taller than a tug. Long barges float by silently, almost unnoticed. Standing along the banks, one can only imagine how exciting it would have been to see the large steamers floating downriver, the big paddlewheels turning, water slapping and splashing as black smoke billowed from their stacks. The high-pitched sound of the whistle and the tolling of the bell would signal a ship's arrival—echoes of a time and place now lost to history.

Yet even though the grand era of the excursion boats ended after the *Columbia* wreck, steamboats made a comeback, of sorts, on the Illinois River in the mid- to late-1970s. The incomparable

Julia Belle Swain returned to the Peoria shoreline. It was not the original *Julia Belle Swain,* which was long gone–burned in winter quarters on the Monongahela River in 1931–but a new boat, built some 40 years later in 1971, that carried on the famous name. The new *Julia Belle Swain* was impressive and designed to "appeal to steamboat aficionados and the general public alike." Its engine was still steam-driven, and the paddlewheel–relocated from its original side location to the back of the boat for greater efficiency–was still operated by way of original Pittman arms and crank assemblies.

The new ship spent many years in Peoria, offering pleasure cruises on the river. Folk singer and songwriter John Hartford, who was a self-admitted steamboat man before he was a musician, wrote a song about the *Julia Belle Swain,* his favorite legendary ship:

> *When the Julia Belle comes to Peoria,*
> *You know that the summer time is here,*
> *Up on the Illinois River,*
> *It's the very best time of year!*

The new *Julia Belle Swain* eventually left the Peoria area and is now permanently based in La Crosse, Wisconsin. Today, a steamboat named *The Spirit of Peoria* is docked on Peoria's riverfront year-round.

Even in the early days of steamboats, names were not exclusive. For example, on the inland waters there were eleven steamers named the *Columbia,* six of them sternwheelers and five side-wheelers. By 1900 many were running at the same time, only in different areas and rivers. By 1918, the Illinois' *Columbia* was the last boat with that name still on the water. Five of the other *Columbias* ended their careers tragically, mostly due to fires, although no one was killed or seriously injured.

The site of the old Al Fresco Amusement Park just north of Peoria is now a stretch of riverfront land occupied by a private yacht club and a trailer park. It sits across from Route 29 adjacent to Hillside Park between Peoria Heights and Mossville. In 1928, the park's attractions were closed for good. Attendance rates dropped during World War I, but it was ultimately the flow of the river that brought about its demise. When the river was raised by Chicago drainage in the 1920s, portions of the park's land was permanently flooded. Several of the rides were damaged and never repaired. Eventually the famous Figure-Eight Roller Coaster was dismantled, and the park was shut down.

The area continued to thrive for several more decades thanks to a man named Fred Feyler, who leased the land and rented it out to swimmers and picnickers. Business was good, but during World War II, in a flash of patriotic pride, Feyler declared that all men in uniform would be admitted free, somehow neglecting to calculate the number of soldiers that were stationed at nearby Camp Ellis. Hundreds of uniformed men flocked to the park to enjoy the liberated freedom of a day at the beach, and soon the unpaid admissions far outweighed the number of paid ones. Feyler was forced to close the park for good in 1944.

What's left of the steamer *Columbia* today can be found in private collections and local libraries. The American flag that Roscoe Maxey claims he took from the boat the day after the wreck was donated to the Pekin Public Library after his death. Today it sits unseen in an upstairs storage area. Several articles from the *Columbia* can be found at historical societies in the area including the Peoria Historical Society, where a clock, a sign and a broken piece of wood with the words *Columbia* on it were scheduled for display in a new Peoria riverfront museum opening in the fall of 2012. The other half of the wood piece is said to have been used as the roof of a shed in someone's backyard. There are several unconfirmed rumors about where the *Columbia*'s bell ended up. One involves a building in Peoria's warehouse district that once housed a dairy company. The bell was reportedly used to signal lunch break at the old plant. The building was renovated in 2012. No such bell was found.

For those who believe in such things, the question of whether the wreck site is haunted is up for spirited debate, so to speak. In her book *Haunted Peoria,* author Stephanie E. McCarthy writes:

> With the many tragic and gruesome deaths surrounding the

Columbia it is hardly surprising that ghosts have surfaced surrounding the ill-fated ship. One of the many reported stories is that of a phantom steamboat seen in the vicinity of the crash. The ship appears briefly in the heavy fog and just as quickly dissipates. Those sighting the vessel have reported hearing the faint sounds of the calliope just before the boat vanishes. Another popular report is of a ghostly green light that is said to appear in the depths of the river at the place where the boat sank. The story is that the light is from those still searching for an exit or trying to find a loved one on the ship. Legend reports that when occupants see the green light they need to quickly leave the river, as that is the light of those departed trying to pull them to their deaths.

The name Wesley City was eventually replaced by Creve Coeur, named after an old fort in the area. The few coal mines that survived until the mid-1900s have long since been shuttered and the shanties that once dotted the shoreline and housed the mine workers and fishermen are gone. Only a few old houses testify that a settlement once hugged the banks of the river there. The railroad tracks are still on the Tazewell County side of the Illinois. Several train lines run through the Peoria area today but all are used for freight only.

Pekin is still the hub of Tazewell county politics and much of its downtown is a throwback to the earlier part of the last century, with narrow jutted streets and stone and brick buildings. Some of its older residential roads, which still bear the names of its earliest settlers, still have exposed cobblestones.

TODAY WITH A POPULATION of just over 35,000, Pekin remains—like its close neighbor to the north, Peoria—one of the larger cities on the Illinois River and a bustling and thriving community rich in people and history. So it seemed only fitting that at the turn of the 21st century, the town would honor its true resource by beautifying the river's shoreline and opening it up to the community. "It's great to have somewhere to go with the kids," a Pekin resident told a newspaper reporter in 2006 when the newly constructed River-front Park was re-opened.

On that sunny day, Mike Smith, a state congressman from Canton who represented the district, stepped to the podium for the re-dedication ceremony of the *Columbia*'s historical marker. The thousand or so people who filled the park for the arts festival shaded their eyes, then bowed their heads in silence. A bell tolled for each of the 87 victims as Representative Smith read the names aloud.

Several people planned to speak that day, including relatives of those who perished on the boat. At times the gruesome details of the wreck were given as a reminder of the horrors of that night. "There were more women and children killed that night than men," one speaker told the hushed crowd. "The youngest male was two months old. The youngest female three months. The oldest male was 60. The oldest female was 55. The average age of female victims was 25. The average age of males was 22. The women outnumbered the men two-to-one."

A local man played the bagpipes, and an honor guard held the colors. Representative Smith said, "I think this a big part of the history of Pekin and Central Illinois. It is important we do not forget."

One guest of honor could not make it to the ceremonies that day. Lucille Adcock was said to be too frail and ill to attend. She had made it three years earlier for the unveiling of the marker and shared memories of that "horrific" night in 1918. Mrs. Adcock was Lucille Bruder at the time of the tragedy. She and her brother John ran like the wind to make it to the landing just as the boat was about to leave. Lucille wanted to go alone to meet her friends, but her parents insisted she bring her little brother along. Lucille and her co-workers at the steel plant cafeteria had planned a fun night out together to celebrate the end of the week and the Fourth of July holiday. "I was 18 years old," Lucille explained, "I was on the top floor when the boat went down." There she stayed, hanging on to flagpole until a rescue boat arrived. She and her brother were spared. But, she added sadly, "I lost many friends."

Lucille was represented at the 2006 ceremony by her three daughters, Beverly Bowman, Mary Mass and Pat Lohmann. "[My mom] told me that she thought if the boat hadn't been backed up into the channel they could have saved more lives," Lohmann said.

After the ceremony, Lucille's daughters laid flowers in the river. Then they all went to see their mother at the nursing home. That's when they got the sad news. Around 4:30 that afternoon, a few hours after the ceremony ended, Lucille Adcock, age 106, had died peacefully in her sleep. She was the last known survivor of the wreck of the *Columbia*.

THE STEAMBOAT COLUMBIA DISASTER

On July 5, 1918, the steamboat Columbia sank upstream from this spot near what was then Wesley City. What began as one of the season's premier social events ended in tragedy.

The Pekin South Side Social Club sponsored the ornate sternwheeler's ill-fated voyage. Beginning in Kingston Mines, some 500 passengers boarded it for a trip to Al Fresco Amusement Park in Peoria. On the return trip, as festivities were in full swing, a hole was torn in the Columbia's hull and it sank. The deceased were brought to this riverfront for identification. Of the 87 who died, 57 were from Pekin.

Sponsored by the Tazewell County Historical Places Society
and the Illinois Historical Society
July 2003

COLUMBIA HISTORICAL MARKER
PEKIN, ILLINOIS

ACKNOWLEDGEMENTS

FIRST, A NOTE of regret. Despite my efforts and the efforts of others who desperately searched where I could not, no photograph of the pilot George 'Tom' Williams ever turned up. The best glimpse we have is of a man high in the pilothouse peering out below as he prepares for another excursion on the Illinois River. His physical appearance will have to remain in our imagination for now. Perhaps this book will solve the mystery.

The H.W. Humphrey and George W. Barrette booklet titled *The Columbia Disaster* was released shortly after the accident, possibly days, but likely a week or so. Both men were writers and newspapermen from Peoria as far as I can gather. The booklet is a descriptive and oftentimes exaggerated narrative of the first several days after the wreck. There is no mention of the local, state or federal officials who arrived just hours after the accident or Coroner Clary. The captain, pilot and crew are treated as heroes and life savers in the unfolding drama, a stark contrast to what was being echoed across the river in Pekin. Still it is an interesting and informative read and helped me formulate some of the action and timeline of the story. A few of its more sensationalist passages are used for effect within my book. Perhaps the most poignant and sincere moment is on the booklet's first page when Humphery and Barrette write:

> To the honor and memory of those heroes—living and dead— of the steamer *Columbia* disaster, who risked or sacrificed their lives that others might live, this book is respectfully dedicated.

A copy of the twelve-page booklet can be found at the Pekin Public Library and the Tazewell County Genealogical and Historical Society. The Peoria Public Main Library has a delicate original copy in their history room. It's worth a look.

There are many people to thank for the making of *The Wreck of the Columbia*. First and foremost, my sincere gratitude goes to the people at Amika Press and Jay Amberg for taking on this book project. A hearty appreciation goes to John Manos for his expert editing and suggestions. And kudos to Sarah Koz for her brilliant typesetting and spot-on recommendations and Justin Russo for the perfect original cover illustration and design.

A special thank you goes to my wife Connie who encouraged and enlightened me along the way with her thoughts and ideas. Thanks also to my kids Sam and Nora who mostly left Daddy alone while he was lost in his thoughts. Love you guys!

A very gracious thank you goes to many others who helped bring this book from idea to word to print. In no particular order they include Connie and David Perkins and the staff at the Tazewell County Genealogical Society, Bob Killion at the Peoria Historical Society, the staff at the Special Collections at Bradley University, Diantha Sarver at the Chillicothe Historical Society and the helpful staffs at the history rooms at both the Pekin and Peoria Public libraries. Thanks also to the staff at the Morton Library, the Jacksonville, Illinois Library, the materials division of the Abraham Lincoln Presidential Library and Museum in Springfield and the persistent work of the researchers at the U.S. National Archives and Records Administration in Washington, D.C., and the Illinois Regional Archives Depository in Normal. Also the Murphy Library University of Wisconsin-La Crosse for their wonderful steamboat photo collection and the Davenport Library in Davenport, Iowa.

A very personal thank you goes to Dennis Conover, Bob Anton, Greg Batton, Dan Phillips, Doug Stephens, Johnna Ingersoll, Nancy Cloud Loeschner, Carole N. Starrett, Alan Bates, Stephanie E. McCartney, David Tschiggfrie, Norman Kelly, Linda Tillman, Rod Mehl and the staff at the Tazewell County Circuit Clerk's Office.

Finally to the many authors who write books about the past and bring lost and forgotten stories back to life. They are an inspiration to all. I encourage everyone to find a piece of the past and explore. Keep history alive!

SOURCES

1 TROUBLE AHEAD

"Some pilots missed the brake..." Bob Anton, interview with author, 2011.

"It was a question of honor..." Curry. *The River's in My Blood: Riverboat Pilots Tell Their Stories*. Nebraska: University of Nebraska Press, 1963.

"Captain Jack..." Ibid.

2 PLACE IN TIME

"Accidents involving destruction of life..." O'Donnell. *Ship Ablaze: The Tragedy of the Steamboat General Slocum*. New York: Broadway, 2004.

"Sam was on another boat..." Morris, Jr. *Lighting Out for the Territory: How Samuel Clemons Headed West and Became Mark Twain*. New York: Simon & Schuster, 2010.

"For 48 hours, I labored..." Clemons letter to Mollie Clemons, June 18, 1858.

Hugh Barr story. *The Pekin Centenary 1849-1949*. Illinois: Heine Graphics Group, 1949.

3 STEAMBOATS COMING

"The flaming furnaces would give you..." Klein. *Peoria!*. Illinois: Visual Communications, 1985.

"I've heard of flies, mosquitoes, bed bugs and fleas..." Ibid.

Canton, Ohio history. Scott County Ohio Library.

Canton, Illinois history. Callary. *Place Names of Illinois*. Illinois: University of Illinois, 2008.

"Will you have the goodness to take my overcoat..." Gross. *The Wit and Wisdom of Abraham Lincoln*. Barnes & Noble Books, 2005.

"Eventually three fire companies were formed..." *The Pekin Centenary 1849-1949*. Illinois: Heine Graphics Group, 1949.

"Pekin continued to thrive..." Ibid.

4   MOVERS

Walter Blair bio. Blair. *A River Pilot's Log*. The Arthur H. Clark Co., 1939.

"When we consider..." Deenen letters. University of Illinois at Urbana-Champaign.

"Walter Blair did not accompany..." Blair personal articles. *Davenport Democrat and Leader*.

"Carried 114,857 passengers and 16,896 tons of freight..." Ibid.

"Which was nearly what she had cost us..." Ibid.

Blair's story of meeting Mark Twain. "Mark Twain. He was no Great Shakes at the Wheel, Say all the Rivermen–With One Exception." *Coronet Magazine,* Eskew, 1940.

"Wooden, hinged breast board..." Anton, interview with author, 2011.

5   HIT BOTTOM

"The wet cigar stub..." Loeschner, interview with author, 2011.

"Let this be a lesson..." Loeschner. *Josie*. Lulu, 2008.

6   MIDNIGHT CRUISE

"Day clothes were looser..." Green. *The Uncertainty of Everyday Life 1915-1945*. Arkansas: University of Arkansas, 2000.

"Many working class families chose..." Ibid.

"It was far lighter..." Ibid.

"A common occurrence..." Anton, interview with author, 2011.

"Americans were asked to ration..." Green. *The Uncertainty of Everyday Life 1915-1945*. Arkansas: University of Arkansas, 2000.

"One thousand various articles manufactured..." *Peoria 1915 City Directory and Blue Book*.

"Green walls of the shoreline…" Klein. *Peoria!*. Illinois: Visual Communications, 1985.

7 SURPRISE TICKET

Most of the stories in this chapter are from newspaper articles or letters. Carole Starrett personally transcribed the story of Aunt Minnie and the homemade fudge.

"The Gehrig name and band…" *The Pekin Centenary 1849-1949*. Illinois: Heine Graphics Group, 1949.

8 FRANKIE FOLSOM

"Pekin baseball fans…" *Pekin Daily Times,* Monday, September 3, 1917.

9 AL FRESCO

"The city is a delight…" *Peoria 1915 City Directory and Blue Book.*

"It would be difficult to find among all the names of cities…" Ibid.

"Both Peoria and Illinois were names of pure Indian origin…" Callary. *Place Names of Illinois.* Illinois: University of Illinois, 2008.

"Below is the busy city…" *Peoria 1915 City Directory and Blue Book.*

"I never was so frightful in my life…" Cartmell. *The Incredible Scream Machine: A History of the Roller Coaster.* Amusement Park Books, 1988.

"Before you can remember…" Ibid.

10 FULL AHEAD

"A pilot can't stop with merely thinking…" Twain. *Life on the Mississippi.* Boston: James R. Osgood & Co., 1883.

11 FALLEN BEAMS

"Crumpled like a match stick box…" *Chicago Tribune,* 1918.

13 BLACKING OUT

Story of Lisle and Leo. "They Remember." *Peoria Star,* July 6, 1968.

15 MORE HELP

"The best trip up…" Ad in Peoria newspaper, 1918.

16 ON THAT TRAIN

"I was on fire to ascend those heights…" Way Jr. *Pilotin' Comes Natural.* New York: Rinehart & Co., Inc., 1943.

17   IN SHOCK

"The 'White House Crossing'..." David Perkins. Tazewell County Genea-logical and Historical Society, 2011.

18   HE'S TALKING

"Excessively negative tone..." Collier-Hillstrom. *The Muckrakers and the Progressive Era.* Omnigraphics, 2009.

"There are in body politic..." Ibid.

"Any excess..." Ibid.

"Hysterical sensationalism..." Ibid.

"Muckraking was plainly going out of style..." Ibid.

"Autobiographies should be brief..." East bio. Peoria Public Main Library, History Room.

20   WHEELS OF JUSTICE

"[If you] ever come upon a floater..." Robert P. Smith, interview with author. Tazewell County Genealogical and Historical Society, 2010.

"We believe the conditions of the excursion..." Taylor. "The *Eastland* Disaster." *The Survey,* August 7, 1915.

"Opportunities of its people..." McNeese. *The Progressive Movement: Advocating Social Change.* New York: Chelsea House, 2007.

"Impossible to operate the boat..." Taylor. "The Eastland Disaster." *The Survey,* August 7, 1915.

"No passenger boat is safe..." Ibid.

"When he left the room..." Ibid.

"Now look back and think of the time..."and "I hear from the watchdogs in the press..." Ibid.

"I am willing..." and "I have been mistreated..." Ibid.

21   A PAINFUL GROAN

"I've got a body..." and "I've got another..." Several newspaper stories recount these words said by rescuers.

"The bodies were stacked up like cordwood..." Humphrey and Barrette. *The Columbia Disaster.* 1918.

"Hastily constructed slabs..." *Chicago Tribune,* 1918.

"Time and time again..." Humphrey and Barrette, *The Columbia Disas-ter.* 1918.

"We simply could not handle white…" Anna Mogga in a newspaper interview years later.

22 HOT WATER

"Promote closer relations…" The Transportation Club of Peoria website, transclubofpeoria.com.

23 ANOTHER BODY

"One saloon keeper in Manhattan…" Zacks. *Island of Vice: Theodore Roosevelt's Doomed Quest to Clean up Sin-Loving New York.* New York: Doubleday, 2012.

"Small man with wiry glasses…" Okrent. *Last Call: The Rise and Fall of Prohibition.* New York: Scribner, 2011.

24 HERO DIVER

"Tall, burly and chiseled-looking…" Bonansinga. *The Sinking of the Eastland: America's Forgotten Tragedy.* Illinois: Citadel, 2005.

25 THE STORM

"Most likeable miss…" *Pekin Daily Times,* 1918.

"The buckles were so full of human hair…" Perkins. Tazewell County Genealogical and Historical Society, 2011.

26 SPECIAL PRAYERS

"Of the peculiar ways…" *Peoria Journal-Transcript,* July 8, 1918.

"In fact, a bomb that was set off…" Blum. *American Lightening: Terror, Mystery, the Birth of Hollywood, and the Crime of the Century.* New York: Crown, 2008.

27 PICNIC DAY

"Does your husband wear a gold watch…" Harry Brown's story is a composite from various newspaper sources.

"The Homer Smith stayed in Ohio…" Way Jr. *Way's Packet Directory 1848-1994.* Ohio: Ohio University Press, 1995.

28 OVER THERE

"Please take good care…" Peare. *The Woodrow Wilson Story: An Idealist in Politics.* Ty Crowell Co., 1963.

"There is such a thing…" Ibid.

"One by one they arrived..." *The Pekin Centenary 1849-1949*. Illinois: Heine Graphics Group, 1949.

"Roy King was a Pekin native..." Ibid.

30   SAD SCENARIO

Walter Soady's letters from home. Collection, Tazewell County Genealogical and Historical Society courtesy of the Soady family.

"But [at the drug store]..." Smith-Soady. *Pekin Daily Times*, July 8, 1981.

"Many were wrapped in bandages..." O'Donnell. *Ship Ablaze: The Tragedy of the Steamboat General Slocum*. New York: Broadway, 2004.

31   SHIFTY POSITIONS

Most of the testimonies were taken directly from newspaper coverage. Although the proceedings were transcribed for future trials, no official notes, records or documents exist.

33   THIS THEORY

"He would bring someone to shore..." *The Columbia Disaster*. Tazewell County Genealogical and Historical Society.

"He had no hope..." Ibid.

"Dad never let me..." Ibid.

34   ADMIRALTY LAW

"Concluded investigation *Columbia* disaster..." Greene telegram. Department of Commerce, U.S. National Archives and Records Administration.

"I am thoroughly satisfied..." Greene letter. Department of Commerce, U.S. National Archives and Records Administration.

"We continued to take depositions..." Ibid.

"While most of the statements..." Ibid.

"We could have closed this investigation..." Ibid.

"Referring to the newspaper charges..." Redfield letter. Department of Commerce, U.S. National Archives and Records Administration.

Hartnett's letters and Hoovers response are also from the U.S. National Archives and Records Administration

"The court is bound to do by precedent..." Kremer. *Peoria Journal-Transcript*.

35   FLANKING IN

"The white-bearded one..." Way Jr. *Pilotin' Comes Natural*. New York:

Rinehart & Co, Inc., 1943.

Testimony of former pilots and crew from newspapers *Peoria Star, Peoria Journal-Transcript* and *Pekin Daily Times.*

36   SENSATIONAL ORDER

"One night while attending..." Oakley. "The Stroller." *Peoria Penny Press,* April 26, 1973.

"Give me a song..." Tucker. *Some of These Days: The Autobiography of Sophie Tucker.* Sophie Tucker, 1945.

"Joe Weil of Peoria taught me how to play poker." Ibid.

"Barker was a successful grocer..." Underground@Springdale. *The Barker Family: a Century Long Springdale Story.*

37   DEAD WOOD

"Hours of preparatory work..." *Peoria Journal-Transcript.*

"After a breathing spell..." Ibid.

38   TAKING THE STAND

Witness testimony from various newspaper sources.

39   THE PLEA

"He then asked to be excused for a moment..." *Peoria Journal-Transcript.*

40   STICKY ISSUES

"According to the testimony taken in this case..." Bower and Downs. *Remarks.* Department of Commerce, U.S. National Archives and Records Administration.

"In navigating a steamer..." Ibid.

"In this particular instance..." Ibid.

"The officers and crew of the steamer..." Ibid.

"Accept the thanks of the Bureau..." Redfield letter. Department of Commerce, U.S. National Archives and Records Administration.

"At least 50 of the largest manufacturers..." *Peoria Journal-Transcript.*

"For the men, a stag dinner..." Ibid.

41   PEGGED AHEAD

"We further suggest and urge..." Records, Tazewell County Circuit Clerk.

"Theodore, Theodore, darling..." Morris. *Colonel Roosevelt.* New York: Random House, 2011.

42   LEGAL BATTLE

"Many birds dwell in the trees..." Roosevelt. *Theodore Roosevelt: An Auto-biography*. The Macmillan Company, 1914.

"Herman Mehl, alias Herman Mehl..." Records, Tazewell County Circuit Clerk.

"I have gone down the aisle..." Green. *The Uncertainty of Everyday Life 1915-1945*. Arkansas: University of Arkansas, 2000.

"Ethel P. Hines of East Peoria..." *Peoria Evening Star.*

43   BEYOND CONTROL

"San Sebastian was one of the first..." Kolata. *Flu: The Story of the Great Influenza Pandemic of 1918*. New York: Touchstone, 2001.

"The most recent theory..." Barry. *The Great Influenza*. New York: Penguin, 2003.

"More Americans were killed in a single year..." Kolata. *Flu: The Story of the great Influenza Pandemic of 1918*. New York: Touchstone, 2001.

"In 2002, studies conducted..." Barry. *The Great Influenza*. New York: Penguin, 2003.

44   LOCK AND DAMS

"No evidence of unseaworthiness was found..." Bower and Downs. Department of Commerce, Steamboat Division, U.S. National Archives and Records Administration.

"Things like the [*Columbia*] accident..." *Peoria Evening Star,* 1991.

"If women are not represented..." Hill. *Women's Suffrage*. Omnigraphics, 2006.

"Ellen Wilson was his ideal..." Peare. *The Woodrow Wilson Story: An Idealist in Politics*. Ty Crowell Co., 1963.

45   DEAD DOCKET

"His conviction was posthumous..." Bonansinga. *The Sinking of the Eastland: America's Forgotten Tragedy.* Illinois: Citadel, 2005.

"The captain of the *General Slocum*..." O'Donnell. *Ship Ablaze: The Tragedy of the Steamboat General Slocum*. New York: Broadway, 2004.

46   NO MORE GOOD MORNINGS

"I say any man is a damn fool..." Way Jr. *Pilotin' Comes Natural*. New York: Rinehart & Co, Inc., 1943.

"No woman ought to ever marry a man..." Ibid.

"As he neared the point of the slough..." Burtnett. Burtnett Columns Collection. Chillicothe Historical Society and Museum.

"Daisy recalled..." Loeschner, *Josie*. Lulu, 2005.

"Fred owned and operated..." Rod Mehl, interview with author, April 2012.

"Lawrence is very sick..." Clary obituary. *Pekin Daily Times,* 1933.

EPILOGUE

"There were more women and children killed..." Conover, personal notes, 2006.

"I was 18 years old..." Adcock. *Pekin Daily Times,* 2004.

KEN ZURSKI is a radio broadcasting veteran who has spent the past 25 years doing news and traffic on various radio stations throughout Chicagoland and the Peoria area. He is currently the operations manager and principal anchor at Traffic One in Peoria. Ken lives in Morton, Illinois with his wife Connie and two children, Sam and Nora. An avid reader of history, Ken is currently at work on a new book about another forgotten story.

660

15

Made in the USA
Charleston, SC
29 December 2012